Albert Boyden

History and alumni record of the State Normal School

July, 1876

Albert Boyden

History and alumni record of the State Normal School
July, 1876

ISBN/EAN: 9783337140656

Printed in Europe, USA, Canada, Australia, Japan

Cover: Foto ©Paul-Georg Meister /pixelio.de

More available books at **www.hansebooks.com**

HISTORY

AND

ALUMNI RECORD

OF THE

State Normal School,

BRIDGEWATER, MASS.

TO JULY, 1876.

BY
ALBERT G. BOYDEN, A. M., PRINCIPAL.

BOSTON:
NOYES AND SNOW.
1876.

CONTENTS.

Origin of the School,	9
Government of the School,	14
Board of Education,	22
Visitors of the School,	23
Mr. Tillinghast's Administration,	25
The School,	25
The Model School,	35
Mr. Tillinghast's Idea of a Normal School,	36
The Work Done by Mr. Tillinghast,	38
Memoir of Mr. Tillinghast,	41
The Assistant Teachers,	58
Alumni Record,	59
Mr. Conant's Administration,	80
The School,	80
The Progress of the School,	86
Memorial Addresses on Mr. Conant,	87, 96
Assistant Teachers,	100
Alumni Record,	101
Mr. Boyden's Administration,	112
The School Buildings,	112
The School,	123
Notes by the Way,	133
Instructors,	136
Alumni Record,	138
Roll of Honor,	161
Statistical Summary,	165
Normal Lyceum,	171
Bridgewater Normal Association,	173
Alphabetical Index,	176

PREFACE.

During the last sixteen years, the writer has often been asked "What are the Normal Schools doing?" "What have they accomplished?" "How many of the pupils ever teach?" "How long do they teach on the average?" "Does it pay to educate young ladies in the Normal School, when so many of them do not teach, or get married so soon?" These and similar questions have been asked by all classes of persons, by those occupying high educational positions, and by members of Legislative committees when appropriations have been asked for to supply the increasing wants of the school. It has been said that "half of the persons who attend these schools never teach, and of the other half the majority teach but a short time."

At the Conventions of the Alumni, old friends rush together, and after the hearty hand-shaking, begin to inquire about each other and about the absent classmates and friends, "Where have you been?" "What have you been doing?" "Where's Mr. Brown?" "What is he doing?" "Where's Miss Smith?" "Is she teaching, or is she married?" And so the inquiries go on, in scores of groups, through the whole list of former classmates.

This Centennial year was seen in the near future when these inquiries would again be presented for an answer, and the facts would be wanted on record to go down to posterity. Incited by what was thus heard and seen, the writer determined to record the leading facts in the history of the school, and to gather and preserve answers to the most prominent questions respecting the past members of the school, so that all may know what the school has done, and the Alumni have the pleasure of learning some of the things they would like to know about their Normal friends.

A brief account of the origin of the school is first presented, showing what years of earnest effort were necessary to secure the establishment of the Board of Education, and the opening of the first Normal Schools. This is followed by the Rules and Regulations originally adopted by the Board of Education for the government of all the Normal Schools, with the modifications that have since been made in these regulations; a complete list of the members of the Board of Education, and of the Visitors of the school; an account of the school under each of the three Principals; statistical summaries showing the number of workers, and what they have done; the Roll of Honor, presenting the noble band of patriots who went forth to fight for freedom and free institutions; a brief history of the Normal Lyceum, and the Normal Association; and an Index of all the names in the Alumni Record.

The historical part of the book has been prepared from original sources;—the records of the Board of Education and files of papers and letters preserved by them; an account of the action of Plymouth County in the establishment of the school, furnished by Hon. Artemas Hale, of Bridgewater, who was a prominent leader in the movement; and from the records kept by the Principals of the school. The account of the school has been given in three administrations for the purpose of presenting a more definite picture of the life of the school as it was known by the Alumni.

The Alumni Record has been prepared from the answers to circulars sent to each person whose address could in any way be found. It presents the Alumni in classes as they entered the school, with their residence at the time of admission; the time they were in school; the time they have taught; their present occupation; and their present address; and the date of the death of those deceased, so far as known.

Circular letters of inquiry were first sent out early in 1873. The responses to these were so few and tardy that the whole matter was dropped. At the Convention in 1874, the desire for more definite information about the Alumni was so fully expressed, the writer determined to resume the work and push it to completion. The gathering of the information presented in the Alumni Record has been attended with unexpected difficulties. Class histories, of which much has been said at the Conventions, were found to be myths, except in four instances, and class secretaries could not be found in a large majority of the classes. Circular letters were sent again in 1875, to all whose address could be obtained. Twenty-five hundred of these printed letters of inquiry were sent out. Some of them were forgotten by the recipients, others went to the waste basket; some did not want to put themselves on record; but a large number gladly responded fully. A large number still remained who had not been found. Letters and postal cards were sent to relatives and friends, to classmates, to post-masters, to any persons supposed to be most likely to give the desired information. In some instances it was found that the inquiry had been sent to one long since dead, but this fact was brought to life by the inquiry. Our thanks are specially due to many of the Alumni for their aid in obtaining information about others, and to post-masters for their kindness in forwarding letters and answering inquiries about persons in their towns. Sometimes five or six letters or postals have been sent out to learn about one Alumnus, obtaining as a result, in some cases, the desired information, in others, no clue whatever. These and other difficulties have been met. They are merely mentioned in explanation of the delay in bringing out the book, and of some omissions, and a few errors that may be found. Except in a very few instances, the statements given in the Alumni Record have come directly from the persons of whom they are made, or from near relatives who know the facts.

In one way or another we have succeeded in obtaining some record of more than three-fourths of all who have attended the school. The present members of the school are included in the total of the Alumni, but are not counted in giving the number heard from. We wish the record could have included an account of every Alumnus. The record is not as full as was intended, but is all that could be obtained at this time. The writer cannot hope that in a work offering so many opportunities for error, and undertaken by him in addition to his regular school work and other duties,—the past year unusually pressing,—no mistakes will be found; he trusts, however, that these mistakes are few in number, and not such as will seriously impair the record. It has been impossible for the writer to do all the work of getting the information for the Alumni Record, but for the efficient assistance of one whose modesty forbids the mention of her name, it could not have been completed at this time.

And what does this record show? Aside from its interest in gratifying curiosity, from its making the Alumni better acquainted with each other, and uniting them more strongly as a body, it is hoped that this work will be useful in showing *the vast amount of work* already done by our Alma Mater, though now but thirty-six years of age. A single line states that Mr. A. has taught thirty years. This means that a man *with the mental and moral power* and influence which the thorough training of Mr. Tillinghast gave, has been laboring all these years in form-ing the habits of thought, of feeling, and of action in the large number of young minds who have been under his training. Another line states, Miss J. has taught a primary school thirty-two years in one city. This means that she has taken hundreds of the "little ones," fresh from the hand of the Creator, has wrought at the springs of life, and has given direction to the cur-rent of the whole life. What a grand record has such a teacher! "Inasmuch as ye have done it unto one of the least of these, ye have done it unto me," says the Teacher of all teachers. About one-third of the lady members have married. What educational influence have they exerted as wives and mothers, in their homes, and in the villages and towns where they live? And the men who have left teaching after a few years to engage in other professions, or in busi-ness pursuits, has their influence in the work of education been lost, as they have taken their places on School Committees, in the halls of legislation, and in the town meetings? Let one glance over the thousands of lines in this Alumni Record, and sum up the vast amount of work done in the nine thousand years of teaching reported, let him in imagination trace the lines of its influence through the body politic, and he can but feel that the God of the Pilgrims directed the founding and the carrying on of the Bridgewater State Normal School.

Grateful as this retrospect will be to the Alumni, the Teachers, the Visitors, the Board of Ed-ucation, and the Donors to the Institution must feel the highest satisfaction in the review of what has been accomplished. Would the early friends of the movement wish to recall any of their efforts and sacrifices? Have the Board of Education found better returns for any other like amount of work? Would the Teachers wish that their labors in the past had been less? Could they have cultivated other fields that would have yielded a richer harvest? Has the State found other investments that have paid a larger percentage? Is not such an investment a PAYING ONE?

The days of small things and of severe trial have passed by, the Institution is now recognized as doing an important work. Though it has accomplished so much, it has but just entered upon its usefulness. With the large number of Alumni now at work, scattered all over the country, from the "Pine Tree State" to the "Golden Gates" of the Pacific, each as an educator, and with the annual additions to be made, what shall be accomplished in the next thirty-six years? Let every Alumnus answer.

The work of compiling this History and Alumni Record has been by no means a small one. The Alumni Record ought to be kept as complete as possible. The writer has made arrangements for continuing the record upon the books to be kept at the school.

Is it too much to ask that each Alumnus will annually, on the first of May, send a postal card directed to the Principal of the school, telling where he is and what he is doing? Let every Alumnus do this. The writer will feel amply repaid for his labor in the preparation of this book, if it shall prove satisfactory to the large family of Alumni whose noble career it records, and shall help to unite them more closely to each other and to our common Alma Mater. It is hoped that the pictures of the buildings and the portraits that have been introduced will serve to revive many pleasant associations.

EXPLANATION.

The asterisk following the name in the Alumni Record indicates that the person is deceased. The figure after the residence indicates that the person did not graduate, and shows the number of terms of attendance.

BRIDGEWATER STATE NORMAL SCHOOL.

ORIGIN OF THE SCHOOL.

The free public schools established by the early settlers of Massachusetts have always been cherished by the people, but in the early part of the present century there was a great decline of interest, and a great want of well qualified teachers for the common schools. A few men whose attachment to the cause was earnest and heartfelt, alive to the importance of removing these defects in the system of public instruction, appealed to the people and to the Legislature, through the press and by every form of public address, urging the necessity for the establishment by the State, of a Board of Education and of Normal Schools for the better qualification of teachers for the common schools.

James G. Carter, of Lancaster, was the first to call public attention in Massachusetts to the necessity and advantages of Normal Schools, by a series of articles published in the Boston Patriot, in the winter of 1824–5, with the signature of "Franklin." In these he maintained that "the first step toward a reform in our system of popular education, is the scientific preparation of teachers for the free schools. And the only measure that will insure to the public the attainment of the object, is to establish an institution for the very purpose." He then describes the leading features of an institution for the education of teachers. These essays were ably written and attracted much attention.

After twelve years of persistent effort by Mr. Carter and others, the Legislature passed an act establishing the Board of Education, which was signed by Governor Edward Everett, April 20, 1837. The Governor appointed as members of this Board, James G. Carter, Rev. Emerson Davis, Edmund Dwight, Horace Mann, Rev. Edward A. Newton, Robert Rantoul, Jr., Rev. Thomas Robbins, and Jared Sparks. The Board held its first meeting June 29, 1837, chose Hon. Horace Mann its Secretary, and issued an address to the people of Massachusetts, asking their co-operation, and calling conventions for the discussion of the interests of education, which were held during the autumn of 1837 in every county of the State, except Suffolk.

These conventions stirred the whole community to a higher interest in the whole subject of school education.

The Board of Education immediately recommended the passage of a law providing for the establishment of Normal Schools. In March, 1838, one of the members of the Board, Hon. Edmund Dwight, of Boston, — a name that ought ever to be held in reverence by every friend of the public school system of Massachusetts,—offered, through the Secretary of the Board of Education, to furnish ten thousand dollars, " to be expended under the direction of the Board, for qualifying teachers for our common schools," on condition that the Legislature would appropriate for the same purpose an equal amount. On the 19th of April, the same year, the Legislature passed resolves accepting the proposition. With the sum of twenty thousand dollars at their command, the Board decided to establish these schools for the education of teachers, each to be continued three years, as an experiment. May 30, 1838, the Board voted to locate one of these schools in the county of Plymouth. December 28, 1838, the Board voted to locate the other two at Lexington and Barre. The schools were opened, at Lexington, July 3, 1839; at Barre, September 4, 1839; and at Bridgewater, September 9, 1840.

The people of Plymouth County were the first to make application to the Board for the location of one of these schools. They had become thoroughly interested in the subject, chiefly through the efforts of Rev. Charles Brooks, of Hingham. In 1835, Mr. Brooks, having recently returned from Europe, deeply in love with the Prussian system of Normal Schools, resolved to labor for the establishment of State Normal Schools in Massachusetts, after the Prussian model, hoping, also, that the first one should be located in Plymouth County. He delivered lectures upon the subject before conventions in nearly all the towns in the County, before the Legislature, and in many towns throughout the State.

A committee of the convention of the friends of education, in Plymouth County, presented the application to the Board at their annual meeting, May 30, 1838. The Board immediately voted to establish a Normal School in the County of Plymouth "as soon as suitable buildings, fixtures and furniture, and the means of carrying on the school, exclusive of the compensation of teachers, shall be provided and placed under the control of the Board." The Board suggested that Academy buildings, sufficient for the accommodation of a hundred pupils, and a mansion house, or houses, for their residence, would be deemed adequate to meet the public wants.

ORIGIN OF THE SCHOOL. 11

Measures were immediately taken to comply with the conditions of the Board. To create an interest in the cause among the people of the county, a convention was called, to meet at Hanover, Sept. 4, 1838. The convention was largely attended. The following notice of the proceedings is abridged from the Hingham Patriot.

After an address by Mr. Mann, Secretary of the Board of Education, on "Special Preparation, a Pre-requisite to Teaching," Rev. Charles Brooks introduced a resolution approving of a plan, proposed by a committee of the Association, to raise in the several towns in the county, a sum (ten thousand dollars) sufficient to provide a building, fixtures and apparatus, in order to secure the location of one of the three Normal Schools in Plymouth county.

Mr. Ichabod Morton of Plymouth, who had two years before, offered to meet one-tenth of the expense of the enterprise, "advocated raising up better teachers, who, by a Christian education, could carry the happiness of childhood fresh and whole through life."

Hon. Robert Rantoul, of Gloucester, thought a reformation in our common schools was exceedingly needed, and this change for the better could only be effected by better teachers, well paid, and permanently employed.

Rev. George Putnam, of Roxbury, ably refuted several objections to the Normal Schools, one of which was "that it was some trick of the rich to get advantage of the poor;" and another, "that it may tend to raise the wages of our teachers."

Hon. John Quincy Adams said "I have examined the subject of late, and I think the movements in this county by the friends of education have been deliberate, and wise, and Christian; and I think the plan, contemplated by the very important resolution before the meeting, cannot but find favor with every one who would examine and comprehend it. On this great and glorious cause let us expend freely, yes, *more* freely than on any other."

Hon. Daniel Webster said, "I rejoice at the noble efforts here made of late, and hope they may be crowned with entire success. This plan of a Normal School in Plymouth county is designed to elevate our common schools, and thus to carry out the noble ideas of our Pilgrim Fathers. There is growing need that this be done. The good which these seminaries are to spread through the community is incalculable."

Rev. Thomas Robbins, of Rochester, remarked, "As the offer of the Normal Schools had been first made to the Old Colony, that "Mother of us all,' I hope that the descendants of the Pilgrims will sustain the exalted character of their fathers; and, as in times past, so now, go forward in improvements which are to elevate and bless all coming generations."

An association was formed for raising the proposed fund, and the Legislature of 1839 passed an act incorporating Artemus Hale, of Bridgewater, Seth Sprague, Jr., of Duxbury, Ichabod Morton, of Plymouth, Sylvanus Bourne, of Wareham, Arad Thompson, of Middleborough, and their associates and successors, by the name of the " Plymouth County Normal School, in the County of Plymouth," to provide the buildings for the use of the school. Artemus Hale, of Bridgewater, was President of this Corporation, and was very active and influential in securing the means for the establishment of the school.

These Trustees held meetings in most of the towns of the county, in which the importance of the measure was ably and strongly urged. The towns of Plymouth, Duxbury, Marshfield, Abington and Wareham, voted to make appropriations for the school from the surplus revenue, which had just before been divided by the general government. The amount thus pledged was little more than eight thousand dollars. The Trustees then agreed that the town in which the school should be located should pay the additional two thousand dollars. In several towns individuals agreed to do this, provided the school should be located in their own town. It was decided that the location should be made by disinterested men. Accordingly, Hon. Samuel Hoar, Hon. Robert Rantoul, Jr., and Hon. James G. Carter, were appointed for that purpose. They gave a public hearing at Bridgewater, March 26, 1840. The principal competition was between Plymouth, Middleborough, and Bridgewater, and the respective claims of these towns were urged in the strongest manner possible. The decision was in favor of Bridgewater. At this stage some of the towns which had voted to pay their proportion of the ten thousand dollars, refused to do so, and as the other pledges were made on the condition that the full sum should be raised, the whole matter, as to funds, for which so much time and money had been spent, became null and void. To prevent the failure of an enterprise of so much importance, application was made to the Board of Education to know on what terms they would establish the school at Bridgewater. The Board voted " that the school be established at Bridgewater for the term of three years, on condition that the people of the town put the Town House in such a state of repair as may be necessary for the accommodation of the school, and that they place at the disposal of the Visitors of the school the sum of five hundred dollars, to be expended in procuring a library and apparatus, and that they give reasonable assurance that the scholars shall be accommodated with board within a suitable distance at an expense not exceeding two dollars per week."

The town accepted these conditions, granted the use of the Town House, spent two hundred and fifty dollars in fitting it up, and paid the five hundred dollars for library and apparatus. A school house for the Model School, connected with the Normal School, was built by the Centre School District at an expense of five hundred dollars.

It will thus be seen that the people of Plymouth county were foremost in the endeavor to open a Normal School, that they proposed to raise a fund sufficient to give it a permanent home at the outset, and for nearly two years the friends of the movement made every possible effort to accomplish the desired object. But the time for so large an outlay had not come; the Normal School in Massachusetts was an untried experiment, and it must be content with an humble beginning. This prolonged effort to provide good buildings at the start, made this the last of the first three Normal Schools of the State to be opened, but it was so firmly planted in Bridgewater by these efforts that it has never changed its location.

Horace Mann said of this school, at the dedication of the school house, in 1846, "Its only removal has been a constant moving onward and upward, to higher and higher degrees of prosperity and usefulness."

GOVERNMENT OF THE SCHOOL.

The twenty thousand dollars furnished "for qualifying teachers for our common schools," was placed in the hands of the Board of Education, without any specifications for its expenditure. The object of this provision evidently was to test the utility of State Normal Schools in educating teachers. The particular form of the experiment, and all the details of these institutions were left entirely to the discretion of the Board, and they have continued to have the entire management of these schools. May 27, 1838, the Board adopted the following Rules and Regulations for the Massachusetts Normal Schools, which, with the modifications indicated, are still in force.

VISITORS.

"The Board of Education will choose by ballot, for each school, three of their members to be its Visitors."

"It shall be the duty of the Visitors, or the major part of them, to visit the school under their charge at least once every term, to supervise the administration of its Rules; to be present at, and direct the examination of all candidates for admission, and of pupils leaving the school with the purpose of becoming teachers; to advise with the Principal in all matters of internal discipline; to submit, by their chairman, estimates of the appropriations necessary to be made for the support of their schools; to draw, by their chairman, on the Treasurer of the Board for the sums of money appropriated to their school, as the same shall from time to time be needed to pay expenses; and to report of their doings, and the state of the school, to the Board, once a year at least, and oftener if they have occasion and opportunity."

"The Visitors shall have power to suspend any of the existing regulations of the school, and to establish new ones, to have effect until the next meeting of the Board of Education."

INSTRUCTORS.

"The Board will appoint for each school a Principal Instructor, who shall direct and conduct the whole business of government and instruction, subject to the Rules of the Board and the supervision of the Visitors.

"At all examinations the Principal shall attend and take such part therein as the Visitors may assign to him, and make reports to them at such times and on such points as they may require.

"*Assistants*. The Visitors shall appoint Assistant Instructors when authorized or directed to do so by the Board. The Assistants will be subordinate to the Principal, and perform such duties as he may assign to them."

Conditions of Admission.

" Candidates for admission, *proposing to qualify themselves to become school teachers*, must have attained the age of seventeen years complete, if males, and sixteen years if females, and be free from any disease or infirmity which would unfit them for the office of teacher. They must be well versed in Orthography, Reading, Writing, Arithmetic, Geography and Grammar. They must furnish satisfactory evidence of good intellectual capacity, and of high moral character and principles. Examinations for admission will take place at the commencement of each academic year, and oftener, at the discretion and convenience of the Visitors and the Principal."

Course of Instruction.

"Instruction will be given in the following branches, namely :—
1. Orthography, Reading, Grammar, Composition and Rhetoric, Logic.
2. Writing, Drawing.
3. Arithmetic, mental and written, Algebra, Geometry, Bookkeeping, Navigation, Surveying.
4. Geography, ancient and modern, with Chronology, Statistics and General History.
5. Physiology.
6. Mental Philosophy.
7. Music.
8. Constitution and History of Massachusetts and of the United States.
9. Natural Philosophy and Astronomy.
10. Natural History.
11. The Principles of Piety and Morality common to all sects of Christians.
12. *The Science and Art of Teaching with reference to all the above named subjects.*

"A portion of the Scriptures shall be daily read in the Normal Schools.

"Such of the above studies as are required by the Statutes to be taught in the public schools, shall be the first and most constant objects of attention in the Normal Schools.

"One or more of the above named branches may be omitted in any school, or in certain classes of a school, at the discretion of the Principal, with the consent of the Visitors."

Length of the Course of Study.

"The courses of studies shall be so arranged as to occupy one year, but provision shall always be made for the further instruction of those pupils who, with the advice of the Principal, may choose to continue in the school for a longer period."

Certificates.

"Pupils who shall have been members of any of the Normal Schools for one year or more, and have attended to its rules and studies in a manner satisfactory to the Visitors, shall, on leaving, be entitled to a certificate of qualifications, in such form as the Board, or the visitors, may hereafter prescribe. The certificate to be given by the Principal, under the direction or by order of the Visitors."

The Committee of the Board who reported the above Rules and Regulations, say, in closing their report, "we will not undertake to prescribe rules for the internal discipline, classification, and order of study of the schools. On these points much must be left to the wisdom and genius of the instructor. We want at the head of every school a man of such energy and skill, that having furnished him with school house, scholars, and apparatus, and a bare outline of our plan and wishes, we can trust him to say, with the Principal of the Haarlem school, "I am the Code; there is no other." And indeed, there is no other that will accomplish our designs in a manner satisfactory to the public and to the benefactors of the Normal Schools."

In expenditures the Visitors cannot exceed the sum allotted by the Board, nor can the Board exceed the amount specifically appropriated by the Legislature each year.

Changes in the Government of the School.

Visitors. Since the increase in number of the Normal Schools, the Board have chosen for each school two of their members, instead of three, to be its Visitors, and the Secretary of the Board is a Visitor of each of the schools. The duties of the Visitors have not been changed.

Instructors. The following requirement has been added: "It shall be the duty of the Principal to make a report, at the end of each term, to the Visitors, and, if in their judgment, any do not promise to be useful as teachers, they shall be dismissed."

In May, 1859, the Board of Education voted, "That the Principals of the several Normal Schools shall have power to remove pupils temporarily for misconduct, and shall immediately report every such case to the Visitors for final action."

The following votes were passed by the Board of Education, December 2, 1874:

Voted, "That the Principal of each Normal School shall annually present an account to the Visitors, debiting himself, or herself, with $2.00 per term from each pupil, and crediting himself with the expenditures from this fund. This account shall be audited by the Visitors, and a general statement of the account shall be annexed to their report, and the account shall be placed on file with the Treasurer of the Board."

Voted, "That the principals of the boarding houses shall, at the close of every term, render to the Visitors accounts charging themselves with the full amount of board for each pupil, and with all extras charged, and crediting themselves with the sums expended for meats, vegetables, butter and eggs, groceries, fuel, light, wages, repairs on house, repairs on furniture, incidentals, and the amount brought from the last account; that these accounts be audited by the Visitors, and a general statement of expenditures be presented to the Legislature with the annual report of the school."

Conditions of Admission. From the beginning of the school to the nineteenth term, inclusive, pupils were required to remain in the school at least two terms, which, however, were not necessarily successive.

May 27, 1846, the Board passed an order requiring pupils who should afterward enter the Normal School at Bridgewater, to do so with the avowed intention of remaining at least one year in successive terms. Accordingly, after the nineteenth term, candidates for admission were required to sign the following declaration: "We, the subscribers, on entering the Normal School, declare that it is our intention to become teachers; that we are of the requisite age, and intend to remain in the school for three successive terms." At this time there were three terms, of fourteen weeks each, in the year.

In 1869, provision was made for a four years' course of study. New members are admitted to the shorter course of two years at the commencement of each term, to the course of four years, at the commencement of each Fall term.

Since 1860, candidates for admission have been examined in the History of the United States, in addition to the studies previously required.

Course of Instruction.— December 13, 1849, the Board adopted the following rules in relation to the order and distribution of the studies in the course : —

1. "The Course of Study in each of the Normal Schools, shall begin with a review of the studies pursued in the common schools, namely: Reading, Writing, Orthography, English Grammar, Mental and written Arithmetic, Geography and Physiology.

2. "The attention of the pupils in the Normal Schools shall be directed 1, To a thorough review of elementary studies; 2, To those branches of knowledge which may be considered as an expansion of the above named elementary studies, or collateral to them; 3. To the art of teaching and its modes.

3. "The advanced studies shall be equally proportioned, according to the following distribution, into three departments, namely : 1, The Mathematical, including Algebra, through Quadratic Equations; Geometry, to an amount equal to three books in Euclid; Book-keeping, and Surveying. 2. The Philosophical, including Natural Philosophy, Astronomy, Moral and Intellectual Philosophy, Natural History, particularly that of our own country, and so much of Chemistry as relates to the atmosphere, the waters, and the growth of plants and animals. 3. The Literary, including the critical study of the English language, both in its structure and history, with an outline of the history of English literature; the history of the United States, with such a survey of general history as may be a suitable preparation for it; and Historical Geography, ancient and mediæval, so far as is necessary to understand general history, from the earliest times to the period of the French Revolution.

4. "The art of teaching and its modes, shall include instruction on the philosophy of teaching and discipline, as drawn from the nature and condition of the juvenile mind; the history of the progress of the art, and the application of it to our system of education; and as much exercise in teaching under constant supervision, towards the close of the course, as the circumstances and interests of the Model Schools will allow."

In June, 1853, the Board voted, "that the direct preparation of teachers by actual practice of teaching, under the eye and supervision of the Principal, be regarded as an essential part of the process of qualifying teachers for the public schools, and that the Visitors of the several Normal Schools be directed to see that this principle be carried out in the schools under their charge."

The Board of Education, by a vote passed January 9, 1866, prescribed the following course of study, for the State Normal Schools:

"The design of the Normal School is strictly professional; that is, to prepare, in the best possible manner, the pupils for the work of organizing, governing, and teaching the public schools of the Commonwealth.

"To this end, there must be the most thorough knowledge; *first*, of the branches of learning required to be taught in the schools; and *second*, of the best methods of teaching those branches.

"The *time* of the course extends through a period of two years, and is divided into terms of twenty weeks each, with daily sessions of not less than five hours, five days each week."

Branches of Study to be pursued.

First Term. — 1. Arithmetic, oral and written, begun. 2. Geometry, begun. 3. Chemistry. 4. Grammar and Analysis of English Language.

Second Term. — 1. Arithmetic, completed; Algebra, begun. 2. Geometry, completed; Geography and History, begun. 3. Physiology and Hygiene. 4. Grammar and Analysis, completed. 5. Lessons twice a week in Botany and Zoology.

Third Term. — 1. Algebra, completed; Book-keeping. 2. Geography and History, completed. 3. Natural Philosophy. 4. Rhetoric and English Literature. 5. Lessons twice a week in Mineralogy and Geology.

Fourth Term. — 1. Astronomy. 2. Mental and Moral Science, including the Principles and Art of Reasoning. 3. Theory and Art Teaching, including: (1) Principles and Methods of Education. (2) School Organization and Government. (3) School Laws of Massachusetts. 4. The Civil Polity of Massachusetts and the United States.

"In connection with the foregoing, constant and careful attention to be given throughout the course to Drawing and Delineations on the blackboard; Vocal Music; Spelling, with derivations and definitions; Reading, including analysis of sounds and vocal gymnastics; and Writing.

"The Latin and French languages may be pursued as optional studies, but not to the neglect of the English course.

"General exercises in Composition, Gymnastics, Object Lessons, etc., to be conducted in such a manner and at such times as the Principal shall deem best.

"Lectures on the different branches pursued, and on related topics, to be given by gentlemen from abroad, as the Board of Visitors shall direct, and also by the teachers and more advanced scholars.

"The order of the studies in the course may be varied in special cases, with the approval of the Visitors."

The Board of Education, on February 3d, 1869, voted, "that a Supplemental Course of Study, occupying two years, be introduced into each of the four Normal Schools, which shall comprise the Latin, French, Higher Mathematics, Ethics, Natural Sciences, and English Literature." The object of this advanced course, is to give to young persons of decided ability the opportunity to prepare themselves, thoroughly, to meet the constantly increasing demand for well-trained teachers in the higher grades of the public schools.

Pupils who, on entering the school, have in view the completion of this higher course, may take a part of its studies in connection with a part of the branches in the shorter course, and in this way, at the end of four years, be prepared to graduate from both courses simultaneously. This arrangement gives the students the benefit of the study of the languages in connection with the study of the other branches of the course

Length of the Course of Study. — The course of study was arranged for one year, at the beginning, but during the first six years pupils were required to remain in the school only two terms, and these need not be successive, so that practically, the course of required studies extended through two terms, and after the *second* term scholars were permitted to select their studies.

From the beginning of the twentieth term, August 5, 1846, to the beginning of the forty-fifth term, March 21, 1855, the course of required studies was three successive terms of fourteen weeks each. After the first term, pupils were allowed to select one or two of the permitted studies in addition to the required studies.

From the forty-fifth term, March, 1855, to the beginning of the sixty-fifth term, March, 1865, the required course was three successive terms of twenty weeks each.

Since March, 1865, the required course has been four successive terms of twenty weeks each, and the course has been so full as to occupy all the time of the pupils without any optional studies. Any pupils who desired have extended their course through additional terms, and have thus taken such additional studies as they chose in connection with existing classes.

Since 1869 the advanced course has furnished full opportunity for extending the course of study.

Each extension of the course has been caused by the demand for higher qualifications in the graduates of the school. The pupils have felt the need of more thorough preparation and have gladly improved the opportunity to get it, so that the effect of each extension has been to increase the number of pupils in attendance, and to elevate the character of the school. A course of three years is none too long to meet the demands made upon the graduates of the school at the present time.

Certificates and Diplomas.—Certificates, written and signed by the Principal, were given to those who satisfactorily completed the required course of study until May, 1861, when the Board of Education, having provided a handsomely engraved diploma, voted, "That one of these diplomas be given to each member of the graduating classes in future, for which no charge shall be made. And any graduate desiring a copy on parchment may receive such upon payment of the actual cost."

The diploma is signed by the Secretary of the Board of Education, the Visitors of the School, and the Principal.

THE BOARD OF EDUCATION.

The following is a complete list of the members of the Board from its organization to the present time. The persons are named in the order of their appointment or connection with the Board, and they represent the various religious denominations, learned professions, and political parties.

Names of the members of the Board since its establishment in 1837.

*JAMES G. CARTER,	HENRY B. HOOKER,	RUSSELL TOMLINSON,
*EMERSON DAVIS,	STEPHEN P. WEBB,	ERASTUS O. HAVEN,
*EDMUND DWIGHT,	THOMAS KINNICUTT,	DAVID H. MASON,
*HORACE MANN,	JOSEPH W. INGRAHAM,	JOHN P. MARSHALL,
*EDWARD A. NEWTON,	JOHN A. BOLLES,	EMORY WASHBURN,
*ROBERT RANTOUL, JR.,	GEORGE B. EMERSON,	ABNER J. PHIPPS,
*THOMAS ROBBINS,	CHARLES K. TRUE,	JAMES FREEMAN CLARKE,
*JARED SPARKS,	MARK HOPKINS,	WILLIAM RICE,
GEORGE PUTNAM,	EDWARD OTHEMAN,	JOHN D. PHILBRICK,
CHARLES HUDSON,	ISAAC DAVIS,	SAMUEL T. SEELYE,
GEORGE N. BRIGGS,	ALEXANDER H. VINTON,	GEORGE D. WILDE,
WILLIAM G. BATES,	GEORGE S. BOUTWELL,	GARDINER G. HUBBARD,
JOHN W. JAMES,	HENRY WHEATLAND,	ALONZO A. MINER,
ELISHA BARTLETT,	HOSEA BALLOU,	HENRY CHAPIN,
HEMAN HUMPHREY,	ARIEL PARISH,	CONSTANTINE C. ESTY,
STEPHEN C. PHILLIPS,	CORNELIUS C. FELTON,	EDWARD B. GILLETT,
BARNAS SEARS,	ALONZO H. QUINT,	PHILLIPS BROOKS,
EDWIN H. CHAPIN,	WILLIAM A. STEARNS,	CHRISTOPHER C. HUSSEY.

EX-OFFICIIS.

Governors.	ALEX. H. BULLOCK,	WILLIAM C. PLUNKETT,
	WILLIAM CLAFLIN,	SIMON BROWN,
EDWARD EVERETT,	WILLIAM B. WASHBURN,	HENRY W. BENCHLEY,
MARCUS MORTON,	WILLIAM GASTON,	ELIPHALET TRASK,
JOHN DAVIS,	ALEXANDER H. RICE.	JOHN Z. GOODRICH,
GEORGE N. BRIGGS,		JOHN NESMITH,
GEORGE S. BOUTWELL,	Lieut.-Governors.	JOEL HAYDEN,
JOHN H. CLIFFORD,	GEORGE HULL,	WILLIAM CLAFLIN,
EMORY WASHBURN,	HENRY H. CHILDS.	JOSEPH TUCKER,
HENRY J. GARDNER,	JOHN REED,	THOMAS TALBOT,
NATHANIEL P. BANKS,	HENRY W. CUSHMAN,	HORATIO G. KNIGHT.
JOHN A. ANDREW,	ELISHA HUNTINGTON,	

*Originally appointed in 1837.

THE VISITORS OF THE SCHOOL.

The following is a complete list of the Visitors of the School for each successive year, from its organization to the present time. The persons are named in the order of their appointment by the Board at its annual meeting, and the one first named is the Chairman. The Secretary of the Board of Education has always been one of the Visitors.

1840. THOMAS ROBBINS, JOHN W. JAMES, HORACE MANN.
1841.
1842. } GOVERNOR DAVIS, THOMAS ROBBINS, JOHN W. JAMES.
1843. GOVERNOR MORTON, THOMAS ROBBINS, EDWIN H. CHAPIN.
1844.
1845. } LIEUT.-GOV. REED, S. C. PHILLIPS, H. B. HOOKER.
1846.
1847. } LIEUT.-GOV. REED, S. C. PHILLIPS, E. H. CHAPIN.
1848.
1849. } LIEUT.-GOV. REED, S. C. PHILLIPS, H. B. HOOKER.
1850.
1851. } S. C. PHILLIPS, LIEUT.-GOV. REED, H. B. HOOKER.
1852. H. B. HOOKER, S. C. PHILLIPS, EDWARD OTHEMAN.
1853. S. C. PHILLIPS, EDWARD OTHEMAN, A. H. VINTON.
1854. EDWARD OTHEMAN, A. H. VINTON, EMERSON DAVIS.
1855. EDWARD OTHEMAN, HOSEA BALLOU.
1856.
1857. } HOSEA BALLOU, EDWARD OTHEMAN.
1858.
1859.
1860. } RUSSELL TOMLINSON, ERASTUS O. HAVEN.
1861. ERASTUS O. HAVEN, GEORGE S. BOUTWELL.
1862. ERASTUS O. HAVEN, JOHN P. MARSHALL.
1863.
1864. } ABNER J. PHIPPS, JAMES FREEMAN CLARKE.
1865 to 1869. JAMES FREEMAN CLARKE, JOHN D. PHILBRICK.
1869 to 1875. JOHN D. PHILBRICK, GARDINER G. HUBBARD.
1875. GARDINER G. HUBBARD, PHILLIPS BROOKS.
1876. GARDINER G. HUBBARD, CHRISTOPHER C. HUSSEY.

Secretaries of the Board of Education.

1837 to 1848. HON. HORACE MANN, LL.D.
1848 to 1855. REV. BARNAS SEARS, D.D.
1855 to 1860. HON. GEORGE S. BOUTWELL.
1861. HON. JOSEPH WHITE, LL.D.

OLD TOWN HALL, BRIDGEWATER.

MR. TILLINGHAST'S ADMINISTRATION.

The school was opened September 9, 1840, in the Old Town Hall, with a class of twenty-eight pupils, twenty-one of whom were ladies, under the tuition of Nicholas Tillinghast, as Principal. The next day a convention was held in Bridgewater, at which addresses were delivered by Governor Morton, Horace Mann, and others, and then the school started upon its career.

The Town Hall, pleasantly situated at the corner of Bedford and School streets, was a one-story wooden building, forty feet by fifty, standing upon a brick basement which was occupied as a dwelling. The lot and basement were owned by a citizen, and the Hall by the town. The town granted the free use of the Hall to the Normal School, for a term not exceeding three years. At the expiration of this time the Hall was sold to the owner of the lot, so that for the next three years the school lived in a hired house at a rental of fifty dollars a year.

The interior of the Hall was a large room divided by a matched board partition, without paint, extending through the middle lengthwise, and so constructed that the lower half could be raised and the whole school be in one room, or this half could be lowered, thus leaving the entering class with the Assistant in one room, and the second term pupils with the Principal in the other. A small room for apparatus, and another for a dressing room for the ladies, completed the suite of rooms occupied by the School. The school room was furnished with the primitive style of furniture, a pine board seat with a straight back attached to the desk behind. A high platform on three sides of the room brought the teachers prominently into view before the pupils Here, in this simple laboratory, by the sheer skill and genius of its Principal, the "experiment" of a State Normal School in the Old Colony was successfully performed. "The truth is," said Horace Mann, in 1846, "though it may seem a paradox to say so, the Normal Schools had to come to prepare a way for themselves, and to show by practical demonstration what they were able to accomplish. Like Christianity itself, had they waited till the world at large called for them, or was ready to receive them, they would never have come."

First Period of the School.

The time of Mr. Tillinghast's administration may, with reference to the attendance and the quality of work which could be secured, be divided into two periods. The first period was from the commencement of the School to August, 1846,—the first nineteen terms, —in which pupils were required to attend two terms, which need not be successive. The second was from the beginning of the twentieth term, August 5, 1846, to the close of his administration, June 28, 1853, the end of the thirty-ninth term, during which pupils were required to remain three successive terms of fourteen weeks each.

During the first period the attendance was very irregular. Pupils would attend one term, then remain out and teach one or more terms before returning. The young men were out in the winter, the young women in the summer. Some terms the school would be composed almost entirely of different pupils from those of the term before. A new class was received at the commencement of each term. The average number of the entering class for the first period, was twenty-one. The average number of pupils in school per term, was forty-eight. The largest number for any one term was seventy-nine.

The irregularity of attendance had such a depressing influence upon the work of the school, as to call forth from Mr. Tillinghast, on the 9th of August, 1845, the following letter to Hon. Horace Mann, the Secretary of the Board of Education:

"I hereby transmit to you, to be laid before the proper authority, my resignation of my situation as Principal of this school, to take effect, unless an earlier date is desired, at the close of this term.

"I had the honor, some time since, to lay before the Board of Education my opinion of the extreme disadvantage to *the cause of Normal Schools*, of the rule by which a pupil is allowed to remain here one term, to return at some future, indefinite time; and offered my advice, founded on my experience here, that scholars should be received for no time less than a year. I feel it to be impossible for me to carry on the School effectively in the fluctuations to which it is subject, and therefore feel impelled, for the good of the School, to withdraw from my present situation."

The resignation was not accepted. In May, 1846, the Board of Education passed an order requiring pupils to remain in the School for three consecutive terms.

The movement of the School at this time will be apparent from the following extracts from a catalogue of the School, published in 1844, at the end of its fourth year:

Object of the Institution.—"It seems to be a prevalent error in the community that attendance at Normal Schools will surely make good teachers,—that any one ought to become an efficient instructor by remaining at these Schools for a few months. This institution does not boast of any such powers; but, on the other hand, all it claims to do, and all it can effect, is to afford aid and encouragement to those faithfully striving to learn their duty; to such as,—animated by love for their race,—are willing to devote their best energies to the advancement of the highest interests of man. Such, only, are wanted at this School,—such, only, are suitable to have intrusted to their care the promises of the coming age. It should be distinctly understood that this School has no power to make good teachers of the dull, the idle, and those wholly wanting in enthusiasm, or even interest for the young. A teacher must educate himself; the Normal School will assist him. Its teachers will give him the fruits of their experience; it and they can do no more."

Requisitions for Admission.—"Applicants for admission are required to present themselves on the morning of the first day of the term, at the school room, to undergo an examination in Reading, Spelling, Writing, Geography, Grammar, and Arithmetic. Both sexes are received: males not under 17, and females not under 16 years of age. Each applicant is required to bring a certificate, testifying to his or her good character, industrious habits and intellectual ability. Persons entering the school must do so with the intention of remaining for, at least, two terms, which need not be successive, and of teaching in Massachusetts. Individuals from other States may attend the school by paying tuition according to the rates charged in the Bridgewater Academy; or, by declaring their intention to pursue the business of teaching within the limits of this State, may be exempted from payment of tuition fees."

Course of Study.—"The entering class will, during the term, be required to attend to the following studies: Reading, Spelling, Enunciation, Writing, Geography, Physiology, Composition, Grammar, and Arithmetic. The male portion of the class will receive instruction in their duties as citizens of the State and nation.

"The studies required of those attending for the second term are Reading, Writing, Spelling, Enunciation, De Sacy's General Grammar, and the School and School Master. Pupils may pursue other studies if they choose, and if the Principal thinks it advisable.

"After their second term, scholars are permitted to select for themselves—from the branches taught in the school—those they prefer to attend to. These are, in addition to those already enumerated, Algebra, Plane and Solid Geometry, Plane and Spherical Trigonometry, Surveying, Navigation, Application of Algebra to Geometry, Astronomy, Natural, Intellectual and Moral Philosophy, Natural History, Book-keeping by single and double entry, Logic and Rhetoric.

There are lectures delivered every week before the whole School. upon the duties and employments of teachers. The subject of Natural Philosophy is illustrated by suitable apparatus. A well selected library for the use of the School, is kept in the building occupied by the School."

Regulations.—"The year is divided into three terms, of 14 weeks each. Pupils are required to be present at the commencement, and to remain until the close of the term, unless good and sufficient reasons can be given for not so doing. Most of the class books are furnished to the scholars, at a reasonable rate for their use, to be returned at the end of the term. The entering class are required, at present, to furnish themselves with Webster's Grammar and Mitchell's School Geography. The charge to each pupil for wood, sweeping, &c., together with use of books, rarely exceeds one dollar per term. Certificates will be given by the Principal to such students who have attended the school for one year, as he may judge, from their ability and proficiency to merit them. A certificate will be given to no one who has not attended a full year.

The Permanent Location of the School.

At the end of three years the success of the Normal Schools had been such that they were no longer to be considered an experiment, and the Legislature appropriated a sum sufficient for their support for another three years; henceforth they were to be among the permanent institutions of the Commonwealth, and buildings more suitable, convenient, and permanent were required for them. This school had increased so much that the accomodations were entirely inadequate.

"The idea of providing suitable buildings for the Normal Schools, originated with some thirty or forty friends of popular education, who, without distinction of sect or party, had met in Boston, in the the winter of 1844–'5, to express their sympathy with Mr. Mann, and who desired, in some suitable way, to express their approbation of his course in the conduct of the great and difficult work of reforming our common schools. It was at first proposed to bestow upon Mr. Mann some token evincive of the personal and public regard of its donors; but it was suggested that it would be far more grateful and acceptable to him to furnish some substantial and efficient aid in carrying forward the great work in which he had been engaged, and in removing those obstacles and hinderances both to his own success and to the progress of the cause, which nothing but an expenditure of money could effect. No way seemed so well adapted to this purpose as the placing of the Normal Schools upon a firm and lasting basis, by furnishing them with suitable and permanent buildings; and the persons present thereupon pledged themselves to furnish five thousand dollars, and to ask the legislature to furnish a like sum for this important purpose."

During the session of the Legislature, in 1845, a memorial signed by Charles Sumner, R. C. Waterston, Gideon F. Thayer, Charles Brooks, and William Brigham, was presented, setting forth the utility of the system of Normal Schools, in the training and preparation of teachers, and the want of proper accommodations at two of the schools, in buildings, apparatus, and libraries. The memorial concluded by asking for an appropriation of five thousand dollars, to be placed at the disposal of the Board of Education, for these purposes, on condition that a further sum, of the same amount, to be obtained by contribution from the friends of the cause, should be placed at their disposal for the same object.

The Committee on Education, in the House, to whom the memorial was referred, unanimously recommended that the prayer of the memorialists be granted. March 10th, a resolve was passed authorizing and requesting the Governor, with the advice and consent of the Council, to draw his warrant for the sum of five thousand dollars, in favor of the Board, when the same sum should be placed at their disposal by the memorialists;—the two sums to be spent by the Board, in providing suitable buildings for the Normal Schools, and in purchasing apparatus and libraries therefor.

Charles Sumner gave his bond for the five thousand dollars pledged by the memorialists.

The Board of Education agreed to appropriate twenty-five hundred dollars for the school in Plymouth County, provided the same amount should be raised by individuals.

"The question of location was again to be settled. The people of Plymouth pledged the amount required, and made strenuous efforts to have it removed to that town. The citizens of Bridgewater were also ready to comply with the conditions of the Board, and thought that as they had been at all the expense of the establishment of the school, and had furnished buildings free from rent for three years, when it was considered only as an experiment, that now, when it was to be made permanent, and new buildings were to be erected, it was not fair that Plymouth, which had paid nothing, should be placed on an equal footing with them."

May 28, 1845, the Board of Education met at Boston, to hear the parties and decide upon the location. The citizens of both towns presented the claims of their respective towns with much earnestness. After listening with patience to the arguments of the parties interested, the Board decided that the school should be established at Bridgewater.

Measures were immediately taken for the erection of a suitable building. Plans and specifications were obtained, and proposals for erecting the building were called for; but no contract could be made for the amount at the disposal of the Board, and the matter was delayed for some time, with no prospect of success. At length Mr. Mann came forward and gave his own obligation to make up the deficiency. A contract was then made with Mr. David Bartlett, of Kingston, who executed the work in a very faithful manner.

On settling the cost of the building, it was found to exceed the funds in the hands of the Board of Education, about eight hundred dollars. One hundred of this sum, in addition to a previous subscription, was paid by Hon. Artemas Hale, of Bridgewater, who has always been one of the strongest friends and supporters of the School, and the balance was paid by Mr. Mann. The sum advanced by Mr. Mann was afterward reimbursed from the State Treasury.

The building was a plain edifice, of the Tuscan order, constructed of wood, sixty-four feet by forty-two, and two stories in height. The upper story was divided into a principal school-room forty-one feet by forty, and two recitation rooms, each twenty-one feet by twelve. This story was designed for the Normal School. The lower story was divided into a Model School room, a Chemical room, and two ante-rooms. Blackboards extended entirely around each of the school rooms. The main school room had an entablature. Each room was supplied with neat, new furniture. The location was excellent; upon a corner lot one and one-fourth acres in extent, and having an eastern slope. The light, cheerful, convenient rooms and the pleasant surroundings of the building, made it one of the most attractive school houses in the State.

THE FIRST STATE NORMAL SCHOOL BUILDING IN AMERICA.

ERECTED IN BRIDGEWATER, MASS., IN 1846.

Dedication of the School House.

The completion of the new edifice for the accommodation of the School was signalized by appropriate exercises, on the 19th of August, 1846. Dedicatory addresses were made by Hon. William G. Bates, of Westfield, and His Excellency, Governor Briggs. The audience then adjourned to the Unitarian Church, and listened to an address from Amasa Walker, Esq., of Brookfield, the orator of the Bridgewater Normal Association, which held its annual convention on this day. After these addresses the company partook of a collation in the Town Hall, on which occasion the health of the Secretary of the Board of Education was given by the President of the day, and received by the company with enthusiastic applause. To this sentiment Mr. Mann responded as follows: —

"Mr. President: — Among all the lights and shadows that ever crossed my path, this day's radiance is the brightest. Two years ago, I would have been willing to compromise for ten years' work, as hard as any I had ever performed, to have been insured that, at the end of that period, I should see what our eyes this day behold. We now witness the completion of a new and beautiful Normal School-house for the State Normal School at Bridgewater. One fortnight from to-morrow, another house, as beautiful as this, is to be dedicated at Westfield, for the State Normal School at that place. West Newton is already provided for by private munificence. Each Normal School then, will occupy a house, neat, commodious, and well adapted to its wants; and the Principals of the schools will be relieved from the annoyance of keeping a Normal School in an *ab*-Normal house.

"Let no man who knows not what has been suffered, has been borne and forborne, to bring to pass the present event, accuse me of an extravagance of joy. I consider this event as marking an era in the progress of education, — which, as we all know, is the progress of civilization, — on this western continent and throughout the world. It is the completion of the first Normal School-house ever erected in Massachusetts, — in the Union, — in this hemisphere. It belongs to that class of events which may happen once, but are incapable of being repeated. Coiled up in this Institution, as in a spring, there is a vigor whose uncoiling may wheel the spheres.

"In tracing down the history of these schools to the present time, I prefer to bring into view, rather the agencies that have helped, than the obstacles which have opposed them.

"I say, then, that I believe Massachusetts to have been the only State in the Union where Normal Schools could have been established; or where, if established, they would have been allowed to continue. At the time they were established, five or six thousand teachers were annually engaged in our common schools; and probably nearly as many more were looking forward to the same occupation. These incumbents and expectants, together with their families and circles of relatives and acquaintances, probably constituted the greater portion of active influence on school affairs in the State; and had they, as a body, yielded to the invidious appeals that were made to them by a few agents and emissaries of evil, they might have extinguished the Normal Schools, as a whirlwind puts out a taper. I honor the great body of common school teachers in Massachusetts for the magnanimity they have displayed on this subject. I know that many of them have said, almost in so many words, and what is nobler, they have acted as they have said: — 'We are conscious of our deficiencies: we are grateful for any means that will supply them, — nay, we are ready to retire from our places when better teachers can be found to fill them. We derive, it is true, our daily bread from school-keeping, but it is better that our bodies should be pinched with hunger than that the souls of children should starve from want of mental nourishment, and we should be unworthy of the husks which the swine do eat, if we could prefer our own emolument or comfort to the intellectual or mental culture of the rising generation. We give you our hand and our heart for the glorious work of improving the schools of Massachusetts, while we scorn the baseness of the men who would appeal to our love of gain, or of ease, to seduce us from the path of duty.' This statement does no more than justice to the noble conduct of the great body of teachers in Massachusetts. To be sure, there always have been some who have opposed the Normal Schools, and who will, probably, continue to oppose them as long as they live, lest they themselves should be superseded by a class of competent teachers. These are they who would arrest education where it is; because they cannot keep up with it, or overtake it in its onward progress. But the wheels of education are rolling on, and they who will not go with them must go under them."

The Second Period of the School.

Two weeks after the commencement of the twentieth term, August 19th, 1846, the school entered the new house. It was filled to overflowing at once. One hundred two pupils were in attendance; the main room had desks for eighty-four. Pupils were required to attend three terms in succession, and the school started forward into a more vigorous life. From that day forward it has grown like a thrifty oak, rooting itself more firmly, and stretching its branches more widely in each succeeding year.

The following extracts from the catalogue of the school, published in 1849, will indicate its course during the last seven years of Mr. Tillinghast's administration:

Regulations. No one is received into the school who does not profess an intention of becoming a teacher, and then only under the following rules:

Applicants for admission must present themselves for examination on the *first day of the term.* They must present a *certificate* of good moral character. Males must be at least *seventeen,* and females at least *sixteen* years of age.

No one is received for less than *three successive terms.* Those who enter must pass an examination in Reading, Writing, Spelling, Grammar, and Arithmetic. It is perhaps impossible to state very definitely what will be regarded as a satisfactory examination; but it may be said, that the applicant will be required to read fluently, so as to call words without hesitation; to write legibly, and with sufficient rapidity; to spell correctly, at least two-thirds of the words given out; to be able to discriminate the different parts of speech; to conjugate verbs, to decline pronouns, etc., and to parse simple sentences; to be able to perform arithmetical operations, which may include the use of vulgar fractions.

Tuition is gratuitous to those who intend to become teachers in the Common Schools of this State. The class-books are furnished by the school. Each pupil pays a dollar a term, which covers all the incidental expenses, including the use of books.

Board is to be had in private families at about two dollars per week.

Course of Study. The school year is divided into three terms of fourteen weeks each.

Studies of First Term. Arithmetic, mental and written; Mechanics, Physiology, Grammar, Geography of North America, and the Drawing of Maps.

Studies of Second Term. Arithmetic; Hydrostatics and Pneumatics; General Grammar; Punctuation; Parsing; Physical Geography; Geography of South America and Asia.

Studies of Third Term. Astronomy; Book-keeping; Optics;

Electricity, etc.; Theory and Practice of Teaching; Parsing; Geography of Europe, Africa and Oceanica.

During all the terms, all the pupils attend regularly to Reading, Enunciation, Writing Abstracts, Essays, etc., and Spelling. The above are the *required* studies; no pupil is allowed to omit any of them.

Among the *permitted* studies are Algebra, Geometry, Trigonometry, Surveying, Intellectual Philosophy, Rhetoric, Natural History, Constitution of Massachusetts and of the United States.

After the first term, pupils are allowed to select one or two of these studies.

Those who have finished, satisfactorily, the whole course, are at liberty to choose all their studies.

At the close of each term, the school is examined in the presence of the VISITORS; and every graduate who gives satisfactory evidence of proficiency, is entitled to a certificate.

THE MODEL SCHOOL.

The early plans of the Board of Education provided a Model School, or School of Practice, in connection with each Normal School, composed of children of the neighborhood who were to be taught by the Normal pupils under the eye and direction of their teachers.

This school was kept the first six years in a small school-house erected for the purpose by the Centre School District of the town, just south of the Old Town Hall, in which was the Normal School. This "Model School" house is now the school-house in District No. 7, in Bridgewater. Afterward the Model School was kept in the model school-room in the lower story of the Normal school-house.

From July 28, 1841, to November 8, 1842, the pupils of the Normal School had charge of the Model School. November 30, 1842, at the beginning of the ninth term, Miss Ruby Potter was appointed its Principal, and taught it, with occasional interruptions from ill health, till the end of the eighteenth term, March 10, 1846. During her absence, Mr. Mertoun C. Bryant had, for the most part, charge of the school.

Miss Deidamia Chase was appointed Principal, April 1, 1846, the beginning of the nineteenth term, and continued in charge till her death, September 30, 1847, in the twenty-third term. One of the pupils taught till the end of that term.

Miss Fanny Leonard was Principal from December 1, 1847, the

beginning of the twenty-fourth term, till the close of the Model School, March 12, 1850, the end of the thirtieth term.

The Model School was under the direct and daily supervision of the Principal of the Normal School, and its Principal was appointed by him. The school-room was well furnished and provided with the appliances for good teaching. The Principals were superior teachers. The Normal pupils were required to spend at least two weeks of their senior term in actual teaching, as Assistants of the Principal of the Model School, after a period of careful observation of the methods of the school. The main object was to give the Normal pupils practice in teaching children, under the supervision and criticism of the Principal of the Normal School, and the Principal of the Model School.

From November 30, 1842, the Principal of this school was allowed $250 a year, which, till July, 1846, was made up as follows: The Board of Education paid $100 a year, Mr. Tillinghast paid $100 a year, and the first School District of Bridgewater, paid $50 a year. From July, 1846, a tuition fee was required of each pupil, which, with the appropriation of the Board, was sufficient, till a short time before the close of the school, to pay the teacher's salary.

Practice teaching in the model school was not very attractive to the Normal pupils. Those who had taught before coming to the Normal School felt that they were not specially benefited by this practice, and those who had never taught before, did not become sufficiently interested to appreciate the work, and some parents preferred that their children should not be "experimented with." Mr. Tillinghast was quite willing that the school should be discontinued. It was closed in March, 1850, and has never been revived.

Mr. Tillinghast's Idea of a Normal School.

The following extracts from a letter written by Mr. Tillinghast, in 1851, for publication in Barnard's Journal of Education, give his views of the kind of Normal School required at that time, founded upon an experience of eleven years as the head of this school:

"It seems to me that these schools are doing good. My own scholars have, I think, succeeded as well as I could reasonably expect. Many have failed; indeed, many from whom I looked for success; others have continued to keep schools, but doing no better, for aught that I know, than they would have done without staying a year here; but still I cannot feel disappointed.

"There are, it seems to me, grave defects in the constitution of my school. Four years would, in my judgment, be profitably given to the subjects which we touch on in one. If pupils must be *taught* subjects in these schools, as I think they must for a time, under the best organization, the course ought to extend over three years, at least. I think it would be a better plan for the present, to receive pupils for, say twenty-one weeks, and to give that time to reading, spelling, arithmetic, and geography; and in another twenty-one weeks, to take up reading, spelling, physiology, grammar; so that only a few studies should be in the school at a time, and teachers might go for a term without interfering with their teaching school. The great evil now, in my school, is the attempt to take up so many studies, most persons inverting the truth, and supposing the amount acquired the important thing, and the *study* unimportant. But I should be content if I could bring pupils into such a state of desire that they would pursue truth, and into such a state of knowledge that they could recognize her when overtaken. A very few studies, and long dwelling on them—this is my theory. I have no especial belief in teaching others *methods* of teaching. I do not mean that the subject should be entirely passed by; but that pupils should not be *trained* into, or·directed into particular processes; it seems to me that each well instructed mind will arrive at a method of imparting, better for *it* than any other method. I therefore have tried to bring my pupils to get at results for themselves, and to show them how they may feel confident of the truth of their results. I have *sought* criticism from my scholars on all my methods, processes, and results; aimed to have them, kindly of course, but freely criticise each other; and they are encouraged to ask questions, and propose doubts. I call on members of the classes to hear recitations, and on the others to make remarks, thus approving and disapproving one another; they are called upon to make up general exercises, and to deliver them to their classes, sometimes on subjects and in styles fitted to those whom they address; sometimes they are bid to imagine themselves speaking to children. I find I am getting more into details than I intend, or you wish. My idea of a Normal School is, that it should have a term of four years; that those studies should be pursued that will lay a *foundation* on which to build an education. I mean, for example, that algebra should be *thoroughly* studied as the foundation for arithmetic; that geometry and trigonometry should be studied, by which, with algebra, to study natural philosophy, etc.; the number of studies should be comparatively small, but much time given to them. I, of course, do not intend to write a list of studies, and what I have said above is only for illustration: the teacher should be so trained as to be *above* his text books. Whatever has been done in teaching in all countries, different methods, the thoughts of the best minds on the *science* and the *art* of instruction, should be laid before the neophyte teachers. In a proper Normal School there should be departments, and the ablest men put over them, each in his own department. Who knows more than one branch *well ?*

"I send herewith a catalogue of my school, which will give you some idea of its osteology; what of life these bones have, others must judge. But when shall the whole vision of the Prophet be fulfilled in regard to the teachers of the land, — 'And the breath came into them and they *lived* and stood upon their feet (not on those of any author) an exceeding great army.'

"God prosper the work, and may your exertions in the cause be gratefully remembered."

The work done by Mr. Tillinghast.

Mr. Tillinghast was Principal of this school for thirteen years, a period of service much longer than that of either of his coadjutors in the other two Normal Schools, and he devoted himself unsparingly to the work of establishing it upon broad and deep foundations. By his persistent, thorough, self-forgetting, and noble work, he exerted an influence that will not cease to be felt among the generations of this Commonwealth. No one man has done more to stimulate the thought and improve the work of teaching in this State than Mr. Tillinghast. When he entered upon his work these schools for teachers, simply "had leave to be." The Board of Education had given them the name "Normal Schools," but both the schools and the name were new to the people, and the schools had to demonstrate by the results they produced that they were worthy of support. The State did not fully adopt them till 1845, when the Legislature, in making an appropriation for their support for the third period of three years, christened them "State Normal Schools." The difficulties which had to be overcome would have appalled a man of less heroic temper. The want of a suitable building and the appliances for good teaching was a very great hinderance, and pupils who came from well furnished schools in other places, expecting better things in this school, were greatly disappointed on finding such meagre provisions. The short period of attendance during the first six years of the School made it extremely difficult to carry out a definite course of study, or to improve very much the qualifications of the pupils, yet the school must be judged by its fruits as manifested in these pupils when they went out to teach. The appropriations of the Legislature for the support of the School were insufficient to meet its most pressing wants, especially in providing such assistant teachers as were necessary. During the larger part of the first year, and all of the third year, Mr. Tillinghast conducted the School without any assistant. He had to spend all the school hours in teaching, and work far into the night to prepare for his daily exercises. Courses of Study in the several branches must be wrought out, the subject matter and the methods of teaching must be carefully considered, for he was teaching teachers, and his work must be a model for them. The want of apparatus and of assistants must be supplied by increased skill and effort on the part of the Principal; he must be the *factotum* of the school. Only those who have had a similar experience can appreciate the amount of work which he performed, and it was always thoroughly done.

In addition to all this exhausting toil, he was called upon to make pecuniary sacrifice as well. When he took charge of the school his salary was fixed at fourteen hundred dollars a year, and he was paid at that rate till January, 1844, at which time the Board of Education reduced his salary to twelve hundred dollars a year, on account of insufficient appropriations by the Legislature. Mr. Tillinghast immediately signified his intention to resign, but Mr. Mann's urgent solicitations, and his own interest in the success of the Normal School experiment, induced him to remain at his post. From his salary, thus reduced, he paid one hundred dollars a year toward the salary of the principal of the Model School, that the people of the town to whom this school had been promised as an inducement for them to contribute funds for the Normal School, might not be disappointed by its discontinuance.

From July 1, 1849, his salary was thirteen hundred dollars a year till January, 1851, when it was placed by the Board at fifteen hundred dollars a year. The provision for Assistant Teachers was very small. In March, 1841, the Board of Education appropriated from the small sum granted by the Legislature, six hundred dollars a year for the salary of an assistant; this was continued till July, 1849, when each of the two assistants was allowed four hundred dollars a year. After May 28, 1851, the First Assistant was allowed seven hundred dollars a year, and the Second Assistant four hundred dollars a year. During the later years of his teaching, Mr. Tillinghast's health had become so much impaired by his unceasing toil that he was obliged to hire extra Assistants and pay them from his own salary; though he was constantly at his post, with the exception of a part of one term, till the time of his resignation.

After his death, in 1856, the Legislature of that year, recognizing the justness of his claims upon the State for the deficiency in his salary and the amounts which he had paid for the Model School and for extra Assistants, passed the following:—"*Resolved*, That there be allowed and paid out of the Treasury of this Commonwealth, to Mrs Ruby H. Tillinghast, and William H. Tillinghast, the widow and child of Nicholas Tillinghast, late Principal of the Normal School in Bridgewater, the sum of eighteen hundred ten dollars and eighty-two cents."

Mr. Tillinghast left the school June 28, 1853, and died April 10, 1856, after years of severe physical suffering. He was buried in the Cemetery at Bridgewater, and his tomb-stone bears the following inscription:

"His purity of heart, independence of mind, and elevation of soul, exhibited the value of the truths which he loved to teach.

His Pupils,

To whom he taught the pricelessness of truth, gratefully raise this stone to his memory."

MEMOIR OF NICHOLAS TILLINGHAST.

BY RICHARD EDWARDS.

[An Address delivered before the Annual Convention of the Graduates of the State Normal School at Bridgewater, Mass., on the 30th of July, 1856. Published in Barnard's American Journal of Education.]

FELLOW TEACHERS AND FELLOW PUPILS:—

WE have met in social and friendly gathering for many years. There are doubtless those here who formed a part of that small band, with whose help, the school of which we have been pupils, was first launched upon the voyage of its existence. Year after year, as occasion would permit, they with others have come up to this, the scene of their former labor, to feel the softening influences of early associations upon those hearts which the business and turmoil of life do so much to harden and deaden; or perhaps to renew here where they were first consecrated to a noble profession, their vows of devotion to its trying but exalting and responsible duties. Some of these occasions have been joyous. The familiar salutations of friends, from whom we have been for a season parted, the warm grasp of the friendly hand, the mutual recital of experiences, the sight of the well known village and its landscapes,— these have been the most prominent circumstances of a convention, and have forever associated with our gatherings the most gladdening recollections. But all has not been joy;— there have also been times of sorrow. Death, that spares no band, has not withheld his hand from ours. Again and again our ranks have been thinned by his unerring shafts. One after another, the young, the promising,— those to whom we look for noble deeds in the future, have fallen by our side, and we have mournfully betaken us to our journey alone.

But whatever change may have met our eyes here, we always, except on a single occasion, until one year ago, were cheered by the countenance, and encouraged by the words of one whom we loved as our teacher, and venerated as a noble illustration of the Christian man. At our last meeting, we were informed that ill health kept him in a distant part of the State. To-day, we miss him again, and even the faint ray of hope with which we then solaced ourselves, has been extinguished. Our hearts are saddened by the knowledge that he has departed from our midst, and that while we continue bound to this lower world, our separation from him is final. This, indeed, is a new experience, and one for which, notwithstanding what we knew of the inroads of disease upon his system, we were scarcely prepared. And even with the positive knowledge we now possess, it is hard to realize the saddening truth. It almost seems as if a convention could not be held without his presence. We can scarcely conceive of the scene without the central figure that was wont to give dignity to it, and to kindle the enthusiasm of us all.

But the sad reality must be contemplated, and on the present occasion it is fit that we should express for his memory, in some suitable way, the respect and affection which we all profoundly feel, and to impress upon ourselves the lesson taught us by his life and his death. And in our expressions of respect and sorrow, I am quite sure there will be none of the cold formality which is sometimes exhibited. For if there is any vice which the very remembrance of him would rebuke in a manner more marked than another, it is the vice of pretence,— the ostentatious profession of a sentiment which we do not entertain. No, our grief is real;— our tribute of respect unfeigned. We dare not profane the memory of one so invariably loyal to the truth and truthfulness, with any offering that comes not from the heart!

NICHOLAS TILLINGHAST, the first principal of the State Normal School at Bridgewater, was born at Taunton, Bristol County, Massachusetts, on Saturday the 22d of September, 1804. He was the second son, and seventh child, of Nicholas Tillinghast, Esq., at that time, one of the most prominent members of the Bristol Bar. He early exhibited the germ of inflexible adherence to what he considered the right, and that elevated and correct tone of moral feeling, which, in later years, expanded into the controlling principle of his life.

At a proper age he was sent to the Bristol Academy, at Taunton, where he pursued the studies usually attended to in those days by lads who were to prepare for college. It had probably been the intention of his father to give him a college training, but the father's death, which occurred in April, 1818, left the family in circumstances that induced them to relinquish this project, and the young man was taken out of the Academy, and placed in the office of a lawyer. Here he continued for about two years; and in June, 1820, through the aid of Hon. Marcus Morton, at that time a member of Congress, an appointment to a West Point cadetship was obtained for him.

Thus was the whole course of his life changed; and instead of the smooth and pleasant path of a New England student, he was ordained to enter upon the rough marches and toilsome labors incident to a life in the United States Army. Speculation as to the degree of usefulness he might have attained, if such change had not occurred is vain; perhaps the wisest cannot with any confidence offer an opinion upon the subject. For those whom it intends for high usefulness, Providence always furnishes the necessary culture, whether they be reared in the cot or in the palace; whether they are trained in the cell of the student, or amid the hardships of frontier life. There can be no doubt, however, that the severe mental discipline of the Military Academy, the self-reliance induced by the active duties of the graduated officer, are, to those possessed of moral stamina enough to endure them and make proper use of them, excellent preparations for the business of teaching. They not only contribute mental strength, but accustom the mind to act promptly from its own judgment formed upon the spot; and this readiness in deciding is a valuable attainment to one whose vocation calls him to immediate decision many times in the day, and upon very important questions,— which is in a high degree the case with the teacher.

Mr. Tillinghast's course as a cadet was in keeping with his general character. As a scholar, he does not appear to have been brilliant, but we doubt not he was always reliable. It is something to say of him that he passed successfully the several examinations to which every cadet is subjected. Of his own class, consisting originally of seventy members, only thirty-one were able to come out of the ordeal unscathed, at the end of four years. That he was among the thirty-one will certainly appear to his credit as a scholar, when it is remembered that he was one of the twelve youngest in the class on being admitted. But he occupied by no means a low position in the class thus eliminated. His number on the merit roll was thirteen, "which," in the language of the venerable Col. Thayer, at that time Superintendent of the Academy, "was a highly respectable standing, considering that he was then the youngest but five in his class, and that in scholarship, the difference between him and most of those above him was very slight." Those who have learned all they know of his success as a student at West Point from his own conversation in respect to it, will be surprised to learn that he stood so high; for here, as everywhere, his own estimate of his labor and of its results was very far short of that placed upon them by others. Indeed the standing here indicated is precisely that which, from his character, we should expect to find him occupying. It does not indicate the possession of splendid and showy powers, but rather of a mind solid, reliable, thinking more of the quality than of the quantity of its acquisitions, — acquiring carefully, so that every new truth learned should become a part of the mind itself, and be a support and strength to it when the Academic course should close, and the special stimuli there applied should be withdrawn.

He graduated on the first day of July, 1824, and was commissioned as a second Lieutenant in the Seventh Regiment of Infantry. After serving for three years on the Western frontier, he was attached to the Military Academy as an instructor in Chemistry, Mineralogy and Geology; and having performed the duties of that situation for two years, he again joined his regiment in the West. In August, 1830, he was reattached to the Academy as Assistant Professor of Ethics, and continued to act in that capacity until December 1834, when, being promoted to a captaincy, he again went to the frontiers, and remained in command of a company in Arkansas for nearly two years. He resigned his place in the Army in 1836.

We doubt not that Mr. Tillinghast, while an officer in the Army, discharged his duty faithfully and to the satisfaction of his superiors. But his tastes and feelings were ill-adapted to that mode of life. He found good and noble men among the officers under whom he served and with whom he was associated, but we think we may say with truth that his experience of military life deepened in his mind the dislike for war and all its paraphernalia. He was emphatically a man of peace, in feeling and in principle.

During his residence in the western forests and prairies, he suffered much from diseases incident to those regions, — fever and ague and other complaints; and his friends think that his physical powers were essentially weakened during his stay in Arkansas. His resignation was undoubtedly caused by this circumstance, joined to the distaste for military life, to which allusion has already been made.

From the time of his leaving the army until his appointment by the Board of Education, in 1840, to take charge of the Normal School at Bridgewater, Mr. Tillinghast was a teacher in Boston. For the most of his time he taught a private school, fitting young men for West Point, for engineers, &c. He was also for a short time an instructor in the English High School at Boston, and always entertained a great respect for Mr. Sherwin, the accomplished head of that instituiion.

It was while laboring in this quiet and retiring manner that he was sought out by Hon. Horace Mann, then Secretary of the Board of Education, and invited to accept the Principalship of the School which it was proposed to establish at Bridgewater. After serious consideration, and with great reluctance, he finally consented to accept the post. On this occasion, as always, he distrusted himself. He shrunk from assuming the grave responsibility belonging to the situation. To be a teacher of teachers seemed to him a great thing, and he did not look upon himself as fitted to accomplish great things. Verily the history of man does occasionally furnish examples of a judgment erring on the side of modesty.

In order to understand the importance of the work which Mr. Tillinghast was called upon to do, and the consequences depending upon it, we may find it useful to recall some facts in regard to the establishment of the Normal Schools in Massachusetts. The establishment of these schools was not a measure first proposed by a legislative committee, and put into operation wholly at the State's expense. On the contrary, it was proposed by individuals, and for the first three years of their existence, the State bore much less than half the expense of supporting them. Three years, it was judged, would be sufficient for trying the experiment, — for testing the plan of training teachers for the public schools at the public expense. At the end of three years, of course, the whole expense of their continuance would come upon the State. Under these circumstances, it will be easy to see that the duty of the teachers of the Normal Schools was no sinecure. It was required of these teachers, that, with exceedingly imperfect instrumentalities, they should demonstrate to the frugal voters of the Commonwealth, the utility of a set of institutions that were to take from the State treasury large sums for the erection of school buildings, and ultimately, thousands of dollars annually for their ordinary support. For feeble humanity this would seem to have been task enough; but in addition to all this, they were compelled to encounter a fierce opposition from many teachers, who thought their own field of labor encroached upon by the new, and hitherto unheard of, State seminaries. Surely, under these circumstances, success was a great achievement, and the fact that success was attained, speaks the praise of those earnest teachers more loudly than any words of mine can do it. It may, I know, be urged, with truth, that the schools had good friends in the Legislature and elsewhere, and that the Secretary of the Board was a gentleman of superior ability, extended culture, great influence, indomitable resolution, and unflinching devotion to the cause, in which, at a great personal sacrifice, he had engaged. The earnest support of all these was necessary to the successful establishing of these institutions. If any of them had been wanting, the scheme must have fallen through.

But every friend of popular education has reason to be thankful, that in the trying hour they all stood bravely at their posts; that the Secretary had counted the cost before entering upon the war; that members of the Legislature, regardless of self and self-interest, gave their energies to the support of a measure which has so abundantly improved the character of the public schools; that the teachers, in spite of many obstacles, such as the brief period during which their pupils were under their instruction, the want of suitable buildings and apparatus, and the influence of the opposition already mentioned, still persisted in their noble work, with a faith that removed the mountains in their path, and an industry that knew no fatigue.

But it will be especially useful for us to enquire what means our teacher took to prepare himself for the work which he regarded as of such importance. The school at Barre, which went into operation on the 4th of September, 1839, had been placed under the charge of Professor Samuel P. Newman, of Bowdoin College. Mr. Tillinghast, when he had finally concluded to accept the appointment offered him, proceeded to Barre, and spent six months in observing the methods, and studying the principles adopted by Prof. Newman in his school. During this time, he prepared many manuscripts of lectures and explanations for his own use in his new position. Every subject on which he was to give instruction was carefully thought out, and the results of his thoughts were committed to paper for future use. This work of six months, however, was but the beginning of what may be called his preparatory labor. Every exercise was carefully considered before it was to come on, — usually on the night before; and very frequently it happened that midnight found and left him at his labors. And such watching was not atoned for by morning slumbers, for the early morning was likewise devoted to duty. He was a believer in industry, in the power of earnest work, and maintained that nothing truly valuable can be accomplished without it. When he had thus prepared himself, as well as the brief space of time, intervening between his appointment and the commencement of his labors would permit, he entered upon his duties as Principal of the Normal School at Bridgewater, on the 9th of September, 1840.

Here, and at this time, no doubt, began the great work of his life. Whatever may have been his success in his previous employments, it is not likely that it was such as to make him particularly eminent. But in the Normal School, his position soon became a marked one. Upon the public schools of the Commonwealth, he has exerted a telling influence for their elevation and improvement. This influence is felt not only in those schools which are under the direct charge of his pupils, but also in hundreds of others, where his name was never heard. His spirit, his views, his methods, seem to have become part and parcel of our educational system, — they seem like the waters of a clear stream, to impart their own purity to the wave with which they mingle. They float about in the educational atmosphere, and are inhaled by all who breathe it. There is no especial part of the system which he originated; no institution which he founded or endowed, or to which he gave a name. These may be called the material or corporeal parts of a people's educational means. But he furnished much of what we may consider the soul, — the animating principle that moves this otherwise dead machinery. He built no schoolhouses, but he built the character of many an earnest and successful teacher. And as the teacher is more valuable than the school-house or school system, however valuable these may be, — as the soul is nobler than the tenement in which it dwells, — so was his life a nobler benefaction to the cause of education, than if it had been spent in endowing institutions or framing systems. Travel over our Commonwealth; visit elsewhere hundreds of school-houses of every degree of architectural pretension, from the lowly, weather-stained cabin in the field or forest, to the costly structure that graces the attractive avenue in the city; — and you will find his pupils in them all, and all, without exception, ready to attribute to him the elements of their highest success.

As a teacher, Mr. Tillinghast had many striking characteristics. In the first place, he acquired a power over his pupils, — men and women, — that we think is seldom attained. To mere lookers on, it seemed like a sort of fascination, and even to the objects of it, the pupils themselves, it was often a mystery. For he used none of the arts commonly practiced to secure the good opinion and attachment of men. On the contrary, his manner towards those who were not more or less familiar with him, was sometimes thought to be cold, distant, reserved. Even in his intercourse with his pupils, he was far from habitually adopting that freedom and ease of manner which often makes school so pleasant. And yet, we may venture to say that the instances are very rare, in which a teacher is so earnestly, and at the same time so universally beloved by his pupils as was Mr. Tillinghast. The true secret of this power of his over his pupils, which enabled him to fill them in a great measure with his own spirit, as well as of the remarkable affection which they entertained towards him, — the secret of all this lay in his personal character, in that quiet but unflinching devotion to principle, that heroic and real abnegation of self, which to those who knew him intimately, appeared as the ruling trait of his moral nature. His words, being few, and well considered, were very impressive, and yet, not so much for what he said as for what he *was*, did he exert so positive, so salutary, and so extended an influence. His pupils were fully persuaded of the soundness of his judgment, his unswerving integrity of purpose, his perfect sincerity and scrupulous justice; and in this persuasion, they seemed to surrender themselves unconditionally to his influence. His devotional exercises in the school were always conducted with great simplicity of manner, but with a power which his pupils can never forget. His reading of the Scriptures, and of those brief, earnest and devout prayers, in his calm and serious manner, was an exceedingly impressive exercise. The words sounded through the perfectly quiet room like the voice of inspiration. He did not discard the teaching of religion and morals, by word or by book, but in these departments, he depended mainly upon that silent teaching which a man of strong religious feeling, and pure character will infuse into the very atmosphere of a school-room. One of the natural results of this course was, that when he did employ words for enforcing some religious or moral truth, they made a deep and distinct impression upon the listener's mind, and the precepts imparted were, in many instances, never forgotten. His power was particularly apparent when some delinquency on the part of a pupil, made it necessary to administer reproof. On such occasions, his words were very few, and by no means severe, and yet they very deeply affected those to whom they were addressed. I never knew a pupil of his who did not shrink even from the mildest reprimand from him. The mere knowledge on the part of a pupil, that Mr. Tillinghast disapproved of his course, even where no disapprobation had been expressed, was a burden which very few could endure. I do not think that in the management of his school, he can be said to have been fertile in expedients. He ruled by the force of his own exalted character, by his earnestness and faith. His remedies for delinquency were, in the main, general; he did not resort to one expedient with one person, and to another with the next, but he approached all in the same straight forward and frank manner. This course is not to be commended to every teacher; most of us need to vary our modes of reproof or punishment, according to the character of the individual to be affected. Our moral power is too feeble; it cannot bend the stubborn will, or arouse the slumbering energies of our pupils, without the aid of schemes devised by the intellect. But in Mr. Tillinghast, the moral power was so well developed that it seemed to bear down all opposition before it, without the aid of shifts and expedients, and for himself, his mode of proceeding was undoubtedly the best.

Of his character as a teacher of the intellect, we may also say that it was distinctly marked. His most notable trait in this respect was something similar to what is usually expressed by the word thoroughness. And yet this word does not fully exhibit the idea. There was thoroughness in his teaching, but there was also another element, which if we could coin a word, we might call *logicalness*,—an arranging of the subject taught according to the character and wants of the mind to be instructed. In every operation, there was not only thorough knowledge, but thorough reasoning. Every point was not only to be thoroughly understood, but it was to be understood rationally; it was to be understood not only by itself, but also in its relations. The pupil was himself required to discover if possible, or at least to appreciate, the connection between one part of the subject and another, to see how much of one statement could be inferred from a previous one. Mere thoroughness in the knowledge of facts, or of principles learned and remembered, is a very different matter from the thoroughness that characterized the teaching of Mr. Tillinghast. The one can be accomplished by the industry of the pupil; the other requires, in addition, careful thought and ready skill on the part of the teacher. His great weapon, by the help of which he accomplished his work in the recitation-room, was the asking of questions. And his questions were always framed with a view of ascertaining, in respect to the subject of the lesson *what* the pupil knew, and *how* he knew it, and the casual interrogative was so frequently employed in his exercises, that his pupils were in the habit of calling it the "eternal *why*." He had rare skill in arranging his questions, so as to expose every false opinion, every illogical conclusion. How many times has the glib and fair-seeming explanation been shown to be hollow and unmeaning by his searching interrogatories! How often have ignorance and sophistry been forced suddenly to stand out in their native deformity, as at the touch of an Ithuriel's spear, when in guise of knowledge and wisdom, they had been silently but surely working the destruction of thorough study and good mental habits! And how many teachers rejoice, to-day in having had their eyes first opened by these thorough and faithful recitations!

From this it will appear that Mr. Tillinghast was a teacher, an educator, one who considered his employment an art, to be rightly practiced only by those who in some way have studied its principles. It is scarcely necessary for me to add here that he was entirely indifferent as to where or how such study had been pursued, provided only it had been thorough and efficient. He thoroughly knew what he was to teach,—no man better,—but he also knew how the knowledge must be imparted in order to promote the mental culture of the pupil. His recitations were quiet, he employed in them very few words, and yet they were full of earnest thought both on his own part and on that of the scholars. Indeed, the most noticeable thing about his recitations was their tendency to awaken thought in the pupil. And this we should be prepared to expect from knowing how they were conducted. Every individual was required to stand upon his own feet, and when he made a statement, to make it from his own perception of its truth. There was no trading on borrowed capital,— or if circumstances seemed to indicate that this was attempted,—that something was confidently stated, which had been received by the pupil upon authority, when it ought to have been reached by his own thought, how soon a skillful question, calling for an exhibition of the vouchers, became the occasion of a failure!

It may not be uninteresting to state here that Mr. Tillinghast was of the opinion that it would be neither well nor expedient to make the Normal Schools exclusively professional, in the sense of excluding from them every study except that of the science and art of teaching. Indeed, his own instruction in this latter department was, in a great measure, though not entirely, imparted indirectly and in connection with the teaching of other things. And let it not be thought, on this account, that he considered it of trifling importance. By no means; for a considerable portion of time was devoted entirely to this subject in his own school. But when we speak of Mr. Tillinghast's giving instruction indirectly, we must not forget that he had a power of silent, and perhaps "unconscious" teaching, that produced great and positive results. This we have already attempted to set forth. He taught many things without uttering a word, that in the minds of his pupils, have taken a distinct form, and become to them a sure guide.

But rather than say anything further of my own, concerning Mr. Tillinghast's qualities as a teacher, I will take the liberty of repeating the testimony of another of his pupils, a gentleman eminent in his profession, occupying an important and honorable post connected with the educational interests of another State, and who was for long and intimately acquainted with our beloved teacher. This testimony seems to me so just and well expressed that I introduce it even at the risk of some slight repetition :

"He was a truly religious man, and in the highest and best sense ; for his religion manifested itself in his life and deeds, rather than in his words. He always sought to know the right, and to do it; to seek the path of duty and to follow it, lead where it might.

"He was sincere and true in his dealings with himself and with others, neither doing or saying anything merely for effect. He censured the wrong because it was wrong, and commended the right because it was right, and showed by his life that his own standard of action corresponded to that which he indicated to others.

"He was truly and unaffectedly modest. He forced you to think of the subject he presented rather than of himself. He never pressed himself, his opinions, or his school on the notice of others. He sought no expression of their good opinion, and deprecated not their ill opinion. While at times he may have felt that his school did not receive that attention from without which it deserved, and that his work was not fully appreciated by any save his own pupils, he would by no act or word call attention to it. He was content to labor on, believing that the time would surely come when the result of his work would be made manifest, whether he should be known in it or not.

"He had that high self-respect which led him to respect others. He therefore appealed to worthy motives only. Everything like trickery and deception he despised, in teacher as well as in pupil. Hence he could never tolerate those whom he could not trust. He had a deep sense of personal responsibility, and sought,—with great success,— to inspire others with it.

"His words of reproof were few, yet apt. There was no escaping them. They never came undeserved, they were always direct, always kindly spoken, and always 'told home.'

"Though at first reserved and apparently cold and distant, he was very warm-hearted and generous, sympathetic and kind. Happy indeed were they who came to know him intimately.

"He was industrious, earnest, and devoted. He allowed himself no idle hours, and discouraged all idleness in others. He believed that 'nothing good was ever come by without labor,' and regarded industry as a duty. Hence, he never did his pupils' work for them. He would guide them in the right track, and indicate methods of overcoming difficulties, but nothing more. His suggestions and explanations, and the assistance he rendered never did away with the necessity of thought on the part of the pupil, but rather made it the more necessary. With him no glibness or readiness could conceal or atone for a want of study; nor could self-distrust or diffidence hide the evidence of faithful preparation.

"Almost invariably accurate, he was ever ready to acknowledge any error he had made. The sentence, 'I was wrong in my statement or opinion,' fell from his lips, though very, very rarely called for, as easily as did the contrary one, 'You were wrong.' He never sought to hide, or explain away, or excuse erroneous statement or explanation which he had made; but always endeavored to correct it. He was very successful in exciting a similar spirit in his pupils.

"He had a great analytical power. While he could grasp a subject as a whole, he could also comprehend all its parts, could trace their relations to each other, and could determine the proper place and importance of each. To this power he was indebted, I think, for the great clearness of his explanations.

"He had a great love for thoroughness,— thoroughness in study, in teaching, in everything. Especially was he thorough in investigating and teaching the first principles of a science. In his view, a deficiency there was fatal. He held his pupils to a point till they mastered it, and could appreciate something of its relations. Those accustomed to superficial views, sometimes complained at first of their slow progress; but, when the work was done, and they were prepared for a higher course, they felt its value.

"In his teaching he was strictly inductive; developing his subjects easily and naturally, and removing difficulties, and explaining just enough to stimulate to exertion. He would question closely, and would make his pupils feel their ignorance and need of study, without humiliating them.

"He usually read character very readily and accurately, though he was sometimes deceived. This, however, but seldom happened. He understood his pupils much better than they thought he did, and knew much of their thoughts, feelings and habits of life."

To this testimony I will only add a few considerations in regard to Mr. Tillinghast's character as a man. As has already been intimated, the great distinctive feature of his character was his constant reference to principle, in respect to every act.

His judgment of others, and especially of his friends, was kind and liberal. He was always very lenient toward the faults of his assistant teachers, excusing in them many deficiencies that he would have severely censured in himself, and expressing great satisfaction with their performances, when it was morally certain that he would have regarded similar things in himself as of very little worth.

His practical benevolence, although it made serious drafts upon his moderate salary, was conducted strictly upon the Christian plan,— his left hand never knowing what his right hand was doing. Many a man could tell of substantial aid received from him in greatest need, and the books of benevolent and reformatory associations would show no meagre sums accredited to his name, were it not that the name was most frequently withheld, when the gift was delivered. Where prudence and benevolence came in apparent conflict, and either of them was called to give way, that duty generally fell to the share of the more cautious virtue. All generous reforms had in him a warm sympathizer, and a prompt supporter; and his firm and consistent anti-slavery was not without the usual accompaniments of obloquy and social proscription. Naturally he was a man of strong feelings, both of liking and aversion. He was the firm friend,—not exacting, but liberal,—making his friendships more valuable to his friends than to himself. His aversions were not for persons, but qualities. He was really impatient of certain vices, such as deceit, pretence, the putting on of false appearances, the arrogating to one's self of excellencies to which there was no claim, the doing of things for mere effect, and similar maneuvering. His own conduct was outspoken and straightforward, and his feeling of contempt for the opposite course was very strong. But, he was free from suspicion, very slow to attribute bad motives, unwilling to believe evil of those about him; and it was only upon very strong evidence, that men came under his condemnation.

In his religious feeling, he was habitually earnest and devout; but his devotion did not obtrude itself upon men's observation, and draw attention to itself. It was a modest, firm, constant, deep-seated, calm and trusting devotion. At the time of his death, and for many years before, he held the office of deacon in the Unitarian church at Bridgewater. We believe he was a Christian, for, otherwise, we know not how to interpret that teaching of our Saviour: "By their fruits shall ye know them: a corrupt tree cannot bring forth good fruit."

Mr. Tillinghast's modesty made him exceedingly disinclined to appear before the public as an author, and we are not aware that he ever did so except in two instances. About the time of his appointment to Bridgewater, he prepared a work on Geometry for the use of schools; and, a short time before the close of his connection with the school, he published an excellent collection of prayers for schools, consisting of such as he had himself used, while at Bridgewater. This book is highly prized by his pupils, both on account of its intrinsic merit, and because its perusal serves to recall most vividly the memory of their teacher, in one of the most interesting exercises of their school-days.

In the way of history, little more can be, at present, said. Long continued hard work gradually enfeebled and finally overpowered, a slender physical frame. In July, 1853, he left the school, as it was then hoped, to return to it in the course of a year. But his body had become the prey of that fatal disease, consumption; and, notwithstanding the efforts of skillful physicians, and a winter's residence in Florida, he continued to sink in strength, and, on the 10th day of April, 1856, he died, in the fifty-second year of his age. For some time before his death, he had suffered much from severe fits of coughing, and had some apprehension that he should pass away in one of these convulsions. But, it was not so ordered. He encountered the "king of terrors" calmly and serenely, passing gently from a quiet sleep to the repose of death. He died the death of the Christian, rejoicing in the hope of immortality, and, with his last breath, committing his spirit to the Father who gave it. His remains lie upon the southern slope of the southern hill in the beautiful cemetery at Bridgewater, at a point that overlooks the pleasant village which was so long the scene of his labors,—where the sun smiles upon his rest, as his Heavenly Father smiled, in the hour of death, upon his returning spirit.

We are told, in Scripture, that the limit of our life is three score years and ten, and that the strength which carries us beyond is labor and sorrow. From this declaration, it may be inferred that, as a general rule, the ages of men who duly observe the laws of their being, will approach, more or less nearly, the limit here established. Men, who receive their bodies and souls as gifts from God, which they are to watch and keep with jealous care; who do not poison the life-currents of the one with the artificial stimulants to a depraved appetite, nor shake the foundations of the other by the upheavings of ungoverned passion; 'such men may be expected to approach in their journey, the utmost confines of human life, and to pass away amid the consolations of a green old age.

But, there are, sometimes, crises in human affairs; times when the development of some great principle, or the illustration of some truth not known to the multitude of men, demands that the work of many years shall be crowded into one; or, that the power of truth shall be illustrated in one glorious moment of martyrdom; when, at the call of duty, life must either be shortened by an intense devotion to a great work, or its thread be suddenly snapped as a testimony to the faithfulness of the laborer, and the greatness of the work in which he was engaged. The higher life, the progress of the race, may require the sacrifice of the lower life of the individual. Thus, we believe, passed away the beloved teacher, whose memory we this day, with a sad pleasure, recall. He entered the public educational field when the skies were dark, when the star of hope had scarcely risen, and was obscured by the cloud of an adverse public sentiment; when the Normal Schools were, even by their friends, considered only as an experiment, and one that, in the opinion of many experienced and able statesmen, would prove an entire failure. It was to a cause thus unpromising that he gave the whole energy of his soul. With an untiring industry, he devoted to his school his days and his nights. He engaged in hard and continuous study, not from motives of ambition, but from a deep sense of responsibility in respect to his school, and to its influence in advancing the cause of education. Nor did the necessity for such study arise from a defective education, but from a determination to adapt his instructions to the mental and moral wants of his pupils, and of those whom they, in their turn, were to educate. He was earnestly desirous that, so far as he could exert any influence upon the character of the public schools, that influence should be good, should tend to their elevation and improvement, and to the advancement of the cause of popular education; and this, not for his own sake, that he might acquire a reputation, and occupy an honorable position in the sight of men, but for the sake of the thousands whose hearts and minds are formed, in a great measure, in those conservators of New England virtue and intelligence,—the public schools.

Such were his aims, and the amount of labor which he thought necessary to their accomplishment, could be sustained only by a robust physical frame, and could be performed only by a well-balanced and active mind, guided by the highest principles, and acting under the influence of a determined will. For such a work we believe his mental and moral endowments to have been eminently fit; but, in his physical system, the necessary conditions were not supplied; the sword was too sharp for the scabbard, the energies of the spirit were too mighty for the clay, and the mortal coil was shuffled off. Shall we now say that his life was not sacrificed in the discharge of a high and holy duty; and, shall we doubt that Heaven approved the offering? Every heart instinctively answers, no. The exigency demanded the sacrifice. His example was needed to show us, his pupils, what manner of spirit we must be of; with what forgetfulness of self we must devote ourselves to the noble work whereon we have entered; how, with an eye single to the truth and the right, in spite of difficulties and discouragements, we must still labor on, in patience and in faith, believing that the harvest will surely come, whether we are among the reapers or not.

And, was the work of Mr. Tillinghast worth such a sacrifice? Did he, in his short life, achieve results at all commensurate with the time, the labor, and the life that were devoted to them? Let the appeal be made to every individual who ever enjoyed the benefit of his instructions. My brother, or my sister, whence came your higher views of life and its duties? Who opened to your mind a new world of intellectual life and moral perceptions, of which you had before never had a glimpse? Who stirred your soul to higher aspirations than you had ever felt, and roused it to nobler purposes than you had as yet formed? Who waked up within you a moral energy that, when you do not permit other influences to smother it, makes you ashamed of low views of duty, of feeble and ill-directed effort, and enkindles within you a glowing earnestness in your work? On this point, I am sure that language fails to express what is deeply and clearly felt in the heart of every pupil of his, who is with us to-day. We all feel that the *great* work which he did for us, that which we most highly value, is precisely that which can not be represented in speech. The higher teaching was not conveyed to us in words, and words can not impart it to others. If imparted at all, it must be by the sympathy of spirit with spirit. If therefore, we would do for our pupils what he did for us, we must teach as he taught, by possessing ourselves the qualities with which we would have their characters adorned, and by entering upon our work with a zeal and an earnestness that will bring the minds of our pupils into sympathy with our own; remembering that only from the fullness of our own hearts, and the perfection of our own characters, can we have the instruction to impart; and, only by a glowing and energizing enthusiasm can we make it efficient upon the character of others.

Such, friends and fellow-pupils, so far as my imperfect ability could sketch him, in so brief a time, was the man at whose feet it has been our high privilege as well as our delight, to sit in the attitude of reverent and attentive listeners. I have endeavored to be strictly just, to state not only the precise truth, but also to present that particular combination of truths that would give the justest and truest idea of the man. I have sought to weigh my words, to abstain from unwarranted statements, and excess of panegyric, and I am confident that my expressions fall below what you feel in your hearts. We all feel that we are cherishing the memory of no ordinary man, and that the language of an ordinary occasion is not adapted to our use to-day. It is not only our teacher that has fallen, but a standard-bearer in the great educational army. When we consider his exalted character, and the parental relation in which he stood to us all, with what sincerity, and what loneliness of heart, are we ready to exclaim: —

> "He was a man, take him for all in all.
> I shall not look upon his like again."

On such an occasion as this, it seems eminently fit that the feelings which we have been for years cherishing, without an opportunity for public utterance should be freely expressed. Let us then lay upon his grave the tribute of our respect and affection; and, as we return to the scenes of our accustomed labor, let us learn the lesson of this experience, let us open our minds to receive and to cherish the influence that goes forth from the life and character of our departed friend and teacher, and let us see that our own lives and the teachings we impart, shall not be altogether unworthy of that which we have received.

5.

ASSISTANT TEACHERS.

THOMAS RAINSFORD was appointed March, 1841, resigned May, 1841.
CHARLES GODDARD   "   "   Sept., 1841,   "   May, 1842.
JAMES RITCHIE,   "   "   August, 1843,   "   Nov., 1844.
JOSHUA PEARL,   "   "   Dec., 1844,   "   Feb., 1845.
CHRISTOPHER A. GREEN,   "   March, 1845,   "   March, 1847.
DANA P. COLBURN   "   "   March, 1847,   "   June, 1847.
JOSHUA KENDALL   "   "   March, 1847,   "   March, 1848.
    Graduated from this school in 1846. Taught three winters in country schools; five years in Normal Schools,— as Assistant in this school, and Principal of the Rhode Island State Normal School; — and twenty years in private schools. He is now Principal of a Private School for Boys, in Cambridge, Mass.

NANCY M. BLACKINTON, was appointed March, 1847, resigned Dec., 1847.
    Assistant teacher in Westford Academy two years after leaving this Normal School; Assistant in this school three terms; Assistant Principal of the Dudley Grammar School, Roxbury, one year; married Freeman A. Smith, a member of the fourteenth class in this school; died at Malden, in 1861.

DANA P. COLBURN was appointed March, 1848, resigned July, 1850.
    Mr. Colburn was born in West Dedham, September 29, 1823; graduated from this school in 1844; taught in common schools three years, and in Normal Schools and State Teacher's Institutes twelve years. He was Assistant in this school three years; during the next four years he was an Assistant of Prof. Wm. Russell in his Normal School at Merrimac, N. H., and in his New England Normal Institute at Lancaster, Mass.; and was a teacher in the Providence Normal School. May 29, 1854, he was appointed Principal of the State Normal School of Rhode Island, and continued to have charge of this school till his death, on the 15th of December, 1859. He was the author of a series of arithmetics —" The Child's Book of Arithmetic," " Intellectual Arithmetic," "The Common School Arithmetic," " Arithmetic and Its Applications."

RICHARD EDWARDS was appointed April, 1848, resigned Jan., 1853.
    Mr. Edwards was born near Aberystwith, Cardigan shire, Wales, December 23, 1822. He came with his parents to Palmyra, Ohio, in 1833; taught his first school at Ravenna, Ohio, in the winter of 1843-4; taught at Hingham, Mass., in the winter of 1844-5; graduated from Bridgewater State Normal School in July, 1846; taught in Hingham and Waltham; graduated from Rensselaer Polytechnic Institute, at Troy, N. Y., in 1848; was assistant in this Normal School five years; Master of the Bowditch English High School for Boys, in Salem, from January to November, 1853; Agent of the Mass. Board of Education one year; Principal of the State Normal School at Salem from September, 1854, to October, 1857; Principal of the City Normal School of St. Louis, from October, 1857, to June, 1862; President of the State Normal University, at Normal, Illinois, from June, 1862, to July, 1875. Taught twenty-six years in Normal Schools, and two years in other schools. Author of a series of School Readers. He is now Rev. Richard Edwards, LL. D., Pastor of a Congregational Church in Princeton, Illinois.

ALBERT G. BOYDEN was appointed August, 1850, resigned October, 1853.

EDWIN C. HEWETT was appointed January, 1853, resigned December, 1856.

ALUMNI RECORD.

Class 1. September 9, 1840.

GUSTAVUS D. BATES, Plymouth. T. fifteen years. Principal of Grammar School, Plymouth.
CYRUS BENSON, Jr.,* Bridgewater. 2. Taught twelve years. Died August 8, 1854.
MERTOUN C. BRYANT,* Bridgewater. Taught two years. Supt. Gas Works, Lowell. Died November 19, 1862.
ALBERT CONANT, Bridgewater. Taught five years. Artist, 151 W. Brookline St., Boston.
ALDEN HARLOW, Marshfield. Taught three years. Carpenter. Needham.
JOHN MOOREHEAD, Jr.,* Marshfield. Taught seven years. Died January, 1848.
SAMUEL E. RAYMOND, Bridgewater. Did not teach. Clerk of Gas Co., Lowell.

    Total of teaching for seven, forty-four years. Average, six years.

ELIZABETH BATES, Bridgewater. Did not teach. Mrs. Rev. T. P. Doggett, Quincy.
NANCY C. BESSEY, Duxbury. 2. T. one year. Mrs. J. B. Page, 102 Park Place, New York.
LUCY M. CONANT, Bridgewater. Taught one year. Mrs. Geo. F. Leonard, Bridgewater.
CATHERINE CROOKER,* Bridgewater. Taught twenty-five years. Died Nov. 27, 1873.
APHIA FULLER,* Scituate. 2. Mrs. Warren Sawyer, Boston. Died in 1868.
OLIVE C. GAY,* Bridgewater. Did not teach. Died October 9, 1842.
DESIRE S. HARLOW,* Plymouth. Taught two months. Died June, 1848, at Boston, Institution for the Blind.
SARAH D. HOLMES, Kingston. T. twenty-six years. Mrs. Dr. H. J. Paine, Petaluma, Cal.
JULIA H. H. HOOPER, Bridgewater. Taught eight years. Address, N. Middleborough.
HELEN JAMES, Scituate. Taught seven years. Mrs. Judge Wm. E. Parmenter, Arlington.
JULIA P. KENDALL,* Plymouth. Did not teach. Died May 31, 1873.
FANNY LEONARD, Bridgewater. Taught ten years. Mrs. Thos. Kent, Clifton, Pa.
ABIGAIL MORTON, Plymouth. Taught ten years. Author. Mrs. M. A. Diaz, 117 Myrtle Street, Boston.
SOPHIA L. RAYMOND, Bridgewater. Taught three terms. Mrs. O. Bullard, 198 West Brookline Street, Boston.
CAROLINE E. ROBINSON,* Bridgewater. Died December 3, 1843.
MARIANNA STEPHENS, Plymouth. Taught twenty-seven years. Four in Plymouth, twenty-three in Primary school, Boston. Mrs. Chas. B. Rice, 117 Myrtle St., Boston.
CELINDA TAYLOR, W. Bridgewater. Taught twenty-seven years. Three in Bridgewater, twenty-four in Grammar school, Boston. Mrs. Chas. Seaver, W. Bridgewater.
CAROLINE TILDEN,* Scituate. Taught six years. One year in High School, five years in State Normal School at Lexington. Died May 24, 1848.
JANE A. WASHBURN,* Bridgewater. 2. Taught three terms. Mrs. Dr. S. Worcester. Died December, 1854.
HARRIET A. WHITE, Plymouth. Taught two terms. Mrs. Buell, Waukegan, Ill.

    Total of teaching for nineteen, 151 years. Average, eight years.

Class 2. December 9, 1840.

NATHANIEL T. CUSHMAN, Bridgewater. Taught five years. Farmer. Scotland, Mass.
ALSON A. GILMORE, Easton. Taught three years. Shoe Manufacturer. N. Easton.
JOSEPH HAGAR, Waltham. Taught two years. Physician. E. Marshfield.
CYRUS LEONARD, West Bridgewater. Taught nine years. Farmer. West Bridgewater.
HENRY F. LATHROP, Easton. Did not teach. Farmer. Pittsford, Vt.

BRIDGEWATER STATE NORMAL SCHOOL.

HERBERT SCARBOROUGH, Brooklyn, Conn. 2. Has been an invalid since 1841.
JOHN C. SWEEZY, River Head, L. I. 1. Taught two years. River Head, L. I.
 Total of teaching for seven, twenty-one years. Average, three years.
SUSAN M. BLOOD,* Bridgewater. Taught one term. Mrs. Robert Perkins. Died April 18, 1863.
ANNE R. JAMES, Scituate. Taught thirty-four years,—thirty-two years in Boston. Now teaching Primary School, Poplar St., Boston.
AMY A. PACKARD,* Dartmouth. Taught four terms. Mrs. Reuben Howland. Died Dec. 9, 1852.
RUBY H. POTTER,* Dartmouth. Taught five and one-half years,—three and one-half in Model School, Bridgewater. Mrs. Nicholas Tillinghast. Died April 10, 1860
ELIZABETH SAMPSON,* Plymouth. Taught one term. Mrs. John Kneeland, Boston. Died Dec. 19, 1856.
MRS. HANNAH SPAULDING, Middleboro. 1. Not heard from.
CATHARINE H. WINSLOW,* Dartmouth. 1. Died August 18, 1843.
 Total of teaching for five, forty-one years. Average, eight years.

CLASS 3. MARCH 10, 1841.

GEORGE W. BEAL, Scituate. Taught twenty-six years,—ten in Grammar and High Schools, sixteen in Normal Schools. Principal Normal School, Jersey City, N. J.
THOMPSON B. COLWELL,* W. Bridgewater. 1. Taught sixteen years. Died in Washington, D. C., April 4, 1873.
SETH DEAN, Middleborough. Taught five years. Farmer. Middleborough.
JOSHUA M. EDDY, Middleborough. T. one and one-half years. Farmer. E. Middleborough.
EDWARD H. HARLOW, Duxbury. Not heard from.
JONATHAN E. HARLOW, Middleborough. 2. Taught one and one-half years. Physician. Hingham.
JOHN KNEELAND, Plymouth. Taught thirty years. Master of Grammar Schools in Dorchester and Roxbury. Now Agent Mass. Board of Education. Boston Highlands.
PEREZ TURNER, Scituate. Not heard from.
JOSEPH UNDERWOOD, JR., Charlestown. Taught three years. Physician. Quincy.
 Total of teaching for seven, fifty-three years. Average, seven and one-half years.
CAROLINE A. ASHLEY,* Dartmouth. Taught eight years. Died in 1852.
DIEDAMIA CHACE,* Fall River. Taught six years. Died September 30, 1847.
ISABELLA N. HARTWELL, W. Bridgewater. T. one term. Mrs. David Battles, Brockton.
BETHIA A. HOLMES, Bridgewater. Taught three terms. Address, Bridgewater.
HANNAH F. HOWLAND, Dartmouth. Not heard from. Mrs. — Leach, Long Plain.
HANNAH H. LEACH, W. Bridgewater. 1. T. fifteen years. Mrs. Charles Hartwell, Brockton.
ELIZABETH W. LINCOLN, Wareham. 2. Not heard from.
CATHARINE SCARBOROUGH, Brooklyn, Conn. Taught four years. Mrs. Albert Conant, Boston.
MARTHA A. WITHERELL, Taunton. 1. Not heard from.
 Total of teaching for six, thirty-four years. Average, six years.

CLASS 4. JUNE 9, 1841.

LUCIUS GURNEY, North Bridgewater. Taught two years. Shoe Business, Brockton.
JAMES M. UNDERWOOD,* Charlestown. Physician. Died E. Abington, Jan. 31, 1870.
 Total of teaching for one, two years.
MARY E. BATTELLE,* Needham. Died in Needham, December 14, 1844.
ALICE S. BRADFORD, Plymouth. 2. Not heard from.
HANNAH E. BROOKS, Boston. Did not teach. Mrs. Benj. B. Converse, Dorchester, Boston.
HARRIET DEAN, Raynham. Taught eight years. Mrs. John W. Sterling, Madison, Wis.

LAVINIA W. HARLOW, Middleborough. T. thirteen years. Address, Middleborough.
SARAH A. HOOPER, Bridgewater. T. two years. Mrs. Wales S. Andrews, Bridgewater.
MARIA R. MANN, Wrentham. 2. Taught thirty years. 1505 Race St., Philadelphia, Pa.
LYDIA WASHBURN,* E. Bridgewater. No information.
MARY K. WILLIAMS, Taunton. Taught fourteen years. Address, Raynham.
 Total of teaching for eight, sixty seven years. Average, eight and one-half years.

CLASS 5. SEPTEMBER 8, 1841.

OLIVER FRENCH,* Salisbury. 2. No information.
SILAS S. JOHNSON,* Canton. 1. Died May 11, 1843.
THOMAS S. LATHROP, W. Bridgewater. T. two years. Clergyman. N. Salem, N. Y.
 Total of teaching for one, two years.
ELIZA A. ALLEN, Fall River. Taught two years. Mrs. Albert Bolles, 12 Hathaway St., Fall River.
MELINDA A. CAREY, N. Bridgewater. 2. T. four months. Mrs. Benj. C. Frobisher, Brockton.
JANE G. DEANE, Mansfield. 2. Taught nine years. Mrs. Henry H. Crane, Raynham.
CHARLOTTE M. LEONARD, Bridgewater. Taught five terms. Mrs. Isaac H. Snell, Bridgewater.
SOPHIA LORING,* Pembroke. 1. T. three terms. Mrs. John Shepherd. Died Feb. 18, 1846.
BETSEY TAYLOR, Pembroke. 1. Taught six years. Mrs. Issacher F. Everson, Rockland.
MATILDA TURNER,* Scituate. Taught six years. Mrs. Stephen Curtis. Died Oct. 7, 1847.
 Total of teaching for seven, twenty-seven years. Average, four years.

CLASS 6. DECEMBER 8, 1841.

HENRY W. ALLEN, Pembroke. 1. Not heard from.
CYRUS LATHROP, Easton. Taught two years. Dealer in Iron and Steel, 16 Hamilton St. Boston.
NATHAN F. C. PRATT, Middleboro'. Taught two years. Farmer. N. Middleboro'.
 Total of teaching for two, four years. Average, two years.
HANNAH P. BROWNELL, Westport. 1. Not heard from.
ANNA DELANO, Duxbury. Taught eleven years. Mrs. Thos. J. Elliott, 8 Brighton St., Charlestown.
HARRIET FULLER,* W. Medway. 2. Taught one year. Mrs. A. B. White, Chicopee Falls. Died May, 1874.
VESTA HOLBROOK,* N. Bridgewater. Taught twenty years in country schools.
LUCY T. LEONARD, Randolph. 2. Not heard from.
RUTH P. LINCOLN,* Warren. 1. Taught three terms. Mrs. Wm. G. Tarbell, Brimfield. Died, 1855.
MARIAN A. MANN, W. Medway. 2. T. seventeen years. Mrs. Elihu White, W. Medway.
BETSEY J. SAMPSON, Pembroke. T. six years. Mrs. Richard Edwards, Princeton, Ill.
ANN B. SHOCKLEY, Middleboro'. 2. Taught five years. Mrs. Rev. J. H. Bonham, 22 Bible House, New York.
MARY F. SHOCKLEY, Middleboro'. Taught twenty-four years. Clerk in U. S. Treasury. 1104 L Street, Washington, D. C.
 Total of teaching for eight, eighty-five years. Average, eight and one-half years.

CLASS 7. MARCH 9, 1842.

JOEL S. DRAKE, Easton. 2. Taught one year. Merchant. Easton.
NAHUM S. C. PERKINS, Braintree. 1. Not heard from.
LEWIS L. WHITNEY, Boston. Taught six years. Address, Woburn.
 Total of teaching for two, seven years. Average, three and one half years.
MARY L. BATES,* Bridgewater. Mrs. Chas. Belcher. Died about 1850.

OLIVE S. CARVER,* Bridgewater. Did not teach. Mrs. Wm. H. Ladd. Died, Jan., 1850.
HANNAH R. CROOKER,* Bridgewater. Taught one Term. Died July 25, 1844.
LOIS DEAN, Middleboro'. 1. Taught twenty-one years in Grammar Schools. Middleboro'.
MARY EMERSON, West Dedham. 2. Taught one year. Address, West Dedham.
HANNAH G. HOLMES, Plymouth. 1. Taught twenty-eight years in Plymouth. Address, Plymouth.
SOPHIA SHEPHERD, Roxbury. 2. Not heard from.
ORRA P. WINSLOW, Bridgewater. Taught three years. Mrs. Minot C. Shaw, Elmwood.

Total of teaching for six, fifty-three years. Average, nine years.

Class 8. July 20, 1842.

ISAAC F. ALDEN, Bridgewater. Did not teach. Bridgewater.
EDWARD W. COBB, Abington. 1. T. two and one-half years. Merchant. Savannah, Ga.
THOMAS A. BURDEN, Wrentham. 1. Not heard from.
CHAUNCY CONANT, N. Bridgewater. 2. Taught two years. Horticulture. Barnstable.
ALBERT ELLIS, Walpole. 1. T. one year. Book Trader. 1317 Chestnut St., Philadelphia.
BENJAMIN B. FULLER,* Dover. 2. Died January 5, 1844.
BENJAMIN W. HARRIS, E. Bridgewater. 1. Member of Congress. E. Bridgewater.
EDWARD HOBART, E. Bridgewater. 1. Not heard from.
CALVIN D. KINGMAN, Middleboro'. 2. T. six years. Shoe Manufacturer. Middleboro'.
HENRY L. PIERCE, Stoughton. Member of Congress. Boston.
CALEB C. THOMAS, Marshfield. Taught five years. Farmer. Walpole.
NATHANIEL WALES, N. Bridgewater. 1. Taught two years. Treasurer, Stoughton Boot and Shoe Co.
CYRENIUS WHITE,* Middleboro'. 1. No information.
ASA T. WHITMAN, E. Bridgewater. 1. No information.
DAVID G. WILLIAMS,* Easton. Did not teach. Died December 10, 1845.

Total of teaching for ten, eighteen and one-half years. Average, two years.

SARAH P. BASSETT,* Middleboro'. Taught five years. Mrs. Calvin D. Kingman. Died Jan. 21, 1874.
SUSAN B. BRIGHAM, Boston. 2. Did not teach. Mrs. Henry Keith, Marlboro'.
FRANCES T. HOLLAND, Boston. T. eight years. Mrs. Franklin Blanchard, Palmer.
MARY W. ELLIS, Middleboro. 2. Not heard from.
MARY H. RUST, E. Bridgewater. Taught seven years. Address, E. Bridgewater.
HELEN L. SHAW, Middleboro. 2. Not heard from.
SUSAN G. WALDRON,* Bridgewater. T. two years. Mrs. Hiram Wentworth, Bridgewater. Died Jan., 1875.
JANE E. WHITE,*.Fairhaven. T. two years. Mrs. Oscar Daggett, lost at sea, Aug. 1856·
MARGARET P. WHITE,* Fairhaven. 1. Taught two years. Died May 25, 1857.

Total of teaching for seven, twenty-six years. Average, four years.

Class 9. November 30, 1842.

HENRY DAILEY,* Easton. 2. Did not teach. Died November, 1862.
BETHUEL F. DRAKE, Easton. Did not teach. Salem, Oregon.
FRANCIS B. GARDNER, Swansey. 2. Not heard from.
CALVIN GAY. Bridgewater. Taught one year. Sewing Machine Agent. Chicago, Ill.
JOSEPH W. KINGMAN,* West Bridgewater. 2. Taught three years. Died April 28, 1851.
JAMES E. LEACH,* Bridgewater. T. one year in Providence High School. Died, 1848.
FRANCIS L. B. MAYHEW, Rochester. 2. Not heard from.
EDWARD I. SANFORD, Raynham. 1. Taught two years. Physician. Attleborough.
ALPHEUS D. THAYER,* Bellingham. 2. Taught seven years. Died December, 1850.

Total of teaching for seven, fourteen years. Average, two years.

MR. TILLINGHAST'S ADMINISTRATION. 63

FRANCES M. CHAMBERLIN, Scituate. 1. T. two years. Mrs. Wm. C. Manson, Scituate.
RACHEL S. CLAPP, Scituate. 1. Mrs. James Brewster, Hanson. Not heard from.
JULIA COLLOMORE,* Pembroke. 1. Taught four years. Mrs. J. W. T. Stodder. Died June 20, 1861.
JULIA M. HIXON, Medway. 2. T. three years. Mrs. Nathan S. Chapin, Brooklyn, N. Y.
MARY S. HOWARD, Bridgewater. 2. Mrs. H. C. Hall, Bridgewater. Did not teach.
ELIZA A. HUBBARD, Pawtucket. 1. T. two years. Mrs. Appleton Park, Pawtucket, R. I.
MARY LEONARD, Bridgewater. Taught twenty-five years. Clifton, Del. Co., Penn.
HARRIET N. SHOREY Seekonk. 2. Not heard from.

Total of teaching for seven, thirty-six years. Average, five years.

CLASS 10. MARCH 30, 1843.

ADONIRAM ALDEN,* E. Stoughton. Taught fifteen years in Boston. Died Aug. 22, 1859.
ELBRIDGE G. AMES, N. Bridgewater. Taught thirty years. Brockton.
ELBRIDGE CLAPP Sharon. Taught four years. Merchant. Quincy.
EBENEZER C. CLARK, Rochester. 2. Not heard from.
DANA P. COLBURN,* West Dedham. Taught fifteen years,—twelve in Normal Schools. Died Dec., 1859.
T. OSGOOD CORNISH, Plymouth. 1. Taught two years. Physician. So. Boston.
CHARLES L. HOOPER,* Bridgewater. 2. Taught one year. Died March 14, 1854.
CHARLES C. KENT,* Marshfield. 2. Taught seven years. Died 1866.
DEAN J. LOCKE, Langdon, N. H. Taught four years. Druggist. Lockford, Cal.
OTIS M. OLIVER,* Fairhaven. 2. Physician. Died in New Orleans.
SOLON PALMER, Alstead, N. H. 2. Not heard from.
HIRAM A. PRATT, Easton. Taught six years. Insurance Agent. N. Raynham.
CHARLES E. SAMPSON,* Dedham. 2. No information.
ALLEN TALBOT, Dighton. 2. Taught twenty years. Carpenter. N. Dighton.
GEORGE A. WALTON, S. Reading. Taught twenty-four years,—four in country schools, one in Model School at W. Newton, one in High School, sixteen in Grammar Schools. Author of a Series of Arithmetics. Teacher in State Institutes ten years. Now Agent of Mass. Board of Education. Westfield.

Total of teaching for thirteen, one hundred and twenty-eight years. Average, ten years.

MARIA BOWERS,* Hingham. Taught one year. Died August 19, 1850.
MERIEL FEARING, Hingham. Never taught. Mrs. Joseph H. French, Hingham.
ELVIRA P. STILES,* Boston. No information.

Total of teaching for two, one year. Average, one-half year.

CLASS 11. AUGUST 2, 1843.

WILLIAM P. AIKEN, Fairhaven. 1. Taught three years. Clergyman. Vergennes, Vt.
WILLIAM D. ALLEN, Worcester. 1. Not heard from.
FREDERIC A. BOOMER,* Fall River. 1. Taught seven years. Lawyer. Died July 22, 1871.
BENJAMIN BURT, JR., Freetown. Taught five years. Trader. Amador City, Cal.
JONATHAN CASS, Mendon. 1. Taught six years. Physician and Surgeon to the N. Y. Dispensary. 44 W. 26th St., New York City; country residence, Great Barrington, Mass.
HORACE CHAPIN, Greenfield. 1. Taught twenty-three years. Physician. W. Somerville.
RICHARD M. DEVINS, Charlestown. Not heard from.
GEORGE H. DICKERMAN, Stoughton. 2. T. five years. Address, New Hampton, N. H.
LYSANDER DICKERMAN, N. Bridgewater. 2. Taught three years. Clergyman.
GEORGE B. FULLER, Plympton. 1. Taught four months. Grocer. Plympton.
CHARLES W. HARRIS, Rehoboth. 1. Not heard from.
WILLIAM P. HAYWARD, W. Bridgewater. Taught twenty-seven years. Prin. Grammar School, Salem.
HENRY HEWINS, Sharon. 2. Not heard from.
AHIRA HOLMES, Plymouth. 1. Taught twenty years. Address, San Francisco, Cal.

BRIDGEWATER STATE NORMAL SCHOOL.

CALEB H. HOWARD,* W. Bridgewater. 2. Taught two terms. Died Sept. 11, 1850.
LEWIS LEONARD, Bridgewater. 2. Taught one term. Farmer. No. Middleboro.
NAHUM LEONARD, JR., W. Bridgewater. 1. Taught five years. Supt. State Workhouse, Bridgewater.
GEORGE T. LITTLEFIELD, Randolph. 2. Taught thirty-four years. Master, Prescott Grammar School, Charlestown.
NATHANIEL LOVERING, Boston. Not heard from.
FREDERIC PERKINS, N. Bridgewater. 1. Not heard from.
WILLIAM ROGERS, Bernardstown. 1. Not heard from.
JAMES V. SMILEY, Haverhill. 1. Taught ten years. Bookseller and Stationer. Haverhill.
BENJAMIN H. STROBRIDGE, Middleboro'. Taught six years. Farmer. Myricksville.
DEPENDENCE S. WATERMAN, Roxbury. 1. T. one year. Cashier, Boylston Bank, Boston.
VIRGIL H. WILLIAMS, Easton. 2. Taught four years. Manufacturer of Straw Goods. Foxborough.
JOHN WOOD, Mendon. 1. Not heard from.

Total of teaching for nineteen, one hundred and sixty years. Average, eight years.

JOANN A. BESSEY,* Marshfield. 1. T. five years. Mrs. Moses Clement. Died Sept., 1861.
CAROLINE L. EDSON, W. Bridgewater. T. four years. Mrs. Harvey Kimball, Bridgewater.
ABIGAIL KEITH, E. Bridgewater. 1. T. one term. Mrs. Francis Worcester, Sullivan, Me.
ANNA SCOTT, Portland, Me. Did not teach. Mrs. Abner Lowell, Portland, Me.
CASSANDRA W. SHAW, Middleboro'. 1. Taught five years. Address, N. Middleboro'.
SARAH SNOW, Rochester. 1. Not heard from.
ELIZABETH TAYLOR, W. Bridgewater. 2. Taught one term. Mrs. Frank E. Howard, W. Bridgewater.

Total of teaching for six, fifteen years. Average, two and one-half years.

CLASS 12. DECEMBER 6, 1843.

NATHAN ATHERTON,* Stoughton. 1. Taught two terms. Died Sept. 11, 1848.
ENOS T. DICKERMAN,* Stoughton. 2. Taught three years. Died April 13, 1849.
JOHN A. GOODWIN, Boston. Taught five years in Grammar and High Schools, Supt. of Schools in Lawrence one year, Speaker of Mass. House of Representatives in 1860 and 1861, on School Committee of Lowell twelve years. Address, Lowell.
BERIAH H. LAWTON, Exeter, R. I. 1. Taught two years. Legislator eight years. Farmer. Wickford, R. I.
EDWARD T. MAY, Pomfret, Conn. 2. Not heard from.
PHINEAS G. PARMENTER, Haverhill. 2. Taught twenty-two years. Grammar Schools. In business, Clinton, Iowa.
ALEXANDER H. WILLIAMS, Taunton. 1. Did not teach. Brick Manufacturer. Taunton.
GEORGE B. WILLIAMS, Taunton. 1. Not heard from.

Total of teaching for seven, thirty-three years. Average, five years.

ABBIE M. ATWOOD, Middleboro'. 1. Taught six years. Mrs A. M. Edwards, Middleboro'.
JULIA F. BARTLETT, W. Bridgewater. 1. T. twelve years. Mrs. H. W. Leach, Cochesett.
CAROLINE BASSETT, Bridgewater. 1. T. one year. Mrs. Mertoun Bryant, Bridgewater.
LUCY E. BOYNTON, Scituate. 1. T. four years. Mrs. L. E. B. Cromack, Hammonton, N. J.
LUCRETIA H. BRYANT,* Bridgewater. 1. Taught three terms. Mrs. Samuel Raymond. Died June 15, 1871.
LOUISA C. CAPEN, Stoughton. Taught eleven years. Mrs. Calvin Thayer, S. Braintree.
HANNAH H. CUSHING,* Hingham. Taught one term. Mrs. Andrew Ellison. Died March 28, 1848.
ELIZA A. HARDING, Wrentham. Taught twenty years. Address, Allston.
IRENE F. HARDING, Wrentham. Taught seven years. Mrs. Rev. George W. Bosworth, Haverhill.
MARIA HARDING, Wrentham. Taught four years. Mrs. Simeon Taylor, Allston.
CATHARINE H. HOBART, Hingham. 1. Taught twenty-two years. Intermediate School. Hingham.

CATHARINE R. T. LINCOLN, Hingham. 1. Taught eight years. Address, Hingham.
SARAH G. LINCOLN,* Hingham. 1. Taught five years. Died October 24, 1854.
SARAH O. NICHOLS. Plymouth. 1. Taught nine years. Mrs. Rev. Frederick Wiley, Stonington, Illinois.
M. CATHARINE PRATT, W. Bridgewater. 1. Taught twenty-nine years. Address, West Bridgewater.
ELIZA P. WEBB, Weymouth. Not heard from.
AVERICK S. WHITE, Weymouth. Taught eleven years. Address, Weymouth.

Total of teaching for sixteen, one hundred and fifty years. Average, nine and one-half years.

Class 13. March 27, 1844.

JOSEPH CASE, Swansea. 1. Taught four terms. Hotel Proprietor. Swansea.
DAVID H. DANIELS, Medway. Taught thirty years. Prin. Grammar School, Brookline.
ABIATHAR DEAN, Berkley. Taught three terms. Farmer. Dighton.
GEORGE W. DEAN, Fal. River. Taught three terms. Engineer, U. S. Coast Survey. Fall River.
HENRY L. EATON, So. Reading. Taught one and one-half years. Grocer. Swampscott.
E. GRANVILLE FRENCH, Peterboro', N. H. Taught eleven years. Trader. Epwarth, Dubuque County, Iowa.
WILLIAM R. GORDON, New Hampton, N. H. Taught twenty-four years in Grammar Schools. Insurance Agent, Beverly.
CHARLES N. HALL, Mansfield. 1. Taught three years. Farmer. Mansfield.
PHILLIP C. KING,* Raynham. 1. Taught two years. Died March 11, 1852.
SAMUEL MILLER, Jr., Middleboro'. Not heard from.
JOHN O. SIMONS,* Boston. No information.
DANIEL M. SMITH, Pawtucket. Taught four and one-half years. Produce Dealer. Pawtucket, R. I.
DANIEL G. WALTON, So. Reading. T. one term. County Commissioner. Wakefield.

Total of teaching for eleven, seventy-nine years. Average, seven years.

NANCY M. BLACKINTON,* Wrentham. Taught five years. Mrs. Freeman A. Smith. Died in Malden, 1861.
ELIZABETH BURT, Freetown. T. three years. Mrs. David Hall. Newton Highlands.
CATHARINE J. FULLER,* Wrentham. Mrs. Alonzo Follett. Died, Brooklyn, N. Y., December 1, 1862.
LYDIA PICKETT, Freetown. Taught nine years. Mrs. I. G. Wickersham, Petaluma, Sonoma County, California.
MARY TAPPAN, Boston. T. three years. Mrs. Robert L. Merriam, 99 Court St., Boston.
JOANNA STRANGE, Freetown. Not heard from.
CHARITY WINSLOW, Freetown. Not heard from.

Total of teaching for five, twenty years. Average, four years.

Class 14. July 31, 1844.

JOHN F. ALDEN, Middleboro'. 1. Not heard from.
SILAS D. BRIGGS, Dighton. 1. Not heard from.
JOHN D. EASTLAND, Marblehead. 1. Did not teach. Shoe Business. Marblehead.
EDWIN FRENCH, Berkley. No information.
JAMES H. GAULT,* Boston. No information. Deceased.
DANIEL G. OTIS,* So. Scituate. Physician, Providence, R. I. Deceased.
ALFRED W. PAUL, Dighton. 1. Taught twelve years. Cultivator of small fruits. Dighton.
JAMES PIERCE, Taunton. 1. Not heard from. Address, Myricksville.
FREEMAN A. SMITH, Northampton. Taught three years. Treasurer, American Baptist Missionary Union, Tremont Temple, Boston.
GEORGE D. WILLIAMS, Freetown. Taught fourteen years. Farmer. Freetown.

Total of teaching for five, twenty-nine years. Average, six years.

OLIVE K. BASSETT,* Middleboro'. Mrs. Charles Stevens. Died at Lakeville, 1855.
HARRIET BLACKINTON,* Wrentham. Mrs. Wallace Goodwin. Died in Attleboro'.
CHARLOTTE R. BROWN, W. Bridgewater. 2. T. twelve years. Mrs. Dana Snow, Brockton.
HARRIET S. COLBY, Middleboro'. Not heard from.
MARY F. DWIGHT, Hallowell, Maine. 1. No information.
P. JANE HART, Taunton. 1. No information.
ELMINA HOWARD, W. Bridgewater. Taught nine years. Mrs. E. W. Cobb, Abington.
MARY B. NOURSE, Hallowell, Me. 1. No information.
DORDANIA K. PRATT, Middleboro'. T. four years. Mrs. Thos. J. Pratt, N. Middleboro.
ANNA H. TOWER, Hingham. Taught five years. Dry Goods Dealer. Weymouth.

Total of teaching for four, thirty years. Average, seven and one-half years.

Class 15. December 4, 1844.

VALENTINE COPELAND, Bridgewater. Taught one term. Farmer. Bridgewater.
WALTER H. NEWELL, Dorchester. Taught twenty years. Address,
NATHANIEL T. PERKINS,* Bridgewater. No information. Deceased.
HENRY WILLEY, Geneseo, N. Y. Not heard from.

Total of teaching for two, twenty years. Average, ten years.

EMILY DAMON, Hanson. Not heard from.
MARTHA M. FISHER, Sudbury. Taught three and one-half years. Mrs. John A. Goodwin, Lowell.
CAROLINE R. GALE, Scituate. Taught eight years. Mrs. Alfred James, Weymouth.
MARY K. HAYWARD,* W. Bridgewater. Taught five years. Mrs. Frank E. Howard. Died June 1, 1857.
HANNAH HOWES, Dennis. Taught twelve years. Mrs. Joseph Sylvan, Dennis.
ARIADNA J. HUNT, Duxbury. 1. Mrs. A. J. Baker, W. Bridgewater.
ELIZABETH KENNEDY, Fall River. 1. Not heard from.
AMY LEONARD, Raynham. Taught two years. Address, Taunton.
CELIA A. LITTLEFIELD, Stoughton. Taught twenty years. Address, East Stoughton.
MARIA W. PARKER, Plympton. T. eighteen years. Mrs. Prof. C. S. Richards, Washington, D. C.
MARY SMITH, Orleans. 1. Taught four years. Mrs. Peleg Howes, E. Somerville.
NANCY SMITH, Orleans. 1. Did not teach. Mrs. A. E. Peck, Worcester.
SARAH STONE, W. Bridgewater. 1. Not heard from.
ELIZABETH WADSWORTH, Duxbury. Taught six years. Mrs. Henry B. Maglathlin, Plympton Station.
CORDANA WASHBURN, Taunton. 1. Taught one year. Address, E. Taunton.

Total of teaching for eleven, eighty years. Average, seven years.

Class 16. March 26, 1845.

GEORGE M. BAKER, Marshfield. Taught five years. Insurance Agent. Marshfield.
F. W. BARTLETT, Kingston. 1. Not heard from.
WILLIAM DANIELS, Medway. Not heard from.
HENRY A. JONES,* Weston. No information. Deceased.
JOSHUA KENDALL, Waltham. Taught twenty-nine years. Principal of Private School for Boys, Cambridge, Mass.
WILLIAM H. LADD, Lynn. Taught thirty years. In German Church School, Baltimore, two years. Sub-Master in Harvard Grammar School, Charlestown, two years. Principal of Shepard Grammar School, Cambridge, five and one-half years. Assistant in Chauncy Hall School, Boston, four years. One of the Principals of Chauncy Hall School, Boston, for the last sixteen years.
PHILANDER D. LEONARD, Bridgewater. Taught fifteen years, in Grammar Schools. Teacher. Bridgewater.

AMOS NOURSE,* Bolton. Taught two years. Photographer. Died in Central America.
RUFUS SAWYER, Bolton. Taught twenty-seven years. Prin. Grammar School, Medford.
  Total of teaching for six, one hundred and eight years. Average, eighteen years.
ELMIRA M. JOSSELYN, Hanover. Taught three years. Mrs. J. B. Barstow, Wollaston.
JOANNA A. HATCH, Marshfield. Mrs. Daniel D. Baker, Brooklyn, N. Y.
LIZZIE HOOPER, Dorchester. Taught seventeen years. Address, Bridgewater.
ELLEN POPE, Bridgewater. Taught four years. Mrs. Aaron Perkins, Bridgewater.
JULIA L. WARE, Walpole. 1. Taught two years. Mrs. S. C. Battles, Walpole.
ELIZA W. WESTON, Marshfield. Mrs. Warren Kent, Marshfield.
HELEN M. WESTON, Marshfield. Not heard from.
  Total of teaching for four, twenty-six years. Average, six and one-half years.

Class 17, July 30, 1845.

EDWARD A. H. ALLEN, Northborough. T. twenty-nine years. In Polytechnic Instiute, Troy, N. Y., five years. German School, two years. Academy, fifteen years. Private Schools, seven years. Now Principal of "Sawin Academy," Sherborn.
NATHANIEL T. ALLEN, Medfield. Taught twenty-nine years. In Ungraded Schools, three years. Principal of the Model School connected with the State Normal School at West Newton, six years. Principal in English and Classical School at West Newton for the last twenty years.
GEORGE L. ANDREWS, Bridgewater. Taught six years. Brigadier-General U. S. Army. Now Professor of French Language, U. S. Military Academy, West Point, N. Y.
H. CARLTON CHEEVER, Wrentham. Taught two terms. Editor and Publisher. Springvale, Maine.
WILLIAM CLELAND, Weston. Taught six months. Mercantile business. Natick.
MARTIN G. CUSHING, Boston. Lawyer. Not heard from.
QUINCY E. DICKERMAN, Stoughton. Taught twenty-six years. Sub-Master, Mayhew School, Boston.
RICHARD EDWARDS, Jr., Hingham. Taught twenty-eight years. Normal Schools at Bridgewater, Salem, St. Louis, Normal, Ill. Clergyman. Princeton, Illinois.
FREDERIC JENNEY, Fairhaven. Taught twenty-five years. Address, Fairhaven.
EDWARD H. LINCOLN, Raynham. Taught seventeen years. Variety Store. Raynham.
JOSEPH D. LITTLEFIELD, Randolph. 1. Taught five years. Physician. Titusville, Pa.
SETH LITTLEFIELD,* Randolph. 1. Taught five years. Died, July 19, 1849.
STEPHEN MORSE, Jr., Marlboro', Taught fourteen years, Grammar Schools. Broker, Boston. Residence, Quincy.
CYRUS MORTON, Jr.,* Halifax. Taught three years. Died in Randolph, Feb. 20. 1870.
WELLINGTON NEWELL, Bethel, Maine. Taught six months. Congregational Clergyman, East Charlemont.
JOSHUA G. NICKERSON, Chatham. Taught seven years. Oil manufacturer. 436 Atlantic Avenue, Boston.
HIRAM A. OAKMAN, Marshfield. Taught six years. Custom House, Boston.
NATHAN W. SHAW, Raynham. Taught fourteen years. Farmer and Life Ins. Agent, Raynham.
JAMES STRATTON, Bolton. T. twenty years. In Real Estate Business. Oakland, Cal.
SAMUEL S. WILSON, Charlestown. T. sixteen years. Counsellor at Law. Charlestown.
  Total of teaching for nineteen, 251 years. Average, thirteen years.
MARIETT ALDEN, Bridgewater. Mrs. Jesse H. Wiley, Canton Street, Boston.
PHILENA BURT,* Berkley. No information.
SERENA K. CASWELL, Raynham. Not heard from.
CHARLOTTE C. CHRISTIAN, Bridgewater. T. seven years. Mrs. Fernando Leonard, Boston.
MARIA CRANE,* Canton. Taught nineteen years. Died in Quincy, Sept. 15, 1865.
ELIZA A. CROOKER,* Bridgewater. Did not teach. Died soon after leaving school.

MARY J. DICKERMAN, Stoughton. 1. Not heard from.
CLARA W. EATON, Middleboro'. 1. T. eight years. Mrs. Stillman O. Keith, Bridgewater.
OLIVE D. HATHAWAY, Freetown. Did not teach. Mrs. B. H. Strobridge, Myricksville.
SARAH P. HATHAWAY, Freetown. Taught two years. Mrs. John E. Corey, Brighton.
MARY E. KEITH, Boston. Not heard from.
JANE A. LEONARD,* Bridgewater. Taught two years. Died July, 1859.
ANN C. SPRAGUE, Hingham. Taught seven years. Mrs. Henry Warner, Rockland.
MARY STROBRIDGE, Middleboro'. Did not teach. Mrs. James Pierce, Myricksville.
CLARA B. TUCKER, Canton. Taught twenty one years. Address, Canton.
LUCRETIA M. WALKER, Dummerston, Vt. Mrs. P. F. WALKER, Farley, Dubuque Co., Iowa.
SABA WASHBURN, Bridgewater. Taught one year. Mrs. Fisher Sprague, Portland, Me.
HENRIETTA WILBER,* Raynham. Taught four years. Died January, 1876.

Total of teaching for thirteen, seventy-one years. Average, five and one-half years.

Class 18. December 3, 1845.

SIDNEY C. BANCROF, Salem, T. three years in Grammar Schools. Lawyer. Peabody.
CHARLES W. BELCHER, Stoughton. Not heard from.
GEORGE W. DIX,* South Reading. No information.
CHARLES C. GREENE, E. Greenwich. Not heard from.
ELLIS H. HOLMES, Plymouth. Taught twenty-nine years. Prin. Girl's High School, San Francisco, Cal.
STEPHEN R. ROGERS, Marshfield. 1. Civil Engineer. Lynn.
JOSEPH B. SANFORD, Taunton. T. three years. Attorney-at-Law. 33 School St., Boston.
JOHN S. P. WHEELER, Salem. 1. Asst. Librarian, Congress, Washington, D. C.
ARTEMAS WISWALL, Newton. Taught twenty-six years. Prin. Grammar School, Dudley Ave., Boston.

Total of teaching for five, sixty-two years. Average, twelve years.

HARRIET ALLEN, Taunton. 1. Not heard from.
ELIZA F. BEAUMONT,* Canton. Taught four years. Mrs. Dr. Edw. Newhall, Lynn. Died June, 1870.
JEANETT D. BURGESS, Plymouth. Taught five years. Mrs. John D. Manter, Plymouth.
HARRIET B. CHASE, Providence, R. I. Not heard from.
LUCY F. COLE,* Carver. 1. No information.
SARAH S. CORNISH,* Plymouth. Taught twenty years. Died in Plymouth, Aug., 1868.
HARRIET COVINGTON,* Plymouth. Did not teach. Died November 30, 1846.
ELIZABETH A. DEAN, Taunton. Not heard from.
JULIA A. W. DREW, Halifax. Taught five years. Physician. Mrs. Chas. L. Winslow, Rockland.
BETSEY A. HALL, Mansfield. Taught eight years. Mrs. Willard Ellis, Walpole.
LYDIA D. HATHAWAY, Freetown. Taught three terms. Mrs. James Dearden, Assonet.
ELIZABETH PARKER, Mansfield. Mrs. Isaac Howard, W. Bridgewater.
ELIZABETH POTTER, Providence, R. I. 1. Not heard from.
LYDIA B. TAYLOR, Rochester. 1. Did not teach. Address, Rochester.
MARY E. WARE, Wrentham. T. two years. Mrs. Henry Howard, 47 Green St., Lynn.

Total of teaching for nine, forty-four years. Average, five years.

Class 19. April 1, 1846.

DAVID ATWOOD, Quincy. Not heard from.
THOMAS H. BOGUE, Boston. Not heard from.
ADAM CAPEN, Jr., Stoughton. Taught three terms. Shoe business. Stoughton.
FREDERIC CAPEN, Stoughton. 1. Not heard from.
ALBERT CUSHMAN. Bridgewater. Taught three months. General Agent Red Line Transit Co. Brookline.
CHARLES CUSHMAN, Bridgewater. Bookkeeper. 184 William St., New York City.

MARIUS S. DANIELS, Blackstone. 1. Taught two terms. Grocer. Custom House Street, Providence, R. I.
GEORGE HERRICK, Westford. Taught one and one-half years. Farmer. Pouca, Dixon County, Nebraska.
ELMER H. LOCKE,* Langdon, N. H. T. one year. Died June 28, 1858, in California.
LEWIS G. LOWE, Boston. Taught two years. Farmer and Insurance Agent. Bridgewater.
GEORGE N. MESSENGER,* Wrentham. No information. Deceased.
ISAAC C. OSGOOD, Westford. Not heard from.
HENRY A. RODMAN, Providence, R. I. 1. No information.
CARLTON STAPLES, Mendon. Taught four years. Unit. clergyman, Providence, R. I.

    Total of teaching for six, ten years. Average, two years.

SARAH R. BATCHELDER,* Canton. Mrs. Richard Fuller.
MARY A CASWELL, Raynham. Not heard from.
NARCISSA Y. CHASE,* Berkley. Taught twenty-five years in Country Schools. Died August 11, 1872.
ABBY HALL, Bridgewater. Taught one term.
ROWENA HAYWARD, Raynham. T. three terms. Mrs. Joseph W. White, Raynham.
JOANN JACKSON, Plymouth. Did not teach. Mrs. Lewis G. Lowe, Bridgewater.
HANNAH S. MACOMBER,* Dartmouth. Taught twenty-one years. Died Oct. 17, 1872.
DEBORAH C. MUNROE,* Bridgewater. No information.
SUSAN G. NOYES, Abington. Not heard from.
ANNE S. RAYMOND, Bridgewater. Did not teach. 198 W. Brookline St., Boston.
ELIZABETH B. RUSSELL,* Plymouth. T. twelve years. Died May 7, 1856, at Plymouth.
ZIPPORAH SAWYER, Bolton. Taught twenty-five years. Member of School Committee, Medford.
EMMELINE O. VINTON, Providence, R. I. Not heard from.
MARY B. WHITE, Rochester. Taught twenty-nine years. In Ungraded Schools, four years. Grammar Schools, two years. Primary Schools, eighteen years. Has been Principal of Training School, New Bedford, five years.
ELIZA E. WHITE, Yarmouth. Not heard from.
MARY WILLIAMS, Raynham. Not heard from.

    Total of teaching for eight, one hundred and thirteen years. Average, fourteen years.

CLASS 20. AUGUST 5, 1846.

BENJAMIN H. BAILEY, Northboro'. Taught nine years. Unit. Clergyman. Marblehead.
ABNER H. BELCHER,* Wrentham. 2. Taught one year. Died November 20, 1857.
CHARLES D. DAVIS, Worcester. Taught two years. Care of Estate. Medfield.
JOHN L. DUNN, Northboro'. Not heard from.
HENRY J. EVERETT,* Wrentham. Taught three years. Died, Medfield, July 7, 1871.
JOHN A. LATHROP, Bridgewater. Taught ten years. Address, Bridgewater.
MARTIN V. PRATT, Easton. Taught ten years. Merchant. Evansville, Wis.

    Total of teaching for six, thirty-five years. Average, six years.

ABBY E. ALLEN, Medfield. Taught six years. Mrs. Charles D. Davis, Medfield.
SARAH J. BABCOCK,* New Bedford. T. four and one-half years. Died February 13, 1853.
FRANCES A. BAKER,* Boston. 1. Did not teach. Died Dec. 21, 1847.
MARTHA C. BASSETT, Bridgewater. Taught nine years. Millinery. Mrs. J. C. Meade, Brockton.
ELIZA F. COPELAND, West Bridgewater. Not heard from.
MARY H. COPELAND, Bridgewater. T. three terms. Mrs. Edwin Gushee, Raynham.
CLEMENTINA DIMICK,* Boston. Taught three years. Mrs. E. K. Whitaker, Needham.
MARY A. HALL,* Mansfield. Taught four terms. Died in Mansfield, Feb. 12, 1858.
SARAH J. HILL, Bridgewater. Taught two years. Mrs. A. Waldo Bassett, Bridgewater.
HARRIET A. LEACH,* Bridgewater. T. ten years. Mrs. J. H. Allen. Died June 22, 1868.
RUTH A. MORSE, Rehoboth. Taught five years. Mrs. Artemas Briggs, Princeton, Minn.

ANNA M. SALISBURY, Medfield. Not heard from.
SARAH E. SHANKLAND, Randolph. 2. Taught twenty-eight years. Teaching Grammar School. Randolph.
MARY P. SOUTHWORTH, Duxbury. Did not teach.
SARAH J. TAUNT, Canton. Not heard from.
AMANDA M. WARE, Wrentham. Taught thirteen years. Mrs. Rev. Franklin Davis, Newington, N. H.
MARGARET WASHBURN,* Bridgewater. Did not teach. Mrs. Stillman Alger. Died July 4, 1856.

Total of teaching for fourteen, eighty-three years. Average, six years.

Class 21. December 2, 1846.

JOHN W. ATWOOD, Chatham. T. ten years. Prin. Grammar School, Jersey City, N. J.
FREEMAN NICKERSON, Jr., Chatham. Taught eleven years. Merchant. 91 S. Water St., Chicago, Ill.
GEORGE H. STEPHENS, Needham. Not heard from.
JOB. C. TRIPP, Fairhaven. 1. Did not teach. Treas. Fairhaven Iron Works.

Total of teaching for three, twenty-one years. Average, seven years.

LUCIA CONANT, Barnard, Vt. Taught three years. Mrs. Ellis S. Wood, Pomfret, Vt.
SUSAN H. CASWELL, Bridgewater. 1. Did not teach. Mrs. Richmond Caswell, Middleboro.
ELIZABETH D. F. CORNISH,* Plymouth. Taught three years. Died July 4, 1854.
MARY A. FISHER,* Northboro'. 2. Taught three and one-half years. Mrs. Rev. Horatio Stebbins. Died February 4, 1875, San Francisco, California.
PHEBE MITCHELL, Nantucket. Taught twenty-seven years. Mrs. Joshua Kendall, Cambridgeport.
ABIGAIL M. MORSE, Rehoboth. Taught six years. Mrs. O. G. Stevens, N. Rehoboth.
MARY N. PRATT, Weymouth. Not heard from.
CATHARINE F. SCOTT, Wrentham. Taught twenty years. Mrs. E. D. Hemenway, Wrentham.
ANNIE B. WARE, Milton. Taught twenty years. Mrs. Frederick Winsor, Winchester.

Total of teaching for eight, eighty-two years. Average, ten years.

Class 22. March 24, 1847.

SIMEON BURT, Freetown. T. five years. Canvasser. 601 N. 18th St., Philadelphia, Pa.
JAMES HARLOW, Plymouth. Not heard from.

Total of teaching for one, five years.

EUNICE H. W. COPELAND, Bridgewater. T. one term. Mrs. Rufus Wood, Bridgewater.
CORNELIA M. FULLER, Wrentham. Taught eight years. Mrs. S. R. Jackson, 233 Friendship St., Providence, R. I.
ANN E. LADD, Lynn. Taught four years. Address, Lynn.
ELIZABETH G. LEACH, Bridgewater. T. nine years. Mrs. Joel Tolman, Bridgewater.
M. ELIZA D. MOORE, Taunton. Not heard from.
MARTHA RUSSELL, New Bedford. Taught twenty-nine years. In Private School for Young Ladies, New Bedford.
MARY E. SMITH, Wayland. Taught one year. Mrs. Ezra Alden, Bridgewater.
SARAH M. VOSE, Milton. Taught sixteen years. Private School. In Hyde Park.
ABBY A. WHITE,* Fairhaven. 1. Mrs. Barker. Died Feb. 18, 1857.

Total of teaching for eight, sixty-seven years. Average, eight years.

Class 23. August 4, 1847.

WILLIAM C. DAVOL,* Westport. Taught three terms. Died in Ecuador, July 16, 1873.
EDWIN H. KEITH, Bridgewater. Did not teach. Manuf. of Cotton Gins. Bridgewater.

ALBERT J. MANCHESTER, Tiverton. Taught twenty-six years. Prin. Grammar School. Providence, R. I., 62 John St.
THOMAS METCALF, Wrentham. Taught twenty-seven years. In Grammar Schools, Charlestown and West Roxbury, nine years; High School, St. Louis, five years; has taught in State Normal University, Normal, Ill., thirteen years.
HENRY MITCHELL, Nantucket. U. S. Coast Survey. 8 Pemberton Sq., Boston.
JOSEPH H. SWAIN, Roxbury. Taught two terms. Physician, San Francisco, Cal.
JAMES. D. WHITMORE, Plymouth. Taught twenty-seven years. Grammar and High Schools. Now in High School, New Haven, Conn.

 Total of teaching for seven, fifty-five years. Average, eight years.

LOUISA T. COOK,* Provincetown. Taught four years. Mrs. Capt. Benj. Freeman. Died Feb. 24, 1859.
LYDIA C. DODGE, Lynn. Taught twenty-two years,— fourteen years in High Schools and Academies. Hubbardston.
ANSTRUS HATCH, Marshfield. Not heard from.
MARY C. JOHNSON, Provincetown. T. seven years. Mrs. Wm. W. Smith, Provicetown.
AMELIA LEONARD,* Bridgewater. Taught five years. Mrs. Joseph Sampson. Died March 17, 1865.
MYRA SAMPSON,* Middleboro'. T. two terms. Mrs. Pickens, Middleboro'. Deceased.

 Total of teaching for five, thirty-nine years. Average, eight years.

CLASS 24. DECEMBER 1, 1847.

ALBERT W. FARNSWORTH,* Roxbury. Taught two years. Teller, First National Bank, Malden. Died March 10, 1875.
HIRAM H. PEVEAR, Roxbury. T. four terms. Baptist Clergyman. Cambridgeport.
WILLIAM J. POTTER, Dartmouth. Taught four years. Unit. Clergyman. New Bedford.
ARTHUR SUMNER, Boston. Taught twenty years in Public and Normal Schools. Brooklyn, Alameda County, California.
SILVESTER SWEETSER, Stoneham. 1. Not heard from.
ROWLAND G. WEEDEN,* Jamestown, R. I. Taught three years. Died in Newport, R. I., September 28, 1856.

 Total of teaching for five, thirty-one years. Average, six years.

RACHEL B. ALLEN, Fall River. Taught two years. Mrs. —— Brown.
SARAH BUNKER, Nantucket. Did not teach. Address, Boston Highlands.
HANNAH COOK, Kingston. Taught twenty-six years. Private School. 1511 Clay St. San Francisco, California.
MARY H. THAYER, Milton. 1. Not heard from.

 Total of teaching for three, twenty-eight years. Average, nine years.

CLASS 25. MARCH 22, 1848.

JOHN F. BARNARD, Worcester. Did not teach. Civil Engineer and Railroad Supt., St. Joseph, Missouri.
JOHN N. BROWN, Candia, N. H. Taught five years. Insurance. Boston.
NATHANIEL MORTON, Plymouth. Taught one year. Manufacturer. Plymouth.
W. HENRY WEST, Milton. Did not teach. Merchant. 35 Commercial St., Boston.

 Total of teaching for four, five years. Average, one year.

THALIA ALDEN, Bridgewater. Taught ten years. Mrs. Henry S. Keith, Campello.
LAURA P. HOLLAND, Chelsea. Taught eight years. School Committee. 133 Hawthorne St., Chelsea.
WEALTHY HOLMES, Bridgewater. Taught three years. Mrs. Stephen Morse, Quincy.
ORILLA C. JONES, Weston. Taught two years. Mrs. Benj. Burt, San Jose, Cal.
PHEBE M. MORSE, Rehoboth. Taught eleven years. Mrs. Allen B. Burt, Taunton.

SARAH D. OTTIWELL, New Bedford. Taught twenty-four years. Prin's Assistant, New Bedford High School.
SARAH D. POND, Wentham. T. three years. Mrs. Jefferson C. Farrar, Newton Centre.
HARRIET ROBINSON, Bridgewater. 2. T. two years. Mrs. Morton Alger, Cambridge.
ELIZA G. SMITH, Lexington. Taught one year· Mrs. F. E. Skinner, 117 West Chester Park, Boston.
MARY E. VOSE, Milton. Taught eleven years. Address, Hyde Park.

Total of teaching for eleven, seventy-six years. Average, seven years.

Class 26. August 2, 1848.

ALBERT G. BOYDEN, S. Walpole. Taught twenty-six years in Grammar, High, and Normal Schools. Principal State Normal School, Bridgewater.
MOSES T. BROWN, Manchester, N, H. 1. Taught twenty years. Sup't of Schools, Toledo, Ohio, five years. Prof. of Oratory in Tufts College, and director of Elocution in Boston Schools. St. James Hotel, Boston.
WILLIAM A. CLOUGH, Barnstead, N. H. T. three years. Flour dealer, Concord, N. H.

Total of teaching for three, forty-nine years. Average, sixteen years.

HELEN M. ATKINS, Sandwich. T. six years. Mrs. Chas. H. Burgess, 2nd, N. Sandwich.
ISABELLA W. CLARKE, Newport, Me. T. two years. Mrs. A. G. Boyden, Bridgewater.
MYRA R. CROCKER, Bridgewater. 2. Did not teach. Mrs. Luther Thomas, Bridgewater.
IRENE S. HATHAWAY, Freetown. Taught four years. Mrs. Simeon Borden, Fall River.
ELIZABETH B. HITCH, New Bedford. Taught two years. Mrs. F. M. Fuller, Peabody.
CATHARINE E. TUCKER, Milton. Taught two terms. Address, Hyde Park.

Total of teaching for six, fifteen years. Average, two and one-half years.

Class 27. December 6, 1848.

WILLARD P. CLARK, Medway. Taught one term. Farmer. Rockville.
STILLMAN HOLMES, Plymouth. Taught four terms. Physician. Santa Cruz, Cal.
CHRISTOPHER C. MOORE, Sterling. No information.
IRA MOORE, Newfield, Me. Taught eighteen years. Prin. State Normal School, St. Cloud, Minn., six years. Prin. Public Schools. San Diego, Cal.
HENRY C. RYDER,* Plymouth. Taught one term. Died at the mines in Cal., June 9, 1854.
STEPHEN W. STONE, Newton. No information.
EDWARD WELLINGTON,* Lexington. T. one term. Drowned in Cambridge, July 6, 1852.

Total of teaching for five, twenty years. Average, four years.

HELEN M. ALLYNE, Sandwich. Taught five years. Mrs. Josiah Stanford, San Jose, Cal.
IRENE B. ASHLEY, Dartmouth. Taught one year. Mrs. I. D. Delano, St. Louis, Mo.
ELIZABETH D. BACON,* Harvard. Taught two years. Died May 9, 1857.
SOPHIA M. GARDNER, Swansey. Taught one year. Mrs. Rev. Edward Cowley, 157 E. 60 St., New York City.
SARAH R. MAXFIELD, New Bedford. No information.
SUSAN H. MOORE, Sudbury. Taught thirteen years· Mrs. J. A. Rockwood, Upton.
ELIZABETH POTTER,* Dartmouth. Taught eight years. Died October 21, 1856.

Total of teaching for six, thirty years. Average, five years.

Class 28. March 28, 1849.

E. H. BEALS, Abington. No information.
EDSON W. BURR, Foxboro'. No information.
CHARLES M. CUSHMAN, Attleboro'. T. six years. Bookseller, Minneapolis, Minn.
IRA COPELAND, West Bridgewater. Taught six years. Manufacturer, Brockton.
ELBRIDGE FAUNCE, Dartmouth. Taught twelve years. Farmer. So. Dartmouth.
ELISHA MANN, 2D, Randolph. Did not teach.
JOSEPH B. READ, Dighton. Taught thirteen years. Baptist clergyman. So. Hanson.

MR. TILLINGHAST'S ADMINISTRATION. 73

JAMES SUMNER, Milton. Taught eight years. Lawyer. Mattapan.
BRADFORD TUCKER,* Canton. Taught two years. Died in 1852.
J. FRANCIS WASHBURN,* Newton. 1. Did not teach. Died in 1859.
DANIEL S. WENTWORTH, Webster. Taught twenty-five years. In Grammar Schools, Milton, Dorchester, Watertown, Mass., Chicago, Ill., sixteen years. Has been Principal of Cook County Normal School, Illinois, the last nine years.

Total of teaching for nine, seventy-two years. Average, eight years.

MARY A. A. CARROLL,* Boston. Taught three years. Died March 8, 1853.
SUSAN CHRISTIAN, Bridgewater. T. ten years. Mrs. George W. Folsom, Bridgewater.
MARTHA COPELAND, Bridgewater. Mrs. Nathaniel Hall, Raynham.
FANNY W. FOGG, Newton. Taught eleven years. Newton Highlands.
LUCRETIA HAYWARD, Bridgewater. Taught one and one-half years. Mrs. Daniel Fobes, N. Cambridge.
MATILDA HAVEN, Fall River. Mrs. James M. Hawes, Delaware, O.
JULIETT JOHNSON,* Sudbury. Did not teach. Deceased.
ABBY A. KEITH,* Bridgewater. Died in Brockton.
MARTHA H. KING, Bridgewater. Mrs. G. H. Thompson, Kidder, Mo.
MARTHA S. PRICE, Attleboro'. Taught seven years. Mrs. Rev. J. D. Pierce, N. Attleboro'.
CAROLINE L. TALLANT, Nantucket. Taught ten and one-half years. Sec'y to Rev. E. E. Hale, 215 Highland St., Roxbury.
LOUISA TUCKER, Canton. Taught three years.

Total of teaching for eight, forty-six years. Average, six years.

CLASS 29. AUGUST 8, 1849.

FRANKLIN BRIGGS, Dighton. No information.
JACOB F. BROWN, Ipswich. Taught twenty-six years. Prin. Grammar School. Salem.
SAMUEL W. CLAPP, Dedham. Taught one year. Civil Engineer. Dedham, Mass.
SAMUEL CUSHMAN, JR., Attleboro'. Taught two years. Superintendent of Mines. Denver, Col.
BENJ. B. W. EDMANDS, Charlestown. Taught two years.
DAVIS M'KENDRY, Canton. Taught three and one-half years. Spice Mill. Neponset.
LEWIS WHITING, Hanover. Taught two terms. Physician. Danvers.

Total of teaching for six, thirty-five years. Average six years.

FRANCES W. ALLEN, Attleboro. T. four years. Mrs. Thomas Fellows, Ontario, Kansas.
ADA G. B. BEAL, Milton. Not heard from.
HANNAH H. DEAN, Easton. Taught one year. Mrs. Haskins, Easton.
LEMIRA A. FISH, Pawtucket. Taught two years. Mrs. B. W. Hood, 673 High St., Providence, R. I.
ANNA S. IRESON, Lynn. Taught two years. Mrs. Amos Tapley, Lynn.
HANNAH B. METCALF, Wrentham. T. three years. Mrs. Austin Saunders, Norwood.
SALLIE M. PECK, Attleboro'. Taught fifteen years. Address, Attleboro'.
M. ELIZABETH PERVEAR, Pawtucket. Did not teach. Mrs. Geo. H. Hill, 63 Charles Field St., Providence, R. I.
EUNICE M. READ, Attleboro'. Taught three years. Attleboro' Falls.
ISABELLA E. ROBINSON, Attleboro. Did not teach. Mrs. Joseph Cushman, Attleboro' Falls.
ELIZABETH WESTON, Boston. Taught twenty-five years, in High and Normal Schools. Kennedy's Hall, Boston Highlands.

Total of teaching for ten, fifty-five years. Average, five and one-half years.

CLASS 30. DECEMBER 5, 1849.

CHARLES F. CROCKER, Barnstable. Taught one term.
EDWARD C. DELANO, Fairhaven. T. twenty-two years. Principal, Chicago Normal School.

BRIDGEWATER STATE NORMAL SCHOOL.

ROBERT C. METCALF, Wrentham. Taught twenty-five years in Grammar, High and Normal Schools. Master of Wells Grammar School, Boston.
AARON PORTER, Danvers. Not heard from.
FREDERICK TABER,* Fairhaven. Taught one term. Died Aug. 13, 1866.
BENJAMIN C. VOSE, Milton. T. twelve years. Cashier, Bay State Iron Co., Hyde Park.
WILLIAM H. WARD, Newton. Taught twelve years. Engineer. Worcester.
    Total of teaching for six, seventy-two years. Average, twelve years.
RUTH A. BURT, Berkley. Taught four years. Mrs. Seth C. French, Taunton.
ELIZA CRANE, Canton. Not heard from.
ELIZA E. CUSHMAN, New Bedford. 2. Not heard from.
ANNIE L. FLYNN, Boston. Not heard from.
ELLEN HINCKLEY, Barnstable. 1. Not heard from.
MARY I. MEGGETH, Slatersville, R. I. T. two years. Mrs. Alvin C. Robbins, Millville.
AUGUSTA M. SHAW, Middleborough. Not heard from.
RUTH STOCKBRIDGE, Randolph. T. nine years. Mrs. F. O. White, 22 Akron St., Roxbury.
CAROLINE TUCKER, Canton. Not heard from.
    Total of teaching for three, fifteen years. Average, five years.

CLASS 31. MARCH 27, 1850.

OLIVER F. BRYANT, Woburn. Taught twenty-two years, Grammar Schools. Chauncy Hall School, Boston.
F. H. CHAMBERLAIN, Worcester. 2. Not heard from.
SAMUEL CRANE. Boston. 1. Not heard from.
THOMAS B. EWELL, Newton. Taught three years. Clerk. Cambridge.
LUCIUS KINGSBURY, Andover, Ct. Taught twenty-five years. Principal, High School, Lincoln, Illinois.
EDWIN MAY, Sterling. Taught six years. Farmer. Ironton, Iron Co., Missouri.
CHARLES A. RICHARDSON, Montague. T. six years. Editor, Congregationalist, Boston.
WILLIAM A. WEBSTER, North Brookfield. Taught ten years. Physician. Westford.
    Total of teaching for six, seventy-two years. Average, twelve years.
CAROLINE ALDEN, Bridgewater. Taught four years. Mrs. Linus Darling, Savin Hill.
ELLEN L. ASHCROFT, Dorchester. Not heard from.
ELIZABETH C. BABCOCK, New Bedford. T. ten years. Mrs. Rev. Wm. J. Potter, New Bedford.
CORNELIA BASSETT, Winslow, Maine. Taught four years. Mrs. Ira E. Getchell, No. Vassalboro, Maine.
LUCY A. CARPENTER, Pawtucket. T. three years. Mrs. Lucius Kingsbury, Lincoln, Ill.
REBECCA E. CHASE, Pawtucket. T. twenty-four years. High School. Providence, R. I.
FRANCES A. CLAPP, W. Scituate. Taught four years. Mrs. Joel Bowker, Maplewood.
ELIZABETH CRAFTS, Boston. Taught eighteen years. Teaching. Malden.
MARY J. CRAGIN,* Woburn. Taught eighteen years. In Wheaton Female Seminary, Norton, eight years. St. Louis Normal School, ten years. Died Nov. 30, 1870.
MARY H. DROWN, Attleboro'. Taught one year. Mrs. Ambrose Keith, Bridgewater.
AMY B. DURFEY, Tiverton, R. I. Taught three months. Address, Tiverton, R. I.
CAROLINE ELLIS,* Walpole. T. eight years. Mrs. P. B. Strong. Died Sept. 16, 1874.
C. EMILY FARRINGTON, Franklin. 1. T. two years. Mrs. J. G. Hubbard, Derry, N. H.
CHARLOTTE M. GARDNER, Nantucket. T. twenty-four years. Teaching. Phila., Pa.
MARY A. HALL, Bridgewater. 2. Mrs. Capt. Copeland, Bridgewater.
ALMIRA W. HODGES, Franklin. Taught seven years. Mrs. Rev. Hiram K. Pervear, Cambridgeport.
ANNE C. IDE, Attleboro.' Taught eight years. Mrs. Benjamin Leavitt, Canton.
LOVE S. JONES, Falmouth. No information.
MARY J. SMITH, Nantucket. 1. Mrs. ——— Thacher.
LYDIA H. SWEET,* Attleboro'. Taught two terms. Mrs. A. H. Tucker. Deceased.

LUCY C. SYLVESTER,* Boston. 1. Did not teach. Mrs. Henry H. Ward. Died Dec. 16, 1873.
ALYDIA S. TAFT,* Mendon. 2. Taught twelve years. Died, 1863.
MARY S. WILDER, Dedham. Taught one term. Copyist. Mrs. J. H. B. Thayer, Dedham.
Total of teaching for nineteen, 148 years. Average, eight years.

Class 32. August 7, 1850.

ADIN A. BALLOU,* Milford. Taught one term in this Normal School. Died Feb. 8, 1852.
THOMAS H. BARNES, Waltham. Taught twenty-four years. Master, Bigelow Grammar School. South Boston.
EDWIN S. BEARD, Falmouth. Taught two years. Cong'l Clergyman. Brooklyn, Conn.
JOHN T. COOK, Tiverton, R. I. Taught fifteen years. Farmer. Tiverton, R. I.
JAMES E. KAIME, Pittsfield, N. H. T. seven years in High School. Real Estate Broker. St. Louis.
SAMUEL J. LOVEWELL, Weston. Not heard from.
ALEXANDER McDONALD,* Boston. T. nine years. Died in New York, April, 1867.
JABEZ M. LYLE, Rockport. Taught five years. Secretary. 5 Dey St., New York City.
LEVI S. ROWE, Stoneham. Not heard from.
Total of teaching for seven, sixty-two years. Average, nine years.
OLIVE S. BALLOU, Keene, N. H. Not heard from.
MARY A. KAIME,* Pittsfield, N. H. Taught two years. Mrs. William A. Webster. Died October, 17, 1855.
MARTHA KINGMAN, W. Bridgewater. Taught fourteen years. In Intermediate School, Fall River, one year. English High School for Boys, Salem, two years. State Normal School, Salem, eleven years. Mrs. Prof. Alpheus Crosby, Salem.
SALOME C. LOTHROP, Provincetown. 2. T. nine years. Mrs. Rob't C. Soper, Provincetown.
ELIZABETH PRATT,* Abington. 2. Died May 3, 1851.
LIZZIE A. SHERMAN, Boston. Not heard from.
ELLEN M. WELD, Roxbury. Not heard from.
MARY WESTALL, Providence, R. I. T. fifteen years. Mrs. David L. Daboll, Providence.
SOPHIA H. WHITE,* Littleton. Died at Littleton, 1854.
ANTOINETTE WIGHT, Dracut. T. fourteen years in Public City Schools. Fall River.
REBECCA S. WILMARTH, Attleboro'. Taught. Mrs. Prof. G. C. Caldwell, Ithaca, N. Y.
MARTHA F. WINNING, Chelmsford. Taught twenty-three years. Head Assistant in Hancock School, Boston. 6 Eden St., Charlestown.
ELVIRA WOOD, Middleboro. T. sixteen years. Mrs. James S. Bump, Jr., Middleboro'.
Total of teaching for nine, ninety-three years. Average, ten years.

Class 33. December 4, 1850.

JAMES M. ADAMS, Milford. Not heard from.
HORATIO F. ALLEN, Walpole. Taught fourteen years, Grammar and High Schools. Fire Insurance. Newtonville.
WALTER GALE, Northboro. Taught one year. Newspaper Publisher. Northboro'.
EDWARD A. LYNDE, Sterling. Not heard from.
SAMUEL A. W. PARKER, Jr., Stoughton. Taught two terms. Provision Dealer. Boylston Market, Boston.
SILAS PEABODY, Fall River. T. twenty-two years.' Prin. Grammar School, E. Lexington.
ABRAM WASHBURN, Jr.,* Bridgewater. Did not teach. Deceased.
WILLIAM WATSON, Nantucket. T. twenty-four years. 73 Marlboro St., Boston.
Total of teaching for six, sixty-two years. Average, ten years.
ELLEN M. BARTLETT, Quincy. Not heard from.
A. E. BRIGHAM, Westboro'. 2. Not heard from.
MARY M. ELLIS, Mendon. Taught two years. Mrs. Edward Dudley, Mendon.
PHILINDA D. FISHER, Nantucket. Not heard from.

BRIDGEWATER STATE NORMAL SCHOOL.

FRANCES A. FRENCH,* Andover. 2. Taught two years. Died Nov. 23, 1856.
BETSEY GERRY, Stoneham. Taught twenty-three years. Teaching. Boston Grammar School. N. Woburn.
LUCY E. HALL, Warwick, R. I. Taught seven years. Mrs. Quincy L. Reed, S. Weymouth.
CATHERINE M. HIGGINS, Fairhaven. Taught one year. Address, Chicago, Ill.
ELIZABETH E. LATHROP,* West Bridgewater. T. eleven years. Died Jan. 19, 1873.
ELIZABETH G. MACY, Nantucket. T. sixteen years. Address, Nantucket.
SUSAN A. MITCHELL, Nantucket. 1. Mrs. Defreez, St. Louis, Mo.
SUSAN A. ROWE, Stoneham. 1. Taught two years. Mrs. William Messen.
MARY E. SPRINGER, Attleboro'. T. fourteen years. Mrs. Sam'l P. Lathrop, Attleboro'.
MARY S. STONE, Watertown. Taught five years. Mrs. C. E. C. Breck, E. Milton.
LUCRETIA S. SWAIN, Nantucket. 2. Not heard from.
ELIZA TAFT, Mendon. Taught one year. Mrs. Samuel Adams, Cold Brook, Barre.

Total of teaching for eleven, eighty-four years. Average, eight years.

Class 34. March 26, 1851.

ALONZO B. ABBOTT, Randolph. Taught five years. Supt. Public Schools. Bradford, Ill.
JAMES T. ALLEN, Medfield. Taught twenty-three years. In Grammar School, two years. High School, one year. Polytechnic Institute, Troy, N. Y., four years. Has been in English and Classical School, West Newton, sixteen years.
WILLIAM BELL, Woonsocket, R. I. 2. Not heard from.
SAMUEL M. BROWN, Mansfield. Taught thirteen years. Farmer. Mansfield.
ELKANAH W. DICKERSON, Rumney, N. H. Taught thirteen years. Tobacco Inspector. 39 N. 3d St., Philadelphia, Pa.
EDWIN C. HEWETT, East Douglas. Taught twenty-three years. Grammar, High, and Normal Schools. State Normal University, Normal, Ill.
GEORGE M. SMITH, Walpole. Did not teach. Bookseller. 11 Bromfield St., Boston.
JOHN W. WILLIS, Milford. T. four years. Grammar and High. Physician. Waltham.

Total of teaching for seven, eighty-one years. Average, eleven and one-half years.

SARAH J. BAKER, Nantucket. Taught twenty-five years in Lawrence and Boston. Principal, Dudley Grammar School. Boston Highlands.
SUSY S. BLISH, Boston. 2 Did not teach. Address, York, Penn.
RHODA M. BRIGGS,* Rochester. 2 No information. Deceased.
ELVIRA BROOKS, S. Scituate. Taught nine years. Mrs. Ezekiel T. Vinal, S. Scituate.
PHEBE B. CATHELLE. Rochester. T. sixteen years. Grammar and High Schools. Rochester.
AROLINE S. DARLING, Bridgewater. T. two terms. Mrs. Chas. H. Vose, New Bedford.
CATHERINE DWIGHT, Springfield. Taught five years. Mrs. Geo. Bliss, Jr., 54 W. 39th St., New York City.
MARY A. E. EBERLE, Boston. 2. Did not teach. Mrs. Geo. Faxon, Providence, R. I.
REBECCA W. EDWARDS,* Chelsea. 2. Taught four years in Chelsea. Died, 1856.
ABBY S. FISKE,* Medfield. Taught five years. Mrs. F. W. Goodale. Died Jan. 15, 1862.
CYNTHIA B. FRENCH, Clinton. 1. Mrs. Joseph P. Williams, 75 Union St., Boston.
MARIA E. GARDNER, Fall River. Taught twelve years. In Iowa.
ABBY H. HILL, Sherburne. Taught twenty years. Address, E. Medway.
MARY J. HUNT, Framingham. Taught two years. Mrs. Samuel Tarbox, Benicia, Cal.
CAROLINE E. JONES, Boston. 2. Not heard from.
ELIZA B. LEWIS, Seekonk. Taught six years. Mrs. J. W. Denison, Denison, Iowa.
CORDELIA F. MAY, Plymouth. Taught two years. Mrs. John B. Souther, Melrose.
MARY C. NILES, Roxbury. 1. Taught two years. Mrs. Sylvester Potter, Vinton, Iowa.
ELIZA J. PARISH,* Hinsdale. 1. Mrs. M. M. Wentworth, Hinsdale. Died Nov. 16, 1859.
HANNAH ROSS, Sterling. Taught ten years in Sterling. Address, Sterling.
RUTH C. RYDER,* Provincetown. 2. Taught seven years. Mrs. John T. Small. Died February 20. 1868.
MARY R. THAIN, Nantucket. Did not teach. Mrs. E. D. Marshall, Philadelphia, Pa.

MARIA E. VINAL, Scituate. Taught two years. Mrs. G. H. Webb, Scituate.
ABBIE W. WOODS, Ashby. T. seventeen years. Mrs. Rev. F. A. Fiske, Brookfield, Ct.

Total of teaching for twenty, one hundred and forty-five years. Average, seven years.

Class 35. August 6, 1851.

SAMUEL BIRD, East Bridgewater. 2. Not heard from.
GEORGE A. TABER, New Bedford. Not heard from.
CHARLES L. WASHBURN, Raynham. Taught seven years. Farmer. No. Perry, Me.

Total of teaching for one, seven years. Average, seven years.

AMELIA BRECK, New York City. 2. Taught seven years. Private School. Covington, Ky.
EMILY P. DAMON, Bridgewater. Taught three years. Address, Bridgewater.
MARY P. HAYWARD, Milford. Taught three terms. Mrs. Wm. Fairbanks, Caryville.
MARIA J. HERSEY,* Bangor, Me. No information. Deceased.
MARY R. JOHNSON, Peacham, Vt. 2. Not heard from.
NANCY N. METCALF, Holliston. Not heard from.
M. ADELINE MOWRY, Marlboro. Not heard from.
CAROLINE L. RANDALL, New Bedford. Not heard from.
MARY A. RUGG, Sterling. Taught seven years. Mrs. James Butterick, Sterling.
SARAH H. SHAW, Bridgewater. T. three years. Mrs. Samuel D. Hayward, Bridgewater.
MARTHA A. SMITH, Dighton. Not heard from.
MARY J. TAYLOR, Plymouth. Not heard from.

Total of teaching for five, twenty-one years. Average, four years.

Class 36. December 3, 1851.

JAMES E. ALDEN, Bridgewater. T. ten years. Salesman. 30 Page St., Providence, R. I.
THOMAS R. BRIGHAM, Bridgewater. T. three terms. New Haven, Franklin Co., Mo.
WILLIAM N. CLARK, Sandwich. Not heard from.
S. E. D. CURRIER, Methuen. Taught one term. Lawyer.
JOHN J. DANA, Perry, Me. Taught three years. Farmer. Perry, Dallas Co., Iowa.
GEORGE FARWELL, Waltham. Taught twenty-one years. Teaching. Brockton.
FRANCIS W. GOODALE, Marlboro'. Taught two years. Farmer. Marlboro'.
LYMAN LEAVETT, New Hampton, N. H. Not heard from.
DANIEL H. PRATT, Easton. Taught twelve years. Money Broker. Denver, Col.

Total of teaching for seven, forty-nine years. Average, seven years.

LUCY C. ALLEN, Northboro'. Taught twelve years. Mrs. Powers, Lansingburgh, N. Y.
ELLEN S. BARNES, Berlin. Taught eight years. Mrs. William H. Brown, Princeton.
SOPHIA A. CORNELL, Dartmouth. T. one year. Mrs. Edward Howland, So. Dartmouth.
SARAH W. HOLBROOK, Northboro'. Taught thirteen years. Mrs. Chas. D. Litchfield, Dorchester.
MARY T. JENNEY, Middleboro. 1. T. two years. Mrs. Theo. Leonard, Detroit, Mich.
MARY F. LOWE, Boston. Mrs. ——— Green, Warwick, R. I.
EMILY M. MACOMBER, Dartmouth. Not heard from.
SUSAN S. NICKERSON, Chatham. Not heard from. Mrs. ——— Smith, Chatham.
CLARA A. PARKMAN, Sutton. T. seven years. Mrs. Rev. D. C. Babcock, Phila., Pa.
SARAH H. SANFORD, Dartmouth. Taught seventeen years. Mrs. Archelaus Baker, S. Dartmouth.
MARY U. F. SOUTHWICK, Uxbridge. T. four years. Mrs. Cyrus G. Wood, Uxbridge.
CORNELIA STRANGE,* Freetown. 1. Died in Bridgewater, Feb. 21, 1852.
HARRIET M. TAFT, Uxbridge. Taught four years. Address, Uxbridge.
SARAH F. TAFT, Uxbridge. Taught ten years. Address, Uxbridge.

Total of teaching for ten, 68 years. Average, 7 years.

Class 37. March 24. 1852.

ISAAC H. BULLARD, Walpole. 2. T. one term. Meats and Provisions. S. Walpole.
WILLARD S. COBB,* Mansfield. Taught ten years in Boston. Died April 18, 1869.
CHARLES W. PACKARD, Lancaster. 1. Not heard from.
NOAH SHERMAN, Rochester. Taught five years.
CHARLES H. STANYAN, Chichester, N. H. 2. Not heard from.
ALBERT STETSON, Kingston. Taught eighteen years. Graduated at Harvard College. In Grammar School, three years. In High School, two years. Has been at State Normal University, Normal, Illinois, thirteen years.

    Total of teaching for four, thirty-three years. Average, eight years.

LYDIA P. BROWN, Nantucket. Not heard from.
CATHARINE M. CLAPP, So. Scituate. T. five years. Mrs. R. P. Briggs, W. Scituate.
MARY M. DANA, Perry, Me. Taught two years. Mrs. Chas. L. Washburn, N. Perry, Me.
LIZZIE S. DIKE, Stoneham. Taught five years. Mrs. Nelson Parker, Stoneham.
ABBY S. GILMORE, Medfield. 1. Not heard from.
PHEBE GREENE, Warwick, R. I. T. six years. Mrs. Albert A. Gamwell, Providence, R. I.
CATHARINE M. HOWE, Templeton. Taught eight years. Address, Templeton.
LUCY B. HOWE, Templeton. Taught nine years. Mrs. James M. Huie, Spadra, Cal.
M. FRANCIS HURD,* Brewster. T. one year. Married and died in San Francisco, Cal.
ELLEN L. LEWIS, Rochester. 1. Taught seven years. Mrs. Judah Hathaway, Rochester.
MARY J. MEADER,* Rochester, N. H. Taught five years. Died June 4, 1861.
ELLEN M. PINKHAM, Nantucket. Not heard from.
AMELIA A. SIMPSON, Southbridge. Taught twenty years. Private School. Southbridge.
FIDELIA L. SIMPSON, Southbridge. T. twenty-two years. Private School. Southbridge.
JANE B. SMITH, Hanson. Taught eleven years. Mrs. F. F. Fiske, Mast Yard, N. H.
MARY YOUNG, Barnstable. Taught twenty-three years in Grammar School. Bowdoin School, Boston.

    Total of teaching for thirteen, 124 years. Average, nine and one-half years.

Class 38. August 4, 1852.

WILLIAM A. BOLLES, Marion. Bloomfield, Davis Co., Iowa.
ALPHONSO B. BOWERS, Baldwin, Me. 1. T. seven years. Civil Engineer. Travelling.
CHESTER H. COMEY, Foxboro. T. eleven years. Insurance Broker. Cambridgeport.
JOHN B. DIETRICH, Baltimore, Md. 1. Not heard from.
EDWARD L. HILL, Portsmouth, N. H. Attorney and Counsellor. Danvers.
FRANKLIN JACOBS, Hanover. Not heard from.
JAIRUS LINCOLN, JR., Northboro'. Taught seven years. Farmer. Longmont, Col.
BERNARD PAINE, Randolph. Taught seven years. Cong'l Clergyman. Foxboro'.
J. HENRY ROOT, Newbury. T. twenty-one years. Prin. High School. Bloomfield, N. J.
JAMES D. SAVAGE, Newton. Not heard from.
O. LAPRELETTE WIGHT,* Medfield. Taught one term. Died Sept. 22, 1855.
ALBERT WOOD, Northboro'. Taught two years. Physician, Worcester.

    Total of teaching for eight, fifty-five years. Average, seven years.

ANGELINE BARNEY, Nantucket. Not heard from.
SARAH J. BARTLETT, Northboro. Taught fifteen years. Teaching Private School. Westboro.
ANNIE H. BEAUVAIS, Dartmouth. 1. Taught three years. Mrs. Henry B. Manchester, S. Dartmouth.
MARY J. BIGELOW, Westminster. Taught six years. Mrs. Joseph A. Priest, Littleton.
SARAH A. BRECK, Bridgewater. Address, Covington, Ky.
HANNAH R. CHADBOURNE, Boston. T. six years. Mrs. Joshua R. Clark, Reading.
JANE T. FISHER, Northboro'. T. three years. Mrs. Jairus Lincoln, Longmont, Col.
ELIZABETH GARDNER, Milton. 1. Taught nine years. Address, E. Milton.

MR. TILLINGHAST'S ADMINISTRATION. 79

LUCY HINCKLEY,* Barnstable. T. two years. Mrs. Lucy H, Backus. Died, 1872.
ELVIRA JOHNSON, Northboro'. Taught twenty-three years. Teaching Family School, Northboro.
MARIA D. KIMBALL, Andover. T. twenty-two years. Chapman School, East Boston.
FRANCES P. M'FARLAND. Not heard from.
HELEN L. MUNYAN, Milford. Mrs. Elijah S. Mulliken, Malteville, N. Y.
LYDIA B. RING, Kingston. Taught twenty-two years. Teaching in Kingston.
LIVONIA E. SHAW, Boston. Not heard from.
ANGELINE E. SMITH, Medfield. Taught one term.
ARIADNE D. SMITH, Pawtucket. T. seven years. Mrs. Thomas T. Smith, Millville.
ADELINE STOCKBRIDGE,* Randolph. T. eighteen years. Died in Boston, Jan. 27, 1871.
ELIZABETH C. WASHBURN, Barnstable. T. seven years. Mrs. Henry Norris, Barnstable.
MARY D. WILLIAMS, Middleboro'. T. two years. Mrs. John H. Nelson, Lakeville.

Total of teaching for fifteen, one hundred and forty-five years. Average, ten years.

CLASS 39. JAN. 26, 1853.

N. AUSTIN BURGESS, Kingston. Not heard from.
CHARLES F. FITZ, Newton. Not heard from.
J. RICHARDSON FLETCHER, Chelmsford. Taught one term. Farmer. Chelmsford.
HORACE A. POTTER, Plymouth, Conn. T. three terms. Farmer. Thomaston, Conn.
HENRY F. SMITH, Pawtucket. 1. Did not teach. Dealer in Lumber. Pawtucket, R. I.
HORACE C. SNOW, Newton. 1. Not heard from.
C. J. STEPHENS, Newton. 1. Not heard from.
NATHANIEL WASHBURN,* Bridgewater. 1. Did not teach. Deceased.

Total of teaching for two, two years. Average, one year.

HARRIET A. BLAKE,* Abington. T. eight years. Mrs. H. A. Faunce. Died June, 1859.
RENA BULLARD, Franklin. T. twelve years, Grammar School and Academy. Franklin.
SARAH CRANE, Berkley. Taught twenty-three years. Teaching. East Freetown.
MARY C. FISHER, Canton. Taught ten years. Address, Canton.
ANNIE M. G. FULLER,* Cambridgeport. Mrs. Annie M. Bisbee. Deceased.
OLIVE G. HARLOW, Duxbury. Taught one year. Mrs. T. B. Blackman, Marshfield.
CAROLINE B. HYDE, Cambridgeport. 1. Not heard from
ANNA L. PIERCE,* Cambridge. T. eight years, High School. Died, W. Cambridge, 1863.
FRANCES W. D. WASHBURN, Plympton. Not heard from.
MARIA E. WEBSTER, No. Brookfield. Taught ten years. Address, Westford.
OLIVE F. WENTWORTH, Bridgewater. T. three years. Mrs. Melvin Leonard, Raynham.
HARRIET A. WORTH, Nantucket. T. twelve years. Address, care of E. R. Worth, Malden.

Total of teaching for nine, eighty-seven years. Average, ten years.

MR. CONANT'S ADMINISTRATION.

The School.

MARSHALL CONANT, the second Principal of the school, entered upon his duties at the commencement of the fortieth term, in August, 1853, and continued his service for seven years, till July, 1860. He came to reside in Bridgewater in 1852, and was employed in connection with the Eagle Cotton Gin Company. His interest in all matters pertaining to education was so great that it very soon opened the way to a cordial intercourse with Mr. Tillinghast, and when the latter resigned his position, he recommended the election of Mr. Conant as his successor. Mr. Conant brought to the school a rich harvest of ripe fruits gathered in other fields of labor, and immediately took up the work where his predecessor left it, and carried it forward. The increasing demand for graduates with higher qualifications, induced many of the students to extend their course of preparation beyond the year required to be spent in the school. In 1854 the Board of Education recognized this demand and passed a vote that there should be two long terms a year, instead of three shorter ones, in all the State Normal Schools, and that pupils should still be required to attend three consecutive terms. This vote went into effect in March, 1855.

The following extracts from the Circular of the school indicate the requirements during the last five years of Mr. Conant's administration:

Conditions of Admission.

Applicants for admission to this School must make an explicit declaration of their intention to become teachers.

Males must be at least seventeen years of age, and females at least sixteen.

Each candidate for admission is required to present a certificate of good moral and intellectual character, and must pass a satisfactory examination in the common branches; viz., Reading, Writing, Spelling, Defining, Grammar, Arithmetic, and Geography.

All candidates for admission must present themselves at the Schoolroom *at nine o'clock, A. M., of the first day of the Term.*

Terms.

The year is divided into two terms. The Spring Term commences on the third Wednesday of March; and the Fall Term on the third Wednesday of September. Length of the Spring Term, nineteen weeks; length of the Fall Term, twenty-one weeks.

Course of Instruction.

The course of instruction embraces a period of Three Terms, and the candidate for admission is required to attend these consecutively. If, however, he is found to be qualified to enter advanced classes, his connection with the Institution may be for a shorter period, but not less than two terms.

The first term is considered as preparatory to a strictly Normal course, to which the two other terms are specially devoted. The studies of the first term are, for the most part, those usually taught in the public schools of the State. In the other two terms, the Students, besides attending to many of the higher branches, learn the Theory and Practice of Teaching. Skill in *acquiring* and skill in *imparting* knowledge is a distinctive feature of the course.

Branches of the Course.

Reading; Writing; Spelling; Etymology; Structure of the English Language; English Grammar; Arithmetic; Algebra; Geometry; Physiology; History of the United States, and General History; Geography, both Physical and Political, with the Construction of Maps; Natural Philosophy; Astronomy; Surveying; Book-keeping; Mental and Moral Philosophy; Logic; Rhetoric; Composition; Latin; School Laws of Massachusetts, and Constitution of the United States. Also occasional lessons in Natural History; and weekly lessons in Music, by a skillful teacher.

Those who complete in a satisfactory manner the course of Studies here specified, are entitled to receive the Diploma of the Institution.

Tuition and Expenses.

Tuition is gratuitous to those who design to become Teachers in the Public Schools of the State. To those from *other* States, who do not become teachers in *this*, a fee of ten dollars per Term is charged for tuition.

Board is usually two dollars and seventy-five cents per week, exclusive of fuel and lights; and one dollar and fifty cents is required of every Student at the middle of each Term, to meet incidental expenses.

It is expected also that each Student will furnish himself with a copy of Lippincott's "Gazetteer of the World," and with some other smaller works; the whole cost of which may amount to seven dollars. All other Text-books are furnished to the Student free of charge.

Besides the Text-books, the Institution furnishes nearly five hundred volumes of valuable works for reference in the various departments of education. This collection, though small, is increasing, and is rendering very essential service to the Students of the Institution. And we would invite the friends of education who would like to increase our means of laboring successfully to meet the wants of the State, to remember our Library and Geological Collection. Any donation to these would be most thankfully received, and put to immediate use.

The School is open at all times to the public, and the friends of education are made welcome within it.

Pecuniary Aid.

The State appropriates a thousand dollars a year for each of the Normal Schools, to aid those Students of the Commonwealth who find it difficult to meet the expense of attending one of these Institutions without assistance. This aid is not granted during the first thirteen weeks of the course. Afterward, applicants for aid may expect to receive it as follows: Those who reside not over twenty miles from the School, fifty cents per week; those residing between twenty and thirty miles, one dollar; and those over thirty miles, one dollar and fifty cents per week.

If, however, the number of applicants in any Term should be greater than to allow of these rates of distribution out of the *regular appropriation* for the Term, *that* amount will be distributed in the *proportion* of these rates.

Applications for this aid are required to be made to the Principal *in writing*, with good references.

Provision for pecuniary aid was first made April 30, 1853, by the Legislature passing a resolve appropriating one thousand dollars annually to each Normal School, — to be paid from the moiety of the income of the School Fund applicable to Educational purposes, — to aid those members of the Normal Schools who find it difficult to meet the expenses necessarily incurred by attending the same, the distribution to be left to the discretion of the Board of Education, after consulting the Principal of each school.

The Plan of Study.

From the report of the Visitors of the School, made December 14, 1855, the following paragraphs are quoted as showing Mr. Conant's views, and the plan of study which he arranged for the School. This plan was followed for five years.

"The arrangement made by the Board requiring two long terms a year, instead of three shorter ones, in the Normal Schools, has gone into effect in this school during the past year. The longer period of study to be pursued by the attendants at this school, in addition to other views of progress, has required some advance and extension in the course of study. An attempt has been made to enlarge the scope of these studies, so as to adapt them, as much as possible, to impart mental strength and development, and an accurate and liberal culture, in view of the great object of the school.

"No little difficulty has been experienced in carrying out, at Bridgewater, the expressed will of the Board relative to having a Model School connected with each Normal School. Though the citizens of the town manifest a disposition favorable to the interests of the Normal School, and this disposition is, we think, increasing, still, for various reasons, no connection of the School with any Town School has been formed that has promised either permanence or utility. The Principal has endeavored to establish such a connection as would not only be mutually agreeable, but be especially efficient in accomplishing the main design contemplated — the practical training of the Normal Pupils. But his efforts have been fruitless, and he has ventured to adopt certain methods of practical training within the Normal School itself. The Committee are of the opinion that this plan is worthy of special consideration.

"In his report at the close of the Winter Term, in January, 1855, Mr. Conant observes: 'It has been a matter of much study and investigation with me, how to impart judicious instruction in respect to teaching and management in our common schools, — these instructions having reference more particularly to preparing the graduating class during the last term of their course. After endeavoring to awaken the conscience to *feel* the responsibilities and duties that devolve upon the teacher, I have sought to draw out the experience of such members of the class as have been engaged in the work. Here I have found materials that come in *naturally* to deepen the interest in these instructions, and apparently adapted to make them effectual.

"'I have also selected individuals (each taking his turn) to give exercises in teaching before the class; after which I have called for suggestions and criticisms from its different members, adding also my own. In this way there seems to have been produced something of a very *practical* and available character to aid the pupils in their future work; in its nature, however, not showy.

"'In respect to didactics, it has appeared to me that they must be given more or less at every lesson, and in connection with the subjects in hand. Ways and methods, — authors and their works, — seem to come up then in a natural course, and with impressive distinctness, and thus to be of practical value.'

"During the succeeding term, he introduced the arrangement,

since continued, by which certain recitations are conducted by the more advanced students, in the classes less advanced. This arrangement is noted in the Plan of Study herewith presented.

"In his report at the close of that term in August, he says: 'From further experience, I am more convinced of the adaptation of these methods to giving instruction in regard to teaching and discipline in our public schools. In connection with the careful study of the School Laws of the State, and of the Constitution of the United States, I find it very easy to lead on the minds of pupils to a just conception of the necessity of good *government* in our schools, and of the importance of *real character* in the teacher.'

"And in a report made a day or two since, he remarks: 'So far as I am able to judge, this course of studies appears to be admirably fitted for our special object — that of preparing competent and skillful teachers for our public schools. The feature of it, which seems to promise *much*, is that of requiring pupils by turns to go thoroughly into the practice of teaching. This arrangement gives the Principal an opportunity of rendering more effectual aid in the attainment of good methods; and, in some measure, of making the theory of teaching become a matter of life and reality.

"'As an element looking to the same end, and also for securing more practice in the application of the principles involved in the lessons, I have divided a large class into sections of five or six pupils each, with a leading pupil for each section. These leading pupils conduct a part of the recitation in their own sections, in the presence of the teacher. This affords the teacher an opportunity to discover the special wants of each pupil, and to adapt his instructions accordingly. The design is to have these sections different for two or three of the branches pursued, in order to bring as many of the pupils as possible into the actual business of teaching.'

"A few words may be allowed in fuller explanation of the Plan of Study herewith presented, and in reference to the method of using it.

"The three terms of study in the school, naturally occasion the division of the pupils into three classes, designated as Junior, Middle and Senior. The plan exhibits the branches of study, and the days and hours when they come up in recitation, so that each pupil sees at a glance what his work is, and when it will be required. This plan, in manuscript, is placed under glass in a frame. The right side of the frame is so cut as to allow a piece of Bristol board, on which are written the names of certain advanced pupils as teachers, at certain hours, to be passed in and out at pleasure. This piece of board is represented on the right of the table of studies, and is changed with a change of these pupils."

PLAN OF STUDY AND INSTRUCTION.

MORNING.

HOURS.		MONDAY AND FRIDAY.			
9 to 9 1-4,	- - -	Devotional Exercises.			
	Junior Class.	*Middle Class.*	*Senior Class.*		*Students Teaching.*
9 1-4 to 10.10,	Arithmetic.	Arithmetic.	American History.		Miss Taft, Arithmetic.
10 1-4 to 11.	1st Latin.	2d Latin.	3rd Latin.		
11 1-4 to 12.	Algebra.	Algebra.	Polit. Class Bk. or Const. U. S.		Mr. Copeland, Algebra.

TUESDAY AND THURSDAY.

9 to 9 1-4,	- - -	Devotional Exercises.		
9 1-4 to 10 1-2,	Geometry.	Nat. Phil.	Trigonometry and Optics.	Mr. Tourtellotte, Geometry.
10 3-4 to 12,	Arithmetic.	Arithmetic.	Astronomy.	Miss Taft, Arithmetic.

WEDNESDAY.

8 1-2 to 8 3-4.	- -	Devotional Exercises.		
8 3-4 to 9 1-2,	Physiology.	Logic.	Rhetoric.	Mr. Crooker, Physiology.
9.35 to 10.35,	- -	Composition.		
10.45 to 12,	- - -	Music.		

SATURDAY.

8 1-2 to 8 3-4	- -	Devotional Exercises.		
8 3-4 to 9 1-2,	Physiology.	Logic.	Rhetoric.	Mr. Crooker, Physiology.
9.35 to 10.35,	Algebra.	Algebra.	Geology and Nat. History.	Mr. Copeland, Algebra.
10.45 to 11.40,	Grammar.	Grammar.	Grammar.	Miss Robbins, Grammar.
11.45 to 12.	- - -	Moral Philosophy and Duties.		

AFTERNOON.

*1 1-2 to 1 40,	- - -	Writing and Spelling every P. M.		

MONDAY AND THURSDAY.

1.40 to 2 1-2	Reading.	Reading.	Book-keeping.	Miss Taft, Reading.
2.35 to 3 1-4,	Grammar.	Grammar.	Grammar.	Miss Robbins, Grammar.
3 1-2 to 4 1-4,	Geography.	Geography.	Geography or Indus. Drawing.	Miss Robbins, Geography.

TUESDAY AND FRIDAY.

1.40 to 2 1-2	Reading.	Reading.	Reading.	Miss Taft, Reading.
2.35 to 3 1-4,	Ment. Arith.	Eng. Language.	Theory of Teaching and School Laws.	
3 1-2 to 4 1-4,	Geography.	Geography.	Surveying and Ind. Drawing.	Miss Robbins, Geography.
4 1-4 to 4 1-2,	- - -	General Exercise, every P. M.		

*These are the hours for the Winter Term; those for the Summer Term are a half hour later.

Progress of the School.

During the sixteen terms in which Mr. Conant had charge of the school, the appliances for school work were much improved. He secured the construction of a large alcove for the reference library, in the south end of the main school-room; the addition of a large number of valuable books to the reference library, and to the library for general reading; a set of full length anatomical plates of the human body; large historical, geological, and geographical maps and charts; and valuable pieces of apparatus, some of which he invented and constructed. In the latter part of this period the number of pupils in attendance increased to nearly one hundred, which was more than the building could conveniently accommodate More room and better arrangements were much needed, and Mr. Conant prepared and presented to the Board of Education plans for the enlargement of the building. These plans were not accepted, but the discussion of them prepared the way for success in providing for this improvement.

At the close of the summer term in 1860, Mr. Conant was compelled, by ill health, to resign his place. The Visitors, in their report of the school, speak of him in the following language: " During his long connection with the school, Mr. Conant, by his accuracy of scholarship, his skill as an instructor, his industry and fidelity, had always secured and maintained the high regard of the pupils, and had given entire satisfaction to the Board of Education, and his necessary resignation of office was universally regretted."

A MEMORIAL ADDRESS ON MARSHALL CONANT.

Delivered by A. G. BOYDEN, before the "Bridgewater Normal Association,"
at Bridgewater, July 15, 1874.

The Traveller slowly wending his way up the mountain side, often passes from the bright sunshine into the deep shadow of a massive cloud floating slowly along the summer sky above. Looking out from this shadow he sees with clearer vision the broad landscape in the sunlight beyond. As he toils on, nearing the mountain top at the close of day, he enters a thick cloud which shuts from his view all below, and the night hangs dark and heavy about him. When the day dawns, and the sun comes up, sometimes the cloud that caps the summit lifts for a moment, and he catches a glimpse of the valley in sunlight below, seeming like another world; then the cloud lowers, and all is dark again. Frequently in the early morning, the clouds sink a little below the summit, and the light and dark cumulus masses, rolling and surging in every conceivable variety of form, fill the whole horizon; as the sun tinges these heaving billows, there comes to the eye of the beholder, a scene of the most surprising grandeur; he can only stand and gaze, rapt in wonder at the glorious sight. As the sun rises in the heavens, the clouds gradually descend the mountain slope and disappear, and the observer sees again the broad earth below, in the clear, bright morning light.

So the shadows come into the light of our lives, the lighter, the deeper, and the overwhelming shadow, which makes all around dark, until the soul is lifted to see the heavenly light beyond. The deep sorrow which sooner or later overshadows every household when the loved ones pass to the other shore, brings out in full relief the life, the character, the work, the affection, and the joy of the presence of the departed one. We know the richness of our treasure by its loss. The light is more brilliant when seen from darkness.

The lights and shadows mingle in every life. The great family of brothers and sisters who gather here in biennial convention cannot be exempt from this universal experience. Every time we come home, we welcome new members of the family and mourn the departure of some who have gone from earth. Thirty-four years have passed, since this Institution was opened to the first class of students. Our Alma Mater now extends her sheltering wings over two generations. Father and son, mother and daughter, parents and children now sit side by side, as members of the Bridgewater Normal Association. Eighteen years ago this month, the elder children of the family gathered here to honor the memory of him, whose signal ability and heroic fidelity, laid broad and deep the foundations of this Institution.

Another good and true man came to the head of the school, took up the work and carried it forward. For many years we have listened with delight to the noble man, the warm friend, the beloved teacher, whose genial presence has always given us such cordial welcome. Many hearts were gladdened at our last convention by his encouraging words, while many eyes were dimmed with tears because his failing strength foretold his departure. The master has called him to his reward, and we meet to-day to do homage to his memory, and to gather the lessons of faith, hope and love, which were so beautifully exemplified in his life. The tributes of respect and love which we bring, I am sure will be offerings from the heart, for no words of formal sentiment could be accepted in speaking of one who was ever loyal to truth. By the kind invitation of our President, and because of the intimate personal relations with Mr. Conant which it was my privilege to hold for several years, it becomes my sad, yet pleasant duty to introduce these memorial services by presenting a brief biographical sketch of our teacher and friend.

MARSHALL CONANT, the second Principal of this Normal School, was born in Pomfret, Vermont, on the fifth day of January, 1801. He lived seventy-two years and one month, and died at Bridgewater, Mass., on the tenth day of February, 1873. His father was Jeremiah Conant, a farmer and house carpenter, who, in 1780, went from Bridgewater, Mass., with several companions, and settled in Pomfret, in the wild Green Mountain State. His mother, Chloe Pratt, was also from Bridgewater. She was the second wife of his father. The subject of our sketch was the sixth son in a family of twelve children, eleven of whom lived to mature years.

The home of his childhood was beautifully situated, and should receive a passing notice, for the surroundings of the child give direction to the main lines of thought and help to determine the chief outlines of character in the future man. I will briefly sketch the place as I saw it a few years since. On the brow of a high hill, a part of one of the eastern spurs of the Green Mountains, stands the plain, one story farmhouse in which Mr. Conant was born. As the rays of the rising sun woke the sleeping boy he could look down a winding valley to the eastward, and out over hills and valleys beautifully wooded, and dotted here and there by a farmhouse. On the west rose a higher range of hills, down whose dark green, well wooded slopes, the shadows of the flying clouds played with the sunlight in the afternoon, forming an ever-changing picture of great beauty until the sun sank below the horizon. Then, on that hill-top, under the open sky, in the solemn stillness of the night, one could almost hear a voice, saying, "The Heavens declare the glory of God, and the firmament showeth his handiwork. Day unto day uttereth speech and night unto night showeth knowledge." Living here in this quiet home the first twenty-three years of his life, with a limited circle of associates, with few books to read, taking into his soul all the beauty of the earth by day, and the glory of the heavens by night, it was the most natural result that the young man, with his active brain, became an ardent lover of nature, and found great delight in studying the movements of the heavenly bodies and all the varying phenomena of the heavens.

> "To him who in the love of nature
> Holds communion with her visible forms
> She speaks a various language."

Here was the source of that wealth of illustration which so frequently enlivened his conversation and teaching.

The District School, "as it was" furnished the rudiments of instruction to the children of the neighborhood, and there, with brothers and sisters, the boy took his first lessons, and shared the common boon of New England. At ten years of age, his help upon the farm, in the summer season, had become a valuable contribution to the thrift of the family, so that from ten to fifteen years of age he went to school only the three coldest months of the year, and whatever else was attained at this early period was a self-achievement.

It was the practice of the father to consult with each of his sons in respect to what he desired to do when he should come of an age to act for himself. This son early showed a fondness for mechanics, which manifested itself in making numerous water-wheels and windmills, and using them to operate little trip hammers, crank turners, and saw-mills. He decided to become an Architect, and so it was thought best to adapt his "schooling" to this pursuit. Reading, Writing, and "Ciphering" were therefore his special branches of study at school. Arithmetic was his favorite study; English Grammar was excluded; Geography was not studied in the common schools at this period An abridgement of Morse's large Geography was sometimes used as a reading book by the first class. From the first part of this old book the boy first gained faith in the actual rotation of the earth upon an axis. "The convincing argument for this fact was so mighty in the mind of the lad, that when it came to his mind he threw himself upon his backless bench, grasping around it underneath to prevent being thrown off by the newly felt movement." Here was a pupil who appreciated a new idea when it came to him.

His school days ended with his fifteenth year and he spent the winter following with a house joiner in learning to make doors and sashes. His skill with tools enabled him soon to master this branch of business, and at seventeen years of age, strong and healthy, he was vigorously at work at his trade, receiving the full wages of an experienced workman, and doing his best to improve the condition of his family. When about eighteen years of age, he took cold while at work, which resulted in a severe inflammation of the lungs. His health gave way and his hopes in the directions of his aims were blasted. He never fully recovered from the effects of this illness, which so nearly proved fatal to him. For four or five years succeeding this failure of his health, he was able to do only some slight mechanical work, and occasionally in summer to guide the team in the field. He had come to an epoch in life which changed his whole future course. The deep sympathy of parents, brothers, and sisters sustained him in his weakness. Unable to work at manual labor, mental improvement was now his aim, and he read and studied all that his physical strength would allow between the frequent periods of severe pain.

He took up the study of Lindley Murray's English Grammar, memorized and parsed Pope's Essay on Man, mastered Morse's large Geography, the astronomical part of which opened to him a new world of thought, which made him all the more ardent in his observations of the heavenly bodies. Pike's large Arithmetic, with its introduction to Algebra, and Euclid were constant companions; the latter he carried and studied while driving the team in the field. He now began to see clearly the treasures of Mathematics and Astronomy. "A few old law books, the Bible, Doddridge's 'Rise and Progress,' Watts and Milton, an English Dictionary, and a few school books, were the literary and light-giving treasures of the house." The old Town Library furnished him a few histories and biographies. To get more books he made a wooden clock, that was going well ten years after, and having sold this for eight dollars, he bought a few more volumes. In the autumn of 1823, a small comet made its appearance in the heavens and he immediately set himself to compute its elements; the great difficulties he met in this effort led him into a successful study of Conic Sections and Planetary Motion, and kept his eye intent upon the visible heavens to note the varying aspects of the different planets.

His health was now so far restored as to enable him to realize the hope he had cherished for the previous four years, and he began his life as a teacher at the age of twenty-three, by teaching the winter school in his own district. His wages were $12 a month; he boarded himself and took his pay in corn, except a very small sum coming to the district as its share of the public money. Part of his wages went to the family; part of the corn he sold, and with the proceeds bought a few books, on Mathematics and Astronomy.

The summer following, he computed a lunar eclipse, and was greatly delighted to find his calculations all verified when the eclipse came; soon after, he calculated a solar eclipse with the same success. He taught the same school the next winter. This winter he carefully studied the stars, *noted* his observations, and constructed tables for a systematic method of making his computations. In the Spring he bought more books, and entered upon the study of higher Geometry and the Differential Calculus.

In the fall of 1825, he attended an Academy at Alstead, N. H; the following winter he taught in East Alstead, and boarded around; this occasioned much exposure, so that when the spring opened, the difficulty with his lungs again appeared, and he was confined to the house by sickness a large part of the year. In January, 1828, his father died, he was appointed Administrator of the Estate, and the care of the family devolved chiefly npon him, his older brothers having married and moved away. During the summer of 1828, he calculated an Almanac for 1829, and by the aid of friends, published an edition of 10,000 copies, which sold very readily. In the Autumn, he taught a select school in Pomfret. In the winter of 1829, he taught the village school in Woodstock, Vt., and his success encouraged him to open there the same year a private school, for instruction in the higher branches, which he continued for nearly five years. This period of his life was one of great activity. Needing apparatus for his school which he had not the means to buy, he made for himself an electrical machine, and the Orrery, which all his subsequent pupils in Astronomy so well remember. He added to his previous acquisitions a knowledge of the French and Latin languages, in the winter evenings, gave courses of lectures to his pupils and the village people, and continued his studies in all directions, having obtained access to the library of Dartmouth College. Besides his labors in teaching, he had continued the preparation of an annual Almanac from 1829 to 1834. He was now 33 years of age. He says at this time, "I felt a strong desire for better opportunities of development, I had a strong inclination to go to Massachusetts. I wished to become better acquainted with her institutions and share the amenities of a higher intellectual life."

Early in March, 1834, he came to Boston and was soon established as a teacher in the Boylston Grammar School on Fort Hill. He secured a boarding place not far from the Old Atheneum, in which he spent three or four hours a day, pursuing a course of historic and scientific reading. In September, 1835, he married Miss Roxana Darling, one of his former pupils in Woodstock. After teaching two years in the Boylston School he took a private school for boys, in Roxbury, in which he remained for three years, having a prosperous school and a very happy home among the cultivated people of his acquaintance. An invitation now came to him to take charge of a new Academy in Hillsboro, Ill., which he accepted. In this school he found for pupils young gentlemen and young ladies, earnest in the work of mental and moral culture. The ill effects of the climate, both upon himself and wife, induced him to return to Boston after an absence of two years. Soon after his return from the West he was invited to take charge of the Academy at Framingham, Mass. He began his labors here in September, 1841, and continued them for four years. Then his health again failed and he was obliged to take entire rest for several months, when it was thought best for him to seek out-door employment. He obtained a position upon the Boston Water Works, then just commenced, at the head of the Typographical department. Here he continued four years — up to the completion of the works. The structure, as it went forward, called for extensive research, and presented many interesting problems in Hydraulics, most of which came to the hands of Mr. Conant for solution. Copies of these he retained and afterwards made a book of plans of the whole work, which he prepared for publication. This manuscript was destroyed by fire and could not be reproduced.

The next two years he spent in laying out and constructing the railroad from Dover to Lake Winnipiseogee in New Hampshire. On the completion of this work he returned to West Newton for a few months and then came to reside in Bridgewater, in 1852, where he was employed in connection with the Eagle Cotton Gin Co. The next year, Mr. Tillinghast resigned his position as Principal of this School, on account of failing health and proposed the election of Mr. Conant as his successor. He was elected and entered upon his duties in August 1853, and continued for seven years, till July 1860, when, both himself and wife being much worn with their arduous labors, he resigned his charge of the School and went to Grantville for recuperation. After resting here for two years he was called to Washington in 1862, by Commissioner Boutwell, to aid in organizing the Department of Internal Revenue. He remained a most faithful and efficient officer in this service till the time of his last sickness, with the exception of one year, when he had a leave of absence. He returned to Bridgewater in 1872, no longer able to perform his duties at Washington, his physical strength steadily declining under a most painful illness. With his mind still clear and active, he continued to work, and finished the manuscript for an astronomical publication but a few days before he was released from suffering by an abundant entrance into the better life beyond.

His life extended a little beyond the allotted period of three score years and ten, though not full of physical strength, it was full of activity and good fruits. The first eighteen years, strong and active, with very limited opportunities for intellectual training, he lived among the hills, and communed with nature. Here he observed and thought for himself, learned the principles of piety and a sacred regard for truth; of sobriety, industry and frugality, the prime elements of a good character. The next five years, he was nearly prostrated by sickness, and although periods of suffering were not wanting, nor times of great depression and discouragement, yet his mind was more active than ever, and he came to a kind of calm *sunshine* of *hoping* and *bearing*. Then he asked specially that he might be spared awhile to teach and to do something in the world. Length of days was granted, and he used the time, strength, and opportunities given him to the full measure of his ability.

The next thirty-seven years he passed as a teacher, author, and engineer, alternating these vocations as the varying conditions of his health required. Twenty-six years of this period were devoted to teaching, and more than two thousand pupils came under his instruction. Who can measure the extent of the influence of his noble soul upon the minds of those pupils? He closed his career of teaching when he left this Normal School. He says, "That period of seven years in charge of one of the oldest Normal Schools in the Country, I look back upon as the culminating epoch in my personal history."

During the last ten years of his life, a part of which he sat at the receipt of custom in the National Treasury, many millions of the public money passed through his hands, but no error nor discrepancy was ever found in his accounts. He was not merely a receiver of tribute money, but his high-toned patriotism and loyalty strengthened the hearts of those who guarded the life of the nation in the days of the rebellion.

The difficulties with which Mr. Conant had to contend in preparing for the work of life, were neither few nor small. But these adverse circumstances did not crush his spirit, nor prevent his doing and rising in the world. They only served to develop his manhood, to bring out those sterling qualities which constitute a truly noble character, as they always do in every genuine man. One of the most prominent traits of his character, was his great hopefulness. He loved life, and his imagination pictured great things to be accomplished,—set before him a high ideal of what life should be. He looked on the bright side, and was sanguine of success even to enthusiasm. This trait made him a very genial companion. Scarcely less prominent was his great perseverance in working out the purpose he had formed. He was industrious and devoted, sparing no pains to accomplish his object. He was never idle, and could not tolerate idleness in others. He believed that earnest labor was the price of everything valuable.

He had great self-respect and fully respected others. He was high toned in all his action and appealed only to worthy motives. He was a man of quick sensibilities, keenly sensitive to neglect, and would not obtrude himself upon the notice of others. The artifices often employed to secure power and position he could not use, but was content to work on, believing that the time would come when the result of his labors would be appreciated, and that he should not be left to want. He was sincere in dealing with himself and with others; every form of trickery and deception he despised. Remarkable for his attention to the wants and feelings of others, always courteous, entirely disregarding his own ease and comfort in his readiness to promote the comfort and happiness of those around him, he was a *true gentleman.*

The crowning traits of his character, were his love of truth and his faith; he sought the truth with his whole soul, both in the works and in the Word of God. He was a careful student of the Bible, an ardent lover of its teachings. He was a man of the largest charity, always kind and liberal in his judgment of others. Though unwilling to contend for place and power, he was fearless in advocating the truth. Every good work found in him a generous supporter; he wrought nobly for himself and for others, but not in his own strength alone. He was brought up in a religious community, and before he left his native place he came to a hearty faith in a divine director and guide, a resting of the soul on the Spirit that called it into being and action.

While teaching in Woodstock, he became a member of the Congregational Church in that place, and through life was sustained and guided by a living faith in Jesus Christ as a personal Savior.

Of Mr. Conant as a teacher, I would gladly speak at length, but I must not trench upon the ground of those who follow me, except to bear my personal testimony to the excellence of his teaching. Working with him as an assistant teacher for several years, I was all this time his pupil, for he was constantly disbursing to me from the rich gatherings of his varied experience. His whole mind and strength were given to his teaching; his genial manner, his ready command of language, and his facility in illustration, always secured the attention of his pupils. In his favorite studies of Mathematics, Astronomy, and Mechanics, he was very clear, definite, and original in his methods. By his fidelity, his devotion, his enthusiasm, and the inspiration of his life, he was constantly drawing his pupils to higher fields of thought, and higher attainments. He threw into his work the poetry of pure and holy motive. You who have been his pupils, as you recall the old school-room; will think, I doubt not, in the words of another, " It was good for us to be there ; for unknown to us, were made therein three tabernacles : one for us, one for our school-master, and one for Him, who is the friend of all children, and the master of all school-masters."

· Such was the man, whose memory is so precious to us to-day. I have sketched his life as fully as I could in so brief a time. I have weighed my words, that I might speak the precise truth, and give that combination of truths which would present the clearest and truest view of the man. " The great lesson, the great legacy of his life," is, that the love of truth, a living faith, and hopeful, persevering industry will enable one to overcome all obstacles, to attain the full stature of a noble manhood, according to the measure of the ability which God has given, will bring one to stations of honor and usefulness, and will leave a memory that shall not perish. "What an inspiration to every youth, longing with a generous ambition to do something in the world," is such a life. Not a teacher, only, has finished his earthly career, but one of the best, the noblest of men. Like a shock of corn, fully ripe, he was gathered. Let us bring to-day, our tributes of respect and affection. Let us go hence, to imitate his virtues, and " let his dear memory serve to make our faith in goodness strong."

A MEMORIAL ADDRESS, Read by ELIZA B. WOODWARD,

Before the BRIDGEWATER NORMAL ASSOCIATION, at Bridgewater, July 15, 1874.

When children, grown-up, and scattered, go home to the accustomed family festival, and gather about the familiar hearth-stone; after the first warm greetings, the eyes turn to the vacant seat, vacated since their last reunion, then vainly wander in search of the missing one; and the heart goes out with longing inexpressible.

So, pupils and friends of Mr. Conant, our eyes to-day, search in vain for a speaking face and a venerable form, with us at our last gathering, and our hearts turn to our missing one, our teacher, our friend, our father.

We meet to-day, a bereaved family; we do not hear his hearty greeting, his cheerful, hope-inspiring words; and we look inquiringly into each others faces. And, because I was here when he went away, and heard his gracious words as he waited, ready and anxious to "pass on" to the promised rest, you have asked me to speak to you of him. I cannot do it worthily; but I cannot by refusal, seem unwilling to honor him dead, whom living, I esteemed worthy of the highest honor.

Many years of intimate acquaintance in the school, in his home, by correspondence, and finally in the sick room, gave me the rare privilege of knowing the spirit of the man; of learning the noble purposes which actuated him, and of seeing how truly his life conformed to his high standard. And, as I have read or listened to your words of grateful praise, and to those which have come from loving hearts all over the country, I have felt that the highest which has been spoken has not transcended what was due to the purity, the justice, the truth, the nobility of his character.

"How rare and how blessed it is to know one of whom we can say, 'I bless God upon every remembrance of him.' Such is our blessedness in knowing Mr. Conant. We knew him a christian gentleman, true to every relation in life. He "cultivated the gentle charities," and was as exact in the common duties which no human eye would note, as in the most public, where the eyes of the nation were upon its treasure.

He possessed that broad and liberal culture which we are accustomed to ascribe to foreign travel and study. He never went abroad, but, in all the changes of his varied life, he kept a mind open and receptive. He mingled freely with strangers and intelligent foreigners; and by a wide range of social intercourse, local peculiarities were lost, his character was rounded, and he made so completely a cosmopolitan, that his nationality was frequently the subject of question by those who did not know him well. Yet love of country was almost a passion with him. He always identified himself with the community in which he lived; and as a citizen, devoted himself to securing the greatest good to the greatest number, without regard to personal interests. He was a most enthusiastic and inspiring teacher; he was thorough, exact, and eminently practical, and gave a charm to every subject which he taught by the store of collateral truths by which he surrounded it. He gave his pupils glimpses of treasures which they could mine for themselves in the future; he opened side-doors into choice museums free to be explored by the eager, curious student when the opportunity should come; so he seldom failed to inspire his pupils with a desire to obtain a high, liberal education.

But you knew him as a teacher and a man; so I have brought together a few extracts from your letters of sympathy, which were kindly furnished me by Mrs. Conant, that your own words may tell, as they best can, of the influence which he had upon your lives, and the place he still holds in your hearts.

"It is with no hollow and idle voices that the hundreds of those who have been under his charge at the Normal School rise up and call him blessed. Many a one owes to him an awakening and an inspiration which have changed the whole current of his thought, and ennobled his whole life. — *Alfred Bunker*.

"I call him father, for never, until I came under his paternal instructions, did I have the energies of my mind enlivened, or the dormant powers of my spiritual nature quickened into being. Through his incitement I have been trying for nearly a score of years to be more and more a scholar and a Christian. — *Rev. Nathan Willis*.

"His life impinged upon my own with singular force. In my list of helpers and inspirers he stands among the highest. A tender, generous, courageous life, — a life of steadfast earnestness and deep enthusiasm. Upon the moral side, his were the loftiest ideals; and he held his pupils to them by spontaneous attraction rather than by any conscious effort. — *Rev. John W. Chadwick*.

"He was my best friend and did more for me than I can tell. He was a man of superior ability and knowledge: but, better than this, he was one of the best of men and truest of friends. The happiest and most profitable years of my life were those I passed with him. — *Edward Rice*.

"I am amazed in considering what Mr. Conant, in his weakness, accomplished. Ever since it was my pleasure to know him, it has seemed that his life hung by a very slender cord. That he lived so long was due, largely, to prudence and care; yet, where do we find those who really accomplish so much? His organization was exceedingly delicate, but the latent force within was ever ready to be kindled whenever it might tend to arouse some dormant intellect, or fan the flame already kindled in some mind thirsting for knowledge. His life was filled with work, but there was that confiding trust in the Good Being, that made everything about him bright and cheerful, even though the sky was overcast."—*S. Dwight Eaton.*

The lamented Prof. Alpheus Crosby, who knew him well, wrote thus of him:—

"It is impossible for us to express our high and affectionate appreciation of him who has gone before us,—of his mind, his heart, and his life! Oh, that we all might have our work as well done as he, and be as well prepared for an exchange of worlds!

"Mr. Conant was not only a man of remarkable ability and attainments; but, what is much more, one of the very best men I ever knew, 'Good all the way through;' and, what is not true of all good men, he was a man not only to be esteemed and trusted, but to be really loved."

When the news of Mr. Conant's death reached Washington, a meeting of the officers and clerks of the office of Internal Revenue was held, at which resolutions were unanimously adopted, expressing profound sorrow and a sense of personal bereavement, and the feeling "that, in the death of Marshall Conant, the office has lost one of the ablest and purest men that have ever been connected with it."

"Is he dead whose glorious mind lifts thine on high?
To live in hearts we leave behind is not to die."

Mr. Conant returned to Bridgewater in his "Sunset hour." He had worked through the early, clouded morning; in the heat and weariness of the noon-tide; through the long, long day: with what courage and hope, how joyously and successfully, we all know. And when the twilight shadows began to lengthen about him, he turned to this as the place where he would review the work of the day, search his own heart, and then lie down for his rest.

He had felt the burden of life slip from his shoulders, and knew that he should never take it up again. No one with health and hope of life can realize what that meant to him whose life had been so full of joyous labor, and for whom this wonderful creation teemed with beauty, mystery, and the grandest subjects of study.

But he bravely turned from all which had so gladdened his life; and, with but one earthly longing and regret, accepted the weary watching and waiting for the dawn of the new day whose sun should never set. Those last days of physical suffering, in which the soul longed for quiet and release, are sacred; but, as he had been in his active life, so he was now in his weakness, the Christian gentleman, — patient, thoughtful of the comfort and feelings of others, and maintaining always a perfect mastery over himself.

His mind was clear; and, though his thoughts were reaching forward and taking hold of the highest things of God, his heart clung fondly to his earthly friends, and his face responded to every word and look of love. No friend or neighbor entered his room without receiving the cordial, old-time recognition; and many a benediction fell from his lips as messages of affectionate remembrance were brought to him from the absent.

Many times during the last blessed afternoon of his life, his lips murmured: "The Lord will deliver him that trusteth in Him." "The Lord will deliver." His deliverance came, and — "He is not, for God took him."

ASSISTANT TEACHERS.

ALBERT G. BOYDEN. from August to November, 1853.
EDWIN C. HEWETT, was appointed January, 1853, resigned December, 1856. A member of the thirty-fourth class. Graduated from this school March 9, 1852. Taught in the High School, Pittsfield, one year. Assistant teacher in Bridgewater State Normal School, three years. Principal of the First Grammar School, Worcester, two years. Has taught in State Normal University, Normal, Ill., the last eighteen years.
MRS. SARAH M. WYMAN, of Ashby, was appointed Nov., 1853, resigned, February, 1854.
JAIRUS LINCOLN, JR., was appointed March, 1854, resigned July, 1855. A member of the thirty-eighth class; graduated from this school, November 8, 1853; taught in Medfield the winter following his graduation; Assistant in Bridgewater State Normal School, one year and a half; taught Grammar Schools five years; now farmer and stock raiser in Longmont, Colorado.
LEANDER A. DARLING, was appointed September, 1855, resigned August, 1857. A member of the forty-second class; graduated from this school, March 13, 1855; assistant in this school two years; taught Grammar Schools, four years; Principal Young Ladies Institute, Charlestown, nine years; has been Principal of Normal School at Tougaloo, Miss., one year.
BENJAMIN F. CLARKE, was appointed December, 1856, resigned August, 1857, A member of the forty-fourth class. Graduated from this school, February 19, 1856; taught the Hacker Grammar School, Salem, three months; Assistant in Bridgewater State Normal School eight months; taught in Private School, Providence, R. I., three years; graduated from Brown University; has taught in Brown University the last thirteen years; Professor of Mathematics and Civil Engineering.
ALBERT G. BOYDEN, from September, 1857, to August, 1860.
ELIZA B. WOODWARD, appointed September, 1857. A member of the forty-seventh class. Graduated from this school July 28, 1857; Has taught in this school the last nineteen years.
ELIZABETH CRAFTS, from December 13, 1858, to February 15, 1859. A member of the thirty-first class. Graduated from this school, March 11, 1851; has taught seventeen years in Grammar and Private Schools; now teaching in Grammar School in Malden.
WARREN T. COPELAND, was appointed March, 1859, resigned February, 1860; A member of the forty-first class; graduated from this school, November 7, 1854; taught Grammar'schools four years; Assistant in Bridgewater State Normal School one year; taught in Grammar Schools seventeen years; Principal of Huntingdon Grammar School, Brockton.
CHARLES F. DEXTER, was appointed March, 1860, and continued till May, 1863. A member of the fifty-second class. Graduated from this school February 21, 1860; Assistant in this school three years; now Merchant in Chicago.

ALUMNI RECORD.

CLASS 40. AUGUST 3, 1853.

WILLIAM A. BARRELL, East Bridgewater. Taught eight years. Paymaster. Everett Mills. Lawrence.
THOMAS B. BLACKMAN, Pembroke. Taught one year. Farmer. Marshfield.
HENRY BLANCHARD, Charlestown. 2. Did not teach. Clergyman. Worcester.
JOSIAH V. BISBEE, North Bridgewater. Not heard from.
WILLIAM D. BURDITT, Northboro'. Taught two years. Apothecary. Marlboro'.
JAMES B. EVERETT, Canton. Taught five years. Physician. Everett.
DYER FREEMAN, JR.,* Webster. Taught over seven years. Died in New Orleans, Jan. 13, 1867.
HORACE B. FULLER, Lincoln, Me. Bookseller. 14 Bromfield Street, Boston.
EBENEZER GAY, JR., Bridgewater. Taught eighteen years. Episcopal Clergyman. Tomkins Cove, New York.
EDWIN GOSS,* Sterling. Taught one year. Died in Sterling, December 15, 1857.
ORANGE H. GREEN, Westminster. 1. Not heard from.
CHARLES B. JOHNSON,* Northboro'. Taught seven years. Died May 9, 1864.
J. W. McMAHAN,* Perry, Maine. Died in Perry, Maine.
JOHN M. RICE, Northboro'. Taught twenty-one years. In Public Schools, five years. In Lawrence Scientific School, Cambridge, three years. In Naval Academy, thirteen years Professor of Mathematics, United States Naval Academy. Annapolis, Maryland.
HIRAM W. WENTWORTH, Bridgewater. Taught five years. Merchant. New Bedford.
GEORGE WHITAKER, Needham. Taught two years. Presiding Elder, Methodist Conference. Westfield.

Total of teaching for thirteen, seventy-seven years. Average, six years.

GRACIA M. BEMIS, Springfield, Vt. Mrs. Abijah B. Going. Springfield, Vt.
MARTHA A. BRIGHAM, Bridgewater. 1. Taught three years. Mrs. Geo. A. King, Concord,
ALVIRA E. BURDON, Sutton. Taught thirteen years. Address, Whitinsville.
JUDITH J. DERRICK, Nantucket. Taught six years. Mrs. George G. Fish, Nantucket.
HELEN A. GARDNER, Nantucket. T. eight years. Teaching. Roxbury High School.
LOUISA JENKINS, Woolwich Me. T. twelve years. Teaching. Williamstown, N. J.
CAROLINE L. JOHNSON, Northboro'. Taught eighteen years. Mrs. Thomas C. Holmes, Rochelle, Ill.
ABBIE F. MILLER, Northboro'. 2. Not heard from.
MARY E. MORSE, Attleboro'. Taught four years. Mrs. Elisha Crocker, Jr., Brewster.
CORDELIA H. RAYMOND, Dartmouth. 2. Not heard from.
HELEN M. READ, Kingston. Taught two years. Mrs. Leander L. Jones, W. Barnstable.
ELLEN RIDEOUT, Salem. Taught six years. Address, Salem.
MARY E. SCOTT, Milford. Taught one term. Mrs. William Tebb, 7 Albert Row, Regent's Park, London, England.
RUTH A. THAXTER, Bridgewater. 2. T. one term. Mrs. Wm. H. Taylor, E. Weymouth.
JULIA A. WENTWORTH, Bridgewater. . T. six years. Mrs. Solomon Keith, Bridgewater.
MRS. JANE C. THOMPSON, Rochester. T. twenty-two years. Teaching. New Bedford.

Total of teaching for thirteen, ninety-one years. Average, seven years.

Class 41. November 30, 1853.

WARREN T. COPELAND, Bridgewater. Taught twenty-two years, Grammar, High and Normal Schools. Principal, Grammar School, Brockton.
LEANDER WATERMAN, East Bridgewater. Taught twenty-one years, Grammar Schools; Master, Andrew School, Boston.

    Total of teaching for two, forty-three years. Average, twenty-one and one half years.

MARY F. BOND,* Charlton. Taught two years. Mrs. F. J. Campbell. Died, Sept., 1873.
SUSAN H. COLEMAN, Nantucket. T. thirteen years. Mrs. Rev. S. D. Hosmer, S. Natick.
MORGIANA CUSHING, Hingham. T. one term. Mrs. Luke H. Bowers, N. Abington.

    Total of teaching for three, fifteen years. Average, five years.

Class 42. March 22, 1854.

ELBRIDGE P. BOYDEN, Walpole. Taught eight terms. Farmer. S. Walpole.
HENRY C. BULLARD,* Milford. Taught sixteen years in Grammar Schools. Died, 1872.
LEANDER A. DARLING, Middleboro'. Taught seventeen years. Principal, Tougaloo Normal School, Miss.
REUBEN W. GUNNISON, Goshen, N. H. Not heard from.
ALFRED N. HARDY, Greenfield, N. H. Taught five years. Farmer. Greenfield, N. H.
VIRGIL THOMPSON, Middleboro'. T. two years. Physician. 234 W. 11th St., N. Y. City.
LEVI F. WARREN, Weston. Taught twenty-one years. Grammar Schools in Salem and Newton. Principal, Grammar School, West Newton.

    Total of teaching for six, sixty-nine years. Average, eleven and one-half years.

LOUISA M. CLARKE, Canton. Taught five years. Address, Hyde Park.
EMMA DAVIE, Plymouth. Taught nineteen years. Teaching. Plymouth.
LIZZIE F. ROBBINS, Plymouth. Mrs. Nathaniel Morton, Plymouth.
ISABELLA G. ROBBINS, Plymouth. Taught one term. Copyist. Boston.
LUCIA R. ROBBINS, Kingston. Taught fourteen years. Teaching, Grammar School, Toledo, Ohio.
REBECCA D. ROBBINS, Kingston. Taught six years. Mrs. L. W. Finney, Plymouth.

    Total of teaching for six, forty-four years. Average, seven years.

Class 43. August 2, 1854.

GUILFORD D. BIGELOW, Harvard. Taught sixteen years. Address, Allston.
WILLIAM H. CUMMINGS, Holderness, N. H. Taught eight years. Farmer. Halifax.
HENRY T. PRATT, Bridgewater. Did not teach. Printer. Bridgewater.
FRANCIS TOURTELLOTTE, Thompson, Conn. Physician. Winona, Minn.

    Total of teaching for four, twenty-four years. Average, six years.

LOUISA BURRELL, Quincy. Taught six years. Clerk, Quincy Bank. Quincy.
CAROLINE H. DARLING, E. Constable, N. Y. Taught five years. Mrs. Edward G. Durant, Racine, Wis.
CAROLINE E. DEWING, Needham. Taught twenty years. Grammar Schools. Teaching. South Framingham.
EMILY F. JOHNSON, Newburyport. Not heard from. Mrs. D. Ricter, Williamsport, Pa

    Total of teaching for three, thirty-one years. Average, ten years.

Class 44. December 4, 1854.

BENJ. F. CLARKE, Newport, Me. Taught eighteen years. High and Normal Schools. Prof. Math. and Civ. Eng. Brown University, Providence, R. I.
WILLIAM P. CONANT, West Danvers. Not heard from.
O. BALFOUR DARLING, Lexington. Taught five terms. Farmer. Lexington.

JOHN A. EMERY, Chatham. Taught four years. Lawyer. Pittsburg, Penn.
GEO. W. LOCKE, Lexington. T. seventeen years. Prin., Grammar School. Fall River.
JOHN NUTTING, Marblehead. Taught nine years. Shoe Business. Marblehead.
GRANVILLE B. PUTNAM, N. Danvers. Taught seventeen years. Graduated at Amherst College. In High Schools, four years. In Grammar, thirteen years. Master, Franklin Grammar School. Boston.
G. MELVILLE SMITH, Boston. Did not teach. Atty. at Law. St. Louis. Mo.

Total of teaching for seven, sixty-three years. Average, nine years.

SOPHRONIA A. BAKER, Wellfleet. T. three years. Mrs. C. W. Rich, 164 Bloomingdale St., Chelsea.
LIZZIE B. CHRISTIAN, Bridgewater. T. four years. Mrs. Wm. E. Jewell, Randolph.
HARRIET M. KEITH, Bridgewater. 2. Did not teach. Mrs. Chas. Jewett, Bridgewater.
PAMELA KEITH, Bridgewater. Taught two terms. Music Teacher. Bridgewater.
SUSAN MORSE, Weston. Taught one year. Geneva, Kane Co., Ill.
MARY W. PERKINS, Bridgewater. T. seven terms. Mrs. Ezra Goodspeed, Bridgewater.
ARVILLA L. ROBINSON, Bridgewater. Taught three years. Mrs. Thomas L. Andrews, Bridgewater.

Total of teaching for seven, fourteen years. Average, two years.

CLASS 45. MARCH 21, 1855.

BENJAMIN T. CROOKER, Bridgewater. Taught two years. Surgeon and Apothecary. Bridgewater.
LABAN G. DUNHAM, Attleboro'. 1. Not heard from.
JAMES H. EATON, Candia. N. H. Taught nine years. Treas., Essex Bank. Lawrence.
HENRY R. EDWARDS, Lincoln, Me. 1. Taught four years. Farmer and Lumberman. Lincoln, Me.
WILLARD S. EVERETT, Canton. Taught five years. Physician. Hyde Park.
JOSEPH H. KEITH, Bridgewater. 2. T. three years in Private School. New Orleans, La.
L. VIRGIL MORSE, Attleboro'. Taught one term. Merchant. Omaha, Neb.
FRANCIS NICHOLS, Sturbridge. Taught two years. Physician. Hoboken, N. J.
E. F. SPAULDING, Francestown, N. H. T. four years. Physician. 7 Princeton St., Boston.

Total of teaching for eight, twenty-nine years. Average, four years.

JULIA M. BLAKE, Framingham. Not heard from.
MELVINA R. BLANCHARD,* S. Weymouth. 1. Died August, 1855.
AMANTHA J. BORDEN, New Bedford. 1. Taught three years. Mrs. Volney Tupper, New Bedford.
MARY E. BRADFORD, Kingston. Taught one year. Mrs. Thos. E. Lanman, Brookline.
HARRIET CLOUD,* South Weymouth. T. four years. Mrs. J. H. Fairbanks. Deceased.
PHEBE CONANT, Bridgewater. Taught one year. Mrs. James C. Leach, Bridgewater.
SATIRA W. CONNER, S. Dartmouth. T. six years. Mrs. Frederic S. Allen, New Bedford.
ANN MARIA EATON, Framingham. Taught six years. Address, Framingham.
MARY EDSON, West Bridgewater. Taught one year. Address, Bridgewater.
EMILY H. FISHER, Franklin. Taught eighteen years. Mrs. Eben M. Swan, 168 Chatham St., Lynn.
MARY A. HAYWARD, Bridgewater. Taught five seasons. Mrs. Lloyd A. Field, Taunton.
LAURA D. HOLMES, Bridgewater, T. eight years. Mrs. Isaac F. Kingsbury, Chestnut Hill.
H. MARIA LEACH, W. Eaton, N. Y. T. ten years. Mrs. Dr. Emory Potter, Experiment Mills, 1857.
EUNICE G. MACY,* Nantucket. 2. Taught one term. Died March, 1857.   [Pa.
LYDIA E. MORSE, Rehoboth. Taught one year. Mrs. D. B. Walker, Odell, Ill.
MARY NICHOLS, West Woburn. T. sixteen years. Teaching, Bigelow School. S. Boston.
ADELIA R. POOR,* Lawrence. Taught ten years. Mrs. Frank Wood. Died Oct., 1867.
CAROLINE SAMPSON, Bridgewater. Taught seventeen years. Teaching, Primary School. Bridgewater.
MARIA D. SAMSON, Pembroke. Taught three years. Mrs. Leander Waterman, Boston.

ELLEN E. SHEDD, Bridgewater. Taught five years. Mrs. Alfred F. Gage, Waltham.
MARY E. WALKER, Taunton. Taught nineteen years. Care of Wm. L. Walker, Taunton.
SARAH S. WELD, Roxbury. Not heard from.
SARAH V. WILDE, Randolph. Taught seventeen years. Teaching. Randolph.
  Total of teaching for twenty, one hundred and fifty-one years. Average, eight years.

CLASS 46. SEPTEMBER 19, 1855.

ANDREW M. FOLGER, Nantucket. Taught seven years. Clergyman. Windsor, Vt.
SAMUEL P. GATES, Ashby. Bookkeeper and Treasurer, Savings Bank. Bridgewater.
EDWARD R. HAYWARD, Easton. Taught one year. Farmer. Easton.
GEO. M. HOOPER, Bridgewater. Taught one year. Brick manufacturer. Bridgewater.
JOHN HUMPHREY,* Athol. Taught three years. Was fatally wounded, and sunk with the Cumberland, Hampton Roads, March 8, 1862.
DAVID S. JEWELL, Newton. T. four years. Agent of Cotton Mills. Suncook, N. H.
HENRY R. LYLE, Gloucester. Taught two terms. Oil Business. Titusville, Pa.
HOWARD MORTON, Plymouth. 2. Did not teach. Farmer. Churchill, Kansas.
A. LEWIS PUTNAM, Danvers. Taught four years. Merchant. Provincetown.
WALLACE A. PUTNAM,* Danvers. Taught two years. Major Putnam. Died June 20, 1864, of wounds received in battle.
LUTHER RUGG, 2d,* Sterling. Taught ten years. Drowned, Oct. 6, 1867.
SIMSON S. SANBORN, Abington. T. fifteen years. Grammar and High Schools. Barnstable.
EDWIN P. SEAVER, Northboro'. Taught fifteen years. Grad. Harvard College; Prof. of Mathematics in Harvard College. Head Master, English High School. Boston.
ELBRIDGE TORREY, S. Weymouth. Taught three years. Torrey, Bright & Co., 350 Washington St., Boston.
NATHAN E. WILLIS,* Bridgewater. Taught eleven years. Graduate, Amherst College. Sub-Master, English High School, Boston. Pastor Cong'l Church, Marion, Ala. Died Sept. 24, 1874.
  Total of teaching for fifteen, seventy-seven years. Average, five years.

MARTHA W. BARTLETT, S. Plymouth. 2. T. nineteen years. S. Plymouth.
ELIZA H. CLARKE, S. Plymouth. Taught six years. Mrs. Thomas S. Bates, New Bedford, 63 No. Third St.
LIZZY CLARKE,* S. Plymouth. T. two years. Mrs. S. S. Holmes. Died May 21, 1862.
JULIA A. COFFIN, W. Tisbury. T. eight years. Postmistress. West Tisbury.
LUCY COPELAND, West Bridgewater. T. fourteen years. Teaching. Campello.
PERSIS S. CROWELL, E. Dennis. Taught two years. Grammar School. Mrs. John H. Addy, E. Dennis.
DELIA P. DAY, Wrentham. Taught four years. Address, Spencer.
FRANCES A. DEWEY, Hanover, N. H. Taught seven years. Mrs. James A. Henderson, Jefferson, Iowa.
L. PARTHENA DEWEY, Hanover, N. H. Taught four years. Mrs. Newton J. Smith, Toulon, Ill.
SARAH E. FISHER. No. Woburn. Taught nineteen years. Teaching. Lewis School, Boston.
ELLEN M. HAWES, No. Wrentham. Not heard from. Mrs. Wm. Wheeler, Worcester.
AMANDA A. HOWLAND, Saratoga. 2. Taught five years. Mrs. Willett L. Carroll, 160 Vincennes Ave., Chicago, Ill.
HARRIET G. LASELLE, Worcester. 2. Taught two years. Mrs. Charles Cole, Taunton.
J. C. MAHAFFEY, Derry, N. H. 2. Taught one year. Mrs. E. H. Keith, Bridgewater.
MARIA H. ORCHARD,* New Hamburg, N. Y. 1. Died, 1857.
MARY PROCTOR, E. Braintree. Mrs. Frederic E. Fowle, Arlington.
SARAH H. RUGG, Sterling. Taught seven years. Mrs. Charles A. Rice, Westboro'.
CAROLINE E. SOULE, E. Middleboro'. Taught twelve years. Address, E. Middleboro'.
DELIA M. UPHAM, Nantucket. T. seventeen years. Teaching. Comins School, Boston.
CARRIE F. WATSON, Kingston, R. I. Taught twenty years. Address, Kingston, R. I.
FANNIE W. WEBB, Belleville, N. Y. T. six years. Address, 105 Elm St., New Bedford.
  Total of teaching for eighteen, one hundred and fifty-five years. Average, nine years.

Class 47. March 19, 1856.

GEO. B. BUFFINGTON, Somerset. Taught seventeen years. Grammar Schools. Atty's Office. Fall River.
WILLIAM DAMON, Hanson. Not heard from.
GEO. GOULD, Dedham. Did not teach. Music Printer. 221 Washington St., Boston.
T. W. J. HOLBROOK, South Braintree. 1. Not heard from.
CHAS. H. PEABODY, Danvers. Taught one year. Farmer. Danvers Centre.
AMOS A. POPE,* Danvers. Taught seven terms. Died, Sept. 15, 1864.
WILLIAM RANKIN, Jr., Rochester. Taught thirteen years, Farmer. Brockton.
    Total of teaching for five, thirty-four years. Average, seven years.
LYDIA A. ARNOLD,* Norton. Taught two years. Mrs. Joseph Hyde, Bridgewater. Died, Aug. 29, 1870.
SOPHRONIA ATHEARN, West Tisbury. Mrs. Joel Nichols, San Francisco, Cal.
JEMIMA F. AUSTIN, Nantucket. Taught sixteen years. Eleven years in public schools. Principal Clark Institute for Ladies. San Francisco. 228 Capp St.
ELLEN D. BRIGGS, Scituate. 2. Taught ten years. Mrs. Luther Paul, Newton Centre.
MARY A. BRIGHAM,* Bridgewater. Died, 1858.
HANNAH C. BRYANT, W. Bridgewater. Taught four years. Mrs. Benj. T. Clark, Boston Highlands.
BETSEY T. CAPEN, Stoughton. Taught nineteen years, Girls High School, Boston. Prof. of Chemistry. Wellesley College.
ELVIRA S. CRANE, Dorchester. Taught eight years. Mrs. Eben Bent, Quincy.
ELIZA J. EVERETT, Canton. Taught five years. Canton.
HANNAH FAULKNER,* Malden. Taught one term. Died Jan. 7, 1860.
SARAH B. FISKE, Medfield. Taught two years. Mrs. Rev. Jas. A. Laurie, Duluth, Minn.
MARY R. FOWLE,* Woburn. Taught one year. Died Dec. 19, 1868.
M. MATILDA FOWLE, Woburn. T. five years. Mrs. Frank C. Eastman, Cambridgeport.
SUSAN B. GETCHELL,* Nantucket. Taught twelve years. Mrs. Henry R. Lyle. Died, Dec., 1869.
MARY E. HAWES, Bridgewater. Taught one term. Mrs. Willard A. Barnes, Campello.
LUCY J. HAYDEN,* Bridgewater. Taught ten years. Mrs. Nathan E. Willis, Marion, Ala. Died Sept. 26, 1874.
OLIVE M. HOBART, Hingham. Taught nineteen years. Head Ass't., Russell School. Arlington.
VIRGINIA HUGHES, Bridgewater. T. three years. Mrs. Dr. A. Sumner Dean, Taunton.
HARRIET A. KEITH, Bridgewater. Taught three years. Address, Bridgewater.
ESTHER M. KEITH, Bridgewater. T. seven years. Mrs. Lemuel M. Keith, Bridgewater.
SUSAN B. LOUD, S. Weymouth. 1. Not heard from.
RUTH H. NICKERSON, W. Tisbury. T. ten years. Mrs. Edward Hiller, Mattapoisett.
MARY G. OSGOOD, Sterling. Taught ten years. Mrs. Luther Rugg, Sterling.
REBECCA D. ROTCH, West Tisbury. Taught nine years. Address, West Tisbury.
HELEN C. SPRAGUE, S. Weymouth. 2. T. two years. Mrs. James Tirrell, S. Weymouth.
LUCY M. THAXTER, Bridgewater. 2. Did not teach. Mrs. Edward McSweeny.
ELIZA B. WOODWARD, Lowell. T. nineteen years. State Normal School, Bridgewater.
    Total of teaching for twenty-four, 177 years. Average, seven years.

Class 48. September 17, 1856.

WILLIAM G. BRUCE, Burlington, Ky. 1. Not heard from.
MASSENA B. HAWES,* Stoughton. Died, 1863, at New Orleans.
NATHANIEL B. HODSDON, Bethel, Me. Taught six years. Prin. of all the Schools. Carmi, Ill.
FREDERICK C. SMITH,* Waterford, Me. Taught four years. Died in Weston, W. Va., April 16, 1862.
LEWIS H. SWEET,* Norton. Taught three years. Killed at Port Hudson, June 15, 1863.
    Total of teaching for four, thirteen years. Average, three years.

AURINA BUGBEE, Worcester. Taught six months. Mrs. J. M. Atwood, Chelsea.
CARRIE F. CUTTER, Bridgewater. T. six years. Mrs. Orville Jones, New Britain, Conn.
LIZZIE B. DAY, Attleboro'. Taught two terms. Address, Attleboro'.
CLARA E. FARRINGTON, Methuen. Taught seventeen years. Mrs. Everett Cummings, Malone, N. Y.
EMILY A. HANNA, E. Randolph. Taught eighteen years. Grammar Schools, Boston. Holbrook.
ELEANOR P. HOOD. Taunton. Taught seventeen years. Grammar School. Taunton.
MARY P. LACKEY, Sutton. Taught three years. Mrs. H. W. Parkis, Slatersville, R. I.
CAROLINE E. MORRISON, Farmington, Me. Taught one year. Mrs. Wm. Randall, Farmington, Maine.
MARY H. PETERSON, Somerset. 2. Not heard from.
DEBORAH ROWLAND,* Oxford. No information. Deceased.
NANCY S. SMITH, Waterford, Me. 1. T. one term. Mrs. C. A. Libby, Fort Fairfield, Me.
ABBIE A. SWEET, Norton. T. three years. Mrs. Chas. H. Walker, S. Braintree.
MARY A. SWIFT, Bridgewater. 2. Mrs. H. F. Barnes.
SARAH H. WIGHT, Medfield. Taught twelve years. Address, Medfield.
ABBY W. WILD, N. Easton. Taught three terms. Mrs. Henry A. Ford, Brockton.
AUGUSTA W. WILLIAMS,* Berkley. Taught five years. Mrs. Dr. Virgil Thompson. Died March 20, 1870.
PAULINE T. WOOD, Middleboro'. T. seventeen years. Grammar School, Malden Centre.
Total of teaching for fourteen, one hundred and four years. Average, seven years.

CLASS 49.   MARCH 18, 1857.

GEORGE A. BLACKMER,* South Plymouth. No information. Deceased.
EDMUND COTTLE, Chilmark. Not heard from.
LUCIAN D. FAY, Marlboro'. Not heard from.
JOHN H. FERGUSON, Chilmark. 1. T. four terms. Lawyer. 7 Commercial Place, N. O.
GEORGE M. GAGE, Gorham, Me. Taught eighteen years in High and Grammar; Principal, State Normal Schools, at Farmington, Me., and Mankato, Minn.; Sup't. Public Schools, St. Paul, Minn.
HORACE GRAVES, Marblehead. T. five years. Lawyer. 361 Fulton St., Brooklyn, N. Y.
A. JUDSON GRAY, Tisbury. 2. Taught four years. Military Inspector and Physician. Fort Laramie, Wyoming Territory.
THOMAS GURNEY, 2D., Hanson. Taught six years. Merchant. Atlantic.
GEO. A. HARRIS, Methuen. 2. Not heard from.
JOSEPH W. JOSSELYN,* Pembroke. T. ten years. Died Oct. 21, 1868, San Leandro, Cal.
SAMUEL T. MERRILL, Barnstead, N. H. 1. Not heard from.
AUGUSTUS REMICK, N. Bridgewater. Physician. Elmwood, Providence, R. I.
AMOS T. RICHARDSON, Dracut. 2. Not heard from.
OWEN B. STONE, Sweden, Me. Taught nineteen years. In High Schools, ten years; in Grammar, nine. Principal, Grammar School. Salem.
JOHN. H. SUMNER, Foxboro'. T. fifteen years. Prin., Grammar School. E. Oakland. Cal.
D. CAPEN WENTWORTH, Bridgewater. 1. Not heard from.
Total of teaching for eight, seventy-nine years. Average, ten years.

JOANNA L. BOYDEN, Medfield. Not heard from.
PHEBE W. BUNKER, Nantucket. Taught seven years. Everett School. Dorchester.
ADDIE O. COOK, Provincetown. Taught one term. Mrs. A. L. Putnam, Provincetown.
LYDIA W. DERBY, E. Randolph. Taught ten years. Mrs. Benj. Wallace, Lockeford, Cal.
ABBY J. ELLIS, Canton. Taught nine years. Mrs. Geo. H. Snow, Canton.
JULIA A. ELLIS, Medfield. Taught nine years. Mrs. Robert Pope, Gardner, Me.
MARY A. FAY, Marlboro'. Not heard from.
SARAH R. FRENCH. E. Randolph. Taught one year. Ass't. Librarian. Holbrook.
SUSAN L. HAMMOND, N. Abington. 2. T. one year. Mrs. Geo. S. Locke, Lockeford, Cal.

E. ANGENETTE KEITH,* Bridgewater. 1. Died, October 27, 1857.
SARAH D. LEAVITT, Bridgewater. 1. Taught one year. Address, Brighton.
ANNA M. NYE,* New Bedford. 1. Did not teach. Mrs. T. G. Bates. Died, 1864.
REBECCA A. NICKERSON, Provincetown. T. nine years. Mrs. J. T. Small, 157 Marion St., E. Boston.
MERCY M. RICH, Provincetown. Taught one year. Mrs. D. F. Lewis, Provincetown.
MARY H. SHAW, Bridgewater. Taught two years. Mrs. J. E. Drane, Waverly, Lafayette County, Mo.
LUCRETIA S. SWAIN, Nantucket. Not heard from.
REBECCA J. STETSON, N. Abington. 1. Not heard from.
SARAH B. THOMPSON, Halifax. Taught two years. Mrs. S. B. Baine, Halifax.
HANNAH A. WASHBURN, Bridgewater. Did not teach. Address, Bridgewater.
  Total of teaching for fourteen, fifty-two years. Average, four years.

Class 50. September 16, 1857.

JEHIEL BARKER, Westport. 1. Not heard from.
GEORGE A. BROCK, Attleboro'. 2. Not heard from.
ALFRED BUNKER, Nantucket. Taught fifteen years in Grammar and High Schools. Sub-Master in Boston, seven years. Address, Boston Highlands.
JOHN W. CHADWICK, Jr., Marblehead. Did not teach. Unitarian Clergyman. Brooklyn, N. Y.
A. SUMNER DEAN, Foxboro'. 3. Taught three terms. Physician. Taunton.
CHARLES W. FELT, Salem. Did not teach. Inventor and Journalist. Harvard.
WILLIAM HASKELL, Beverly. Taught fifteen years. Address, Beverly.
ISAAC F. KINGSBURY, Newton. Did not teach. Assistant Adjutant General, Mass. Rank, Colonel. Chestnut Hill, Newton.
VIRGIL D. STOCKBRIDGE, Canton, Me. Taught three years. Examiner-in-chief Patent Office. Washington, D. C.
TILDEN UPTON,* N. Reading. Taught six years. Died, 1866.
  Total of teaching for eight, forty years. Average, five years.

REBECCA ATKINS, Provincetown. T. one year. Mrs. Charles Loring, Provincetown.
MARY E. COBB, Kingston. Taught five years. Address, Kingston.
MARY F. GOODELL,* Woburn. T. four years. Mrs. J. H. Sumner. Died Sept. 28, 1869.
HARRIET N. KINGMAN, Campello. 2. Did not teach. Address, Campello.
MARTHA B. NEWELL, Bethel, Me. Taught six years. Mrs. T. H. Chapman, Bethel, Me.
EVERLINA E. PAGE,* No. Woburn. 3. No information.
HATTIE F. PERKINS, W. Bridgewater. T. three years. Mrs. Geo. Hayward, Bridgewater.
KATE B. PILLSBURY, Lawrence. Taught three years. Mrs. Rev. J. K. Bragg, Norfolk.
LAURA G. WILLIS,* Bridgewater. T. two years. Mrs. F. H. Ludington. Died, 1862.
  Total of teaching for eight, twenty-four years. Average, three years.

Class 51. March 17, 1858.

WALTER H. ALDEN, Bridgewater. Taught seven years. Address, Bridgewater.
EDWIN A. BABCOCK, Berlin. 2. Did not teach.
SAMUEL J. BLOOD,* Charlton. 2. Taught one year. Died August 30, 1869.
C. FREEMAN CHRISTIAN, Bridgewater. 1. Did not teach. Address, Bridgewater.
FRED. O. ELLIS, S. Boston. T. seventeen years. Sub-Master, Bigelow School. Boston.
WILLIAM B. GROVER, Foxboro'. 2. Did not teach. Merchant. Providence, R. I.
GEO. B. HANNA, E. Randolph. Taught four years. Mining Engineer and Chemist of N. C. Survey. Charlotte, N. C.
ELLIS V. LYON,* Campello. Taught two years. Died at Petersburg, Va., Sept. 24, 1864.
GEO. L. SMALLEY,* Quincy. Taught two years. Died November 23, 1862.
JOSEPH A. TORREY, Salem. Taught two years. Furniture Dealer. Boston.
JACOB P. WASHBURN,* Bridgewater. 2. Died Oct. 23, 1859.

BRIDGEWATER STATE NORMAL SCHOOL.

AMASA A. WHITCOMB, Berlin. 1. Taught three winters. Shoemaker. Berlin.
ISAAC W. WILCOX, Taunton. Taught eleven years. Address, Taunton.
    Total of teaching for twelve, forty-eight years. Average, four years.
EUNICE C. ALDEN, Bridgewater. T. two terms. Mrs. Darius H. Dunbar, Bridgewater.
JOSEPHINE B. ATKINSON, Orleans. Mrs. Chas. H. Thwing, 94 W. Newton St., Boston.
ESTHER A. BOYDEN, S. Walpole. Taught one year. Mrs. David Bentley, Brookline.
LUCIA A. BRADFORD, S. Weymouth. T. one year. Mrs. Wm. Nash, S. Weymouth.
MARY P. BUFFINGTON, Somerset. Taught five years. Address, Fall River.
LUTHERA A. BUMPUS, S. Braintree. 2. Taught seven years. Address, Quincy.
OLIVIA COOK, Woonsocket, R. I. Not heard from.
EUNICE W. FIELD, Peterboro' N. H. Taught fourteen years. Holmes' Primary School, Cambridge.
CAROLINE F. FRENCH, E. Randolph. Taught three years. Asst. Librarian. Holbrook.
SOPHIA H. FRENCH, E. Stoughton. Taught sixteen years. Teaching. E. Stoughton.
MARY A. GROVER,* Newton. Did not teach. Died October 16, 1863.
MARY B. HALL, W. Bridgewater. Taught fourteen years. Mrs. Bliss, Rehoboth.
MARTHA KEITH, Bridgewater. Taught fourteen years. High School. Reading.
ALMARIA KINGMAN, Campello. T. two years. Mrs. F. H. Ludington, St. Louis, Mo.
ANGELIA MASON, Bethel, Me. Taught five years. Mrs. Edmund Clark, Bethel.
RUBY MASON, Bethel, Me. 1. Taught two years. Mrs. L. C. Smith, Hanover, Me.
R. CHARLOTTE MOORE, Lawrence. T. six years. Mrs. J. M. Whipple, Lancaster, N. H.
DORCAS C. MORRISON, Londonderry, N. H. 3. Taught five years. Reader. 18 Avon Street, Cambridge.
LIZZIE MORRISON, Londonderry, N. H. Taught four years. Cashier. 18 Avon Street, Cambridge.
ANN M.-PENNIMAN, S. Braintree. Taught seventeen years. Master's Asst., Shurtleff School. South Boston.
KATE SMITH, Bridgewater. Taught four years. Mrs. G. E. Woodbury, Brockton.
S. AUGUSTA TOWLE, Fitchburg. T. one term. Mrs. S. W. Upton. W. Townsend.
AURELIA G. WHITING, Scituate. 1. Not heard from.
    Total of teaching for twenty, 120 years. Average, six years.

CLASS 52. SEPTEMBER 15, 1858.

DAVID BENTLEY, Upper Stewiacke, N. S. Taught sixteen years. In Grammar and High Schools. Principal of Grammar School, Brookline.
AUGUSTINE CALDWELL, Ipswich. Taught two terms. Clergyman. 82 Portland St. Worcester.
CHARLES F. DEXTER, Mattapoisett. Taught three years in Normal School. Merchant. Chicago, Ill.
HOSAH G. GOODRICH, Danvers. Taught fifteen years. Prin. Gram. School. Hingham.
HENRY T. HARTWELL, Amherst. N. H. Taught seven years. Clerk. 257 Washington Street, Boston.
FRED. L. HOLMES, Plymouth. Taught three years. Market Gardener. Plymouth.
FRANCES H. LUDINGTON, Boston. Taught eight years. Merchant. St. Louis, Mo.
E. WEBSTER NUTTER, E. Bridgewater. Taught four years. Trader. E. Bridgewater.
JONAS REYNOLDS, W. Bridgewater. Taught four years. Boot and Shoe Manufacturer. Brockton.
G. WINSLOW ROGERS, Newbury. 2. Not heard from.
JAMES B. RYDER, Plymouth. Not heard from.
AUSTIN SANFORD, E. Bridgewater. Taught eleven years. Teaching in Young Ladies' Academy. Albany, N. Y.
WALTER H. SEAVER,* Northboro'. Taught two years. Two years in Harvard College. Died March, 1867.
    Total of teaching for eleven, seventy-three years. Average, seven years.

ELIZABETH E. BACKUP, Roxbury. Taught five years. Teaching. Dearborn School, Roxbury.
MARIA H. BLANDING, Wrentham. Taught sixteen years. Teaching. Grammar School, 69 Fort Green Place, Brooklyn, N. Y.
NELLIE S. BROWN, Franklin, N. H. Not heard from.
SOPHIA A. BURGESS. Bolton. Taught two terms. Mrs. T. A. Shedd, Benedict St., E. Somerville.
SARAH E. COBB,* Marion. T. one year. Mrs. Capt. Benj. S. Briggs. Lost at sea.
MARTHA B. CORTHELL,* Hingham. Taught eight years. Mrs. Geo. W. Beale. Died Feberuary 21, 1873.
JANE E. GILMORE, Lowell. T. fourteen years. Supernumerary Teacher. New Bedford.
HANNAH K. HALL, Raynham. T. seven years. Mrs. Horace Bradford, Taunton.
HARRIET E. HOLMES, Plymouth. Taught one term. Mrs. Wm. S. Bartlett, S. Plymouth.
MARIA P. HOWLAND, N. Dartmouth. Taught six terms. Address, N. Dartmouth.
MARTHA HOWLAND, Dartmouth. Mrs. Isaac Howland, Brooklyn, N. Y.
PHEBE T. HOWLAND, New Bedford. Taught four years. Mrs. Hiram Wentworth, New Bedford.
ELIZA A. KENDALL, Ashley. Taught thirteen years. Grammar Schools. Fitchburg.
MARY A. W. KENDALL, Ashley. T. one term. Mrs. G. H. Champney, Ayer Junction.
MARY LINCOLN,* Hingham. Taught ten years. Died April 7, 1869.
ELLEN L. LINDSAY, Winchester. T. three years. Mrs. H. D. Sanford, Bridgewater.
JULIA G. NORTON, Tisbury. Taught ten years. Mrs. William L. Holmes, Long Plain.
EMMA F. PARISH, E. Stoughton. Taught five years. Mrs. W. W. Pettengill, Plymouth.
MARY JANE PATCH, Ashby. 1. No information.
REBECCA R. PETTENGILL, Lawrence. T. five years. Mrs. Morse, Boston Highlands.
MARY A. RANDALL, Easton. T. two years. Mrs. J. H. Leach, 22 Tremont St., Chelsea.
S. ELIZABETH RICE, Ashby. Taught four years. Mrs. Horace S. Brooks, Ashby.
JULIA A. SEARS, E. Dennis. Taught eleven years in Grammar and Normal Schools; Normal School. Nashville, Tenn.
CLEMENTINA SWAIN, N. Y. City. T. ten years. Mrs. H. T. Wing, 147 Pierrepont St., Brooklyn, N. Y.
ANNA M. THOMPSON,* Woburn. 2. Did not teach. Died May 2, 1863.
ORIANA TIDD, Stoneham. 1. No information.
S. MARIA UPTON, Townsend. Taught two years. Mrs. A. A. Greene, Ashby.
Total of teaching for twenty-three, one hundred and thirty-four years. Average, six years.

Class 53. March 16, 1859.

AUGUSTINE W. BISBEE, Rochester. Taught seven years. Farmer. S. Middleborough.
JOHN E. BRYANT,* Woburn. Taught one year. Died in Newbern, N. C., Oct. 1, 1864.
DAVID E. COOK, Provincetown. 1. Taught four years. Fisherman. Chilmark.
FRANCIS T. CRAFTS, Bridgewater. Taught eleven years. Farmer. Milton.
WILLIAM K. CROSBY. Mattapoisett. Not heard from.
WILLIAM G. FAIRBANK, Sterling. T. six years. Sup't. Reform School. Vergennes, Vt.
ABRAHAM G. R. HALE, Stowe. Taught three years. Lawyer. 15 State St., Boston.
W. H. H. HASTINGS, Sterling. Taught one term. Physician to Boston Dispensary. 128 Charles Street, Boston.
JOSEPH W. HAYWARD, Easton. Taught two terms. Physician. Taunton.
WILLIAM HAWES,* Boston. Taught one year. Died in New York.
HENRY C. HOUGHTON, Dorchester. Taught two years. Physician. 50 W. 33d Street, New York City.
WARREN LEIGHTON, Windham, Me. 1. Taught four years. Farmer. West Gray, Me.
HENRY MANLEY, No. Bridgewater. Taught one year. Civil Engineer. City Engineer's Office, Boston.
CHAS. W. McMAHON, Plymouth. Taught ten years. Normal School. Waynesboro', Ga.
ALONZO K. MIRICK,* Sterling. 2. Died Sept. 23, 1862, Washington, D. C.

CYRENUS A. NEWCOMB, Taunton. T. one term. Dry Goods Merchant. Detroit, Mich.
WM. H. OSBORNE, E. Bridgewater. Taught one year. Lawyer. E. Bridgewater.
BENJAMIN W. PARSONS,* Lynnfield. 2. Died August 14, 1864.
JOHN W. PRENTISS, Webster. T. ten years. Supt. Schools. La Grange, Stanislais Co., Cal.
THEODORE RODMAN, Bridgewater. Taught seven years. Public School. Bethel, Del. Co., Penn.
ALBERT E. SMITH, Sharon. Taught one year. Lawyer. Box 289, New York City.
ELISHA M. WHITE, Randolph. Taught one year. Manufacturer and dealer in Surgical Apparatus. 99 Court Street, Boston.

    Total of teaching for nineteen, seventy-one years. Average, four years.

ARABELLA AMES, N. Bridgewater. Taught eight years. Teaching. Brockton.
AUGUSTA ARNOLD, N. Abington. 1. Taught one year. Mrs. H. B. Pierce, Abington.
ADDIE A. BAKER, Brewster. Taught ten years. Mrs. Albert Winslow, 192 Jackson St., Chicago, Ill.
MARY A. BURNAP, Ashby. Taught four years. Mrs. J. C. Spaulding, Holden.
CLARA FISKE, Medfield. Taught four years. Mrs. G. T. Fletcher, Castine, Me.
ABBIE S. HASTINGS, Sterling. Taught two years. Mrs. J. E. Fiske, Grantville.
SUSAN L. HERSEY, Hingham. 1. No information.
HANNAH T. KINGSBURY*, Needham. 1. Died August, 1859.
MARGARET E. LEFLER, Hingham. T. six years. Mrs. Wm. E. Fairbank, Vergennes, Vt.
CORNELIA ROUNSEVILLE Rochester. T. nine years. Mrs. C. H. F. Church, Rochester.
ELLEN SCOFIELD, Stoughton. Taught five years. Mrs. J. E. Norwood, York, Me.
MARY F. TAYLOR, W. Bridgewater. 1. Did not teach. Mrs. G. R. Drake, W. Bridgewater.

    Total of teaching for ten, forty-nine years. Average, five years.

CLASS 54. SEPTEMBER 21, 1859.

JOSIAH F. BAXTER, Plymouth. T. fourteen years. Prin. Grammar School. Winchester.
WILMON W. BLACKMAR, Boston. Did not teach. Attorney. 27 Court St., Boston. Judge Advocate General.
EDWARD I. COMINS, Charlton. T. fifteen years. Prin. Grammar School. Worcester.
JONAS P. HAYWARD, Ashby. Taught three years. Fruit cultivator. Ashby.
CALVIN PRATT, Bridgewater. Taught two terms. Physician. Bridgewater.
PETER C. SEARS, Mattapoisett. Taught two years. Commission Merchant. 181 Jackson Street, Chicago, Illinois.
GEO. A. WHEELER, E. Bridgewater. T. five years. Deputy Sheriff. E. Bridgewater.

    Total of teaching for seven, thirty-nine years. Average, six years.

ELLEN M. BALKAM, Lewiston, Me. Taught ten years. Mrs. Prof. R. C. Stanley. Bates College, Lewiston, Maine.
JANE F. BURT, Berkley. Mrs. S. N. Grosvenor. No information.
MELISSA E. D'ARCY, E. Boston. Taught fifteen years. Teaching in San Francisco, Cal.
ELLEN M. HOLMES,* Bridgewater. Taught ten years. Died December 28, 1875.
SOPHIA F. HOWES, Middleboro'. 2. Has not taught. Watertown.
LIZZIE A. KINGMAN, N. Bridgewater. Taught sixteen years. Perkins Grammar School. Brockton.
MARY S. McINTYRE, Roxbury. 2. No information.
FRANCES M. NORTH, E. Bridgewater. 2. Mrs. A. C. Judkins. 147 Beach St., Boston.
MARY E. RICE, Ashby. 2. T. three years. Mrs. Oliver Baker, 316 Pearl St., Cleveland, O.
SUSAN A. WILLIAMS,* Berkley. Taught five years. Deceased.

    Total of teaching for seven, forty-nine years. Average, seven years.

CLASS 55. MARCH 21, 1860.

CHARLES M. BARROWS, Brimfield. T. fourteen years. Prin. High School. N. Easton.
OTIS J. BROAD, Canton. 1. Did not teach.
HENRY L. CLAPP, Taunton. Taught eight years. Lincoln Grammar School, S. Boston.

MR. CONANT'S ADMINISTRATION.

WILLARD E. CLARKE,* Rochester. Killed at Cedar Creek, Va., Oct. 19, 1864.
THOMAS CONANT, JR., E. Bridgewater. 2. Physician. Gloucester.
GRENVILLE T. FLETCHER, Augusta, Me. Taught fifteen years. Prin. State Normal School. Castine, Me.
AMOS K. HASWELL,* Acushnet. No information. Deceased.
HENRY T. HOWARD,* Rumford, Me. Taught eight years. Died Nov. 22, 1871, at So. Paris, Me.
GEO. T. KEITH, Bridgewater. Did not teach. Civil Engineer. Lawrence.
DANIEL S. PILLSBURY, Hampstead. Taught two years. Bookseller. 680 Sixth Ave. New York City.
ELIAS B. RICHARDSON, Rumford Me. 1. Not heard from.
EDWARD SOUTHWORTH, S. Scituate. 2. T. eleven years. Sub Master, Rice School, Boston. Quincy.
THOMAS H. WEST, Randolph. T. thirteen years. Principal, Grammar School. Randolph.
CHARLES H. WILSON, Derry, N. H. Taught twelve years, Grammar and High School. Lancaster, N. H.

Total of teaching for twelve, eighty-three years. Average, seven years.

MARIA Q. ADAMS, Sharon. Taught five years. Mrs. Erastus Smith, Stoughton.
MARTHA W. BROOKS, S. Scituate. T. thirteen years. Ungraded School. S. Scituate.
REBECCA C. BROOKS, S. Scituate. Taught twelve years. Ungraded School. S. Scituate.
MARY E. DOWSE, Sherborn. Taught four years. Watertown.
J. MARIA FRYE,* Boston. 3. Mrs James Mitchell. Deceased.
MARY E HAMMOND, Mattapoisett. Taught four years. Mrs. L. Pitts, Jr., E. Boston.
SARAH A. HENSHAW, W. Brookfield. Taught nine years. No. 8 Loudon St., Worcester.
HATTIE E. HILL, Sherborn. Taught four years. Mrs. Edward Southworth, Quincy.
MARY A. HOWES,* Bridgewater. 3. Died, Jan. 5, 1869.
MARY F. LEACH, Bridgewater, Taught two terms. Mrs. J. R. Tracy, Raynham.
ELLEN LINCOLN, Hingham. Taught fourteen years. Address, Hingham Centre.
SARAH NEWELL, Dover. Did not teach. 75 Walnut St., Elmira, N. Y.
KATE M. NOYES, E. Bridgewater. T. two years. Mrs. Thomas H. West, Brookville.
SOPHIA E. PRATT, Easton. Taught two years. Mrs. L. W. Morse, Sharon.
ROSE A. ROBERTS, Biddeford, Me. Taught two years. Mrs. P. C. Sears, Chicago, Ill.
H. AUGUSTA ROBINSON, Raynham. T. one year. Mrs. A. C. Southworth, Lakeville.
ELIZABETH RODMAN, Bridgewater. Taught three years. Mrs. S. M. Colcord, 240 Shawmut Avenue, Boston.
ROSINE M. SMITH, Medfield. Taught six years. Mrs. G. T. Higley, Ashland.
MARY A. THAYER, W. Bridgewater. Taught seven years. Superintendent of Schools. W. Bridgewater.
EMMA THOMPSON. Middleboro'. T. nine years. Mrs. L. A. Darling, Tougaloo, Miss.
MARION THOMPSON,* Middleboro'. 2. Did not teach. Died May 28, 1864.
ANN M. WHITNEY, Sherborn. Taught two years. Mrs. Henry Hooker, Ashland.

·Total of teaching for eighteen, ninety-nine years. Average, five and one-half years.

MR. BOYDEN'S ADMINISTRATION.

THE SCHOOL BUILDINGS.

ALBERT G. BOYDEN, the present Principal of the school, was appointed in August, 1860. The number of students had increased so much, under Mr. Conant, that the school building and its furnishings were inadequate to the proper accommodation of the school. Plans for the enlargement and improvement of the building were prepared and presented to the Board of Education. These plans were approved, and the Board made application to the Legislature for the necessary appropriation. By a resolve, approved April 1, 1861, the Legislature appropriated "for the enlargement and repairs of the Bridgewater Normal School building, a sum not exceeding four thousand, five hundred dollars." The Visitors, in their report of the school for 1861, gave the following account of the enlargement:

"The passage of the resolve showed an appreciation of the merits and demands of this school which, during the twenty-one years of its history, has enjoyed a steady prosperity, and has educated 1,286 pupils, nearly all of whom, on leaving the school, entered the ranks of teachers. The Visitors of the school, together with the Secretary of the Board, were appointed a Building Committee, who have endeavored to accomplish as much as possible with the sum appropriated. The building, originally, was a plain structure, 64 feet long by 42 feet wide, and two stories high. To this have been added two wings, each 38 feet long and 24 feet wide, projecting respectively from the centre of the sides of the main building, and of the same height with the main building. The whole makes a structure so symmetrical that, though plain and unornamented, it is doubtful whether any more convenient plan for a Normal School building could be devised. Upon the lower floor are four convenient recitation rooms, two rooms that are used for philosophical and chemical apparatus, one room for mineralogical and geological specimens, and two ante-rooms for the pupils. In the second story the whole of the original structure is devoted to a school-room, which is 63 feet long and 41 feet wide, while opening from it in one wing is a spacious recitation room with an adjoining apartment that may be used for apparatus; and in the other wing a large library room, and a teachers' room.

"It has been deemed desirable that the warming and ventilation of the house should be as nearly perfect as possible. The ventilation is

satisfactory, and new furnaces have been set which warm the entire building. A forcing pump has been placed in the well in the cellar, with pipes and tanks to supply closets and sinks. The building is of wood, the foundation of stone, and it is believed that all of the work is good and satisfactory. It has been done under the special supervision of Mr. Boyden, the Principal of the School, whose interest in the enterprise has led him, without compensation, to devote the entire summer vacation of the school to this work. Notwithstanding this enlargement, the total amount expended by the State for the grounds and building at Bridgewater, is less than the sum expended at either of the other Normal Schools in the State."

The building was scantily furnished before the enlargement, a deficiency which was both more conspicuous and inconvenient afterward. For many years it had received no addition to its furniture except the substitution of a good piano for one nearly worn out. The Legislature of 1862 appropriated two hundred dollars for furniture, which was used in procuring new desks and chairs for the platform of the school-room, and chairs and tables for the class-rooms. In 1864 the school-room was furnished with new oak desks and new chairs, in the place of the pine desks and chairs supplied in 1846, and the building was repainted. The cost of these improvements was one thousand dollars. The Legislature of 1866 appropriated five hundred dollars, which was expended for chemical and philosophical apparatus, and for cabinet cases.

BRIDGEWATER STATE NORMAL SCHOOL, 1861,

The Boarding Hall.—During the first eight years of the school, the price of board for the students was $2.00 a week, including washing. From the end of this period the price gradually increased till in 1866 it was $4.00 and $4.25 a week without washing, fuel, and lights. Board for all the students could not be found at any price. The young men hired rooms for lodging, and formed a club for table board. The Principal was obliged to hire rooms and furnish them with the necessary furniture, in which the young ladies could board themselves, or else allow them to return home for want of accommodations. So urgent was the need of boarding accommodations that an effort was made to form an Association among the citizens of the town for providing a boarding house to be rented for the use of the students. This scheme failed, and application for relief was made to the Legislature of 1867, by the Board of Education, asking for an appropriation of $30,000 for this purpose. The Committee on Education reported a bill for the appropriation of $15,000 for the erection of a boarding hall for the school. This bill failed to pass the House.

The Visitors in their report of the school for 1868, make the following presentation:—" The increase in the number of pupils in attendance makes still more urgent the need of providing better boarding accommodations. A very large proportion are obliged to board themselves, to the great detriment of their health. And even suitable accommodations for self-boarding cannot be obtained. The case is so plain that it does not admit of doubt. A hall for the students is an absolute necessity." A similar want having been experienced at the Framingham Normal School, the Board of Education made a strong appeal to the Legislature of 1869, and secured the passage of the following resolve:—

"*Resolved,* That the Commissioners of the Massachusetts School Fund be, and they hereby are authorized and directed, with the approval of the Governor and Council, to loan from said fund to the Board of Education, a sum not exceeding fifteen thousand dollars, in trust, to be expended by said Board in erecting or otherwise providing and furnishing a boarding house for the accommodation of the pupils of the Bridgewater State Normal School; also a further sum, not exceeding fifteen thousand dollars, to be expended for the same purpose, and in like manner, by said Board of Education at the Framingham State Normal School.

" Said Board of Education shall collect from the occupants of the houses so provided, in addition to other charges, a sum sufficient to cover the interest at six per cent. per annum, on the cost of said buildings and furniture, and a reasonable insurance on the same, and shall pay over said interest money to the Commissioners of the Massachusetts School Fund, semi-annually.

" If said Board of Education shall fail to pay the interest of said sums, as aforesaid, then the Commissioners shall have the power, and, with the approval of the Governor and Council, shall sell said boarding houses, or either of them, with the appurtenances thereto belonging, and the furniture therein, and invest the proceeds of the same as provided by law. *Approved* March 26, 1869.

The plans for the building were carefully matured by the Principal after obtaining information in regard to the plans of several school boarding halls in different parts of the country. After completing the working plans, careful estimates of the cost of the work were obtained, which showed that a building for the accommodation of fifty students could not be erected and furnished for less than $25,000. Another application was made to the Legislature, — the length of the session being specially favorable to this object, — securing an additional appropriation, as follows : —

"*Resolved*, That the Commissioners of the Massachusetts School Fund be, and they are hereby authorized and directed, with the approval of the Governor and Council, to loan from said fund to the Board of Education, in addition to the sums named in the seventeenth chapter of the resolves of the present session, a sum not exceeding ten thousand dollars, for providing and furnishing a boarding house for the State Normal School at Bridgewater; and a sum not exceeding five thousand dollars for a like purpose at the Framingham Normal School; said loans to be made upon the terms and conditions expressed in said resolve, chapter seventeen of the present session. *Approved, June* 12, 1869.

The work was continued without delay and with the following results as given by the Visitors in their report of the school for 1869.

"The most important event in the history of the school for many years past, has been the erection during the last year of a boarding hall for the use of the pupils. The work on the edifice was begun on the 18th of June, and it was completed on the 20th of November. On the 25th of the same month, the management of the establishment was organized, and the rooms were at once filled with boarders. The Visitors of the school, including the Secretary of the Board were appointed by the Board a Committee with full powers to erect the building, furnish it, and put it in running order. This Committee appointed Mr. Boyden, the Principal, Superintendent of the work of building and furnishing, and agent to make all purchases. The arduous and responsible duties thus imposed upon him in addition to his exhausting labors as Principal of the school, he has performed in an admirable manner, and to the entire satisfaction of the Committee, sparing no pains to secure the best results at the least expense. He has rendered to the Committee a full report of his doings as Superintendent, embracing a description of the building and an account of all the expenditures which have been incurred in its erection and equipment.

"After careful deliberation upon the location of the building, it was decided to place it upon the school premises, although the town of Bridgewater offered the sum of one thousand dollars for the purchase of any other lot the committee might select at that price. Several lots were examined, but the cost of grading and fencing them was so great that they were not available, for the means at the command of the committee were only sufficient to erect and furnish the building.

"The building stands about seventy feet from the school house, and fronting in the same direction, near the centre of the school grounds which contain about one and one-fourth acres of land, enclosed by fences, and ornamented by a variety of handsome shade trees. The location proves to be entirely satisfactory.

"The building is a wooden structure, 40 by 80 feet, three stories high above the basement, very pleasant and commodious, and neatly furnished. The basement story, one side of which is wholly above ground, contains the cellars, boiler-room, and laundry. The first story includes the family rooms, the parlor, dining-room, and cook rooms. The remaining stories are divided into students rooms, 10 by 15 feet on the floor, and 10 feet in height—twenty-nine in number; and rooms for the help. The rooms are thoroughly ventilated, carpeted, and supplied with furniture. The whole building is heated by steam.

"Mr. Boyden makes no charge for his extra services as superintendent of this work. The Visitors would, however, ask the Board to refund to him the amount of his travelling expenses while so employed.

"The boarding hall is now fully organized and in successful operation. It is already evident that it will be highly beneficial to the school. It affords the young ladies in attendance good rooms and good board at $1.25 a week less than they have heretofore paid in private families."

The Legislature of 1870 made an additional loan from the school fund to the Board of Education, of a sum not exceeding fifteen hundred dollars, for completing the providing and furnishing of the boarding hall at Bridgewater, thus making the total expended for this purpose, $26,500. In the same resolve a sum not exceeding six thousand five hundred dollars was loaned for the same object for the boarding hall at Framingham, making the total here the same as for Bridgewater.

The boarding hall at Bridgewater was the first one erected by the State for a Normal School. When the first three Normal Schools of this State were opened, a boarding hall was considered one of the necessary buildings. It was now regarded a doubtful experiment, as clearly indicated by the resolve of the Legislature making the appropriation. The interest on the cost of this hall was fully paid according to the conditions of the appropriation. The interest was not paid at Framingham, and the Legislature of 1871 passed a resolve releasing the Board of Education from the payment of interest on the amounts received from the Massachusetts school fund for the building and furnishing boarding houses for the Normal Schools at Framingham and Bridgewater, and from paying the insurance thereon.

During the Fall term of 1870, less than one year after the opening of the boarding hall, the School numbered 142 pupils, only 54 of whom could be accommodated with rooms at the hall. The pressure for rooms and board was as great as before the hall was erected, and required an immediate enlargement of the hall, but the appropriations made for the establishment of a new Normal School at Worcester, and for a boarding hall for the Normal School at Westfield, made it necessary to postpone this enlargement till 1873.

Enlargement of the School Building. The school house, as well as the boarding hall, was too small for the School, having room in the main hall for only 120 pupils. Additional class rooms were needed, and more room for cabinets and apparatus. A resolve of the Legislature, authorizing the expenditure of a sum not exceeding fifteen thousand dollars, for the enlargement and reconstruction of the building, was approved May 12, 1871. The Committee of the Board appointed to take charge of this business, appointed the Principal of the School as their agent, to superintend the work in all its departments.

The plans for the enlargement were carefully matured, after visiting and examining several school buildings recently erected. The building was enlarged by adding a story sixteen feet in height; and greatly improved in external appearance by an observatory on the centre, a new roof with heavier projections and a new cornice, and a band between the first and second stories, with quoins upon the pilasters on the lower story.

The first story contains the ante-rooms for the students, four class rooms, a chemical laboratory, and a room for philosophical apparatus. Upon the second floor are five commodious class rooms, with alcove, and cases for the library and cabinets. The third story contains the main school-room, — a spacious hall, well ventilated, light, and very cheerful, — the senior class-room, and the Principal's room. It is now one of the most pleasant and convenient school buildings in the State.

The work on the building was commenced immediately on the close of the Spring term, and was so far completed at the close of the Summer vacation that the School could go on with its usual work.

Steam Heating Apparatus. The changes in the building created the necessity for new heating and ventilating apparatus. Estimates

BRIDGEWATER STATE NORMAL SCHOOL, 1871.

were obtained for heating and ventilating the building by steam, after the manner which had proved so effective in the boarding hall. The appropriation was found sufficient to procure only ventiducts for this plan. These were put into the construction of the building and portable furnaces were added for use during the winter. During the summer vacation of 1872, a fire-proof boiler house was constructed in the embankment at the southeast corner of the School building, and a complete steam-heating and ventilating apparatus was introduced, at a cost of six thousand dollars, the sum appropriated by the Legislature for the purpose.

Art Room. An appropriation of six hundred dollars was made by the Legislature of 1873 for fitting up an art-room for drawing. This sum was expended in supplying the room appropriated to this purpose with drawing desks of the most approved pattern, and drawing boards and instruments, together with the valuable casts and models which had previously been imported from London, thus affording excellent facilities for teaching drawing.

The Enlargement of the Boarding Hall.—At the commencement of the spring term in 1873, the number of pupils in attendance was 150, and there was as much difficulty in obtaining the requisite boarding places outside the hall, as there was to get suitable boarding places before the hall was built. The necessity for its enlargement was evident beyond question. The Visitors, in their report to the Board in January, 1873, say: "This is the third time that the request for the enlargement of the boarding hall has been brought to the attention of the Board. Last year the request was so far sanctioned by the Board as to allow it to go to the Committee on Education, but with the understanding that it should not prejudice their request for a boarding house for the Westfield school. The Committee recommended to the Legislature and secured provision for the latter, only thinking both projects too much to undertake in one year. This year it is hoped that the moderate request of Bridgewater will at length receive the favorable consideration both of the Board and the Legislature." This hope was realized.

The Visitors, in their report for 1874, present the following statement: "The Legislature of 1873 made an appropriation of $36,000 for enlarging and furnishing the building. and the Legislature of 1874 passed an additional appropriation of $7,600 for the introduction of gas into the building, and various other items not provided for in the first estimates. The Secretary of the Board of Education and Rev. A. A. Miner, D. D., were appointed by the Board a committee, with full powers to enlarge the building, furnish it, and put it in run-

BOARDING HALL, BRIDGEWATER STATE NORMAL SCHOOL.

ning order. This committee appointed the Principal of the school, superintendent of building and furnishing, and agent to make all purchases. The work of enlargement was commenced in July, 1873, and completed in March, 1874. The hall has been fully occupied, and has been in successful operation without any increase of expenses. Mr. Boyden, the Principal, deserves great credit for the faithful, judicious, and efficient manner in which he has superintended all the operations in connection with the building of the boarding hall, without any extra compensation."

The plans for enlargement extended the building so far that there was not room for a carriage way between it and the south line of the school lot. The town of Bridgewater generously donated to the Commonwealth from their adjoining school lot, a strip of land twenty feet wide, and three hundred and twenty feet long, which gave room for easy and convenient approach to the south front of the hall.

The enlargement was made by adding to the south end of the original structure another building, 132 by 40 feet, the wings extending from the hall 46 feet on each side. A piazza extends across the end of the hall on the south front, and a large cupola affords a fine outlook over the surrounding region. The hall is very pleasant and commodious, and will accommodate one hundred and forty students with rooms and board. Two students occupy one room. Each room has two closets, is carpeted, supplied with furniture, including mattress and pillows, heated by steam, lighted by gas, and thoroughly ventilated. One wing of the hall is occupied by gentlemen.

The hall is under the charge of the Principal, who resides in the house and boards with the students. No pains are spared to make the Hall in every respect a home for the pupils. It has a beautiful location, and every room is pleasant. A Reading Room,—supplied with newspapers, periodicals, and some of the best new books,— and a Gymnasium, are provided for the daily use of the students.

The Hall was built and furnished by the State. The boarders are to pay the current expenses, which include board, fuel, light, washing, and the expense of keeping the Hall and its furniture in good condition. The aim is, to make these expenses not more than $80 a term, or $4 a week, for gentlemen; and for ladies not more than $75 a term, or $3.75 a week. Boarders who remain for any period less than half a term will be charged 25 cents a week additional. *The expense thus far has not exceeded the sum specified.*

Payments. $40 for each gentleman, and $37.50 for each lady, at the beginning of the term; and the same amount for each at the middle of the term. The object of this payment in advance is, to secure the purchase of supplies at wholesale cash prices, thereby saving to each boarder much more than the interest of the money advanced.

Furniture. Each boarder is required to bring bedding, towels, napkins and napkin-ring, and clothes bags. Each occupant will want, ordinarily, four pillow cases, three sheets, two blankets or their equivalent, and one coverlet, for a double bed. It is required that every article which goes to the laundry be distinctly and indelibly marked with the owner's name.

The hall has been in successful operation for nearly seven years. There is no longer any question concerning its utility. The habits of regularity, cheerful work, full occupation, with proper recreation, which are here inculcated, tend to the improvement of both body and mind. It has contributed very much to the size, health, happiness, and vigor of the School. The total expenditure by the State for the hall is $70,100.

The Chemical Laboratory. The appropriation of one thousand dollars, made by the Legislature of 1875, for fitting and furnishing a chemical laboratory, and for chemicals and apparatus, was expended for this purpose. The School has now an excellent laboratory, combining the most approved modern ideas, in which twenty-four pupils can work at one time, each pupil himself manipulating the apparatus and dealing with the substances which he studies.

"*The first Normal School-house* ever erected in this hemisphere" still stands as the centre and foundation of the present improved school building. It has increased to the present dimensions as the growth of the School has made it necessary. With all the enlargements and improvements, the School has no more than met the demands of the public. Additional facilities will always be needed to meet the constantly increasing demands of an enlightened public sentiment. The outlays for educational institutions are but "the ounce of prevention," more economical and far more productive of good than the "pound of cure."

THE SCHOOL.

The number of pupils in attendance the fifty-sixth term, at the commencement of this administration, was sixty-seven. The number in attendance the present term, the eighty-seventh, is one hundred sixty-seven. The school has been steadily increasing in numbers up to the present time.

Conditions of Admission.— The History of the United States has been added to the branches in which candidates for admission are examined, and a more extended and thorough knowledge of each branch is now required of the candidates. Each candidate is required to sign the following declaration:

"I hereby engage that if admitted to this school, I will faithfully observe its rules and regulations; and it is my full purpose to remain in the school four consecutive terms, or such a part of this period as is necessary to complete the regular course of study, and afterwards to teach in the public schools in Massachusetts."

The conditions of admission at the present time are these: Gentlemen applying for admission must be at least seventeen years of age; ladies, sixteen. Candidates must present a satisfactory certificate of good moral character; and must be free from any disease or infirmity which would unfit them for the office of teacher; must declare their full intention of faithfully observing the regulations of the school while members of it, and of afterwards teaching in the public schools of Massachusetts;* and must pass a satisfactory examination in Reading, Spelling, Writing, Arithmetic, Geography, the History of the United States, and English Grammar. A greater age and higher attainments than those prescribed, with some experience in teaching, make the course of study in the school much more valuable to the pupil. *These requirements will be strictly enforced.*

Course of Instruction.—The length of the course of study until March, 1865, was three terms of twenty weeks each, and the course included the following branches:

First. Reading, English Grammar (and Analysis), Geography, (Mathematical, Physical, Political, and map drawing), Arithmetic, History of the United States, Algebra, Vocal Music, Physiology, and Hygiene, which are prescribed by law for all the public schools of the State.

Second. Geometry, Natural Philosophy, Chemistry, Book-keeping, Astronomy, Constitution of the United States and General Principles of Government, Rhetoric, and English Literature, which, with the exception of the last, are prescribed by law for the High Schools of the State; and a knowledge of their elements, at least, is deemed essential to a competent preparation for teaching in all the public schools.

Third. The Theory and Art of Teaching, including Mental and Moral Philosophy, General Principles and Methods of Instruction, School Laws of Massachusetts, School Organization and Government.

Exercises in Reading, Writing, Orthography, Composition, Vocal Music, and Gymnastics extend through the whole course.

* Persons intending to teach in other States, or in private schools, are admitted by paying fifteen dollars a term for tuition.

Botany, Surveying, Geology, Latin and other languages are optional.

The primary object of the course of instruction is to secure a thorough investigation of the principles of the studies pursued, and of the best modes of teaching them. All the exercises of the school are conducted with constant regard to preparation for the work of instruction in the public schools.

The Extension of the Course of Study.—In 1863 a committee of the Board of Education invited the Principals of the Normal Schools to meet them with the Secretary of the Board "to consider if any plan seems feasible for increasing the amount and elevating the character of the instruction afforded by said schools." After a day spent in free and full discussion of the topic, "it was the unanimous opinion that it was not advisable to enlarge the general course of study, but that a more thorough mastery of that course in all its steps, and a considerable extension of it in several important branches of study, in order to meet the increasing demands of the schools for thoroughly educated teachers, is greatly desirable. This can only be accomplished by extending the time of the regular course." The committee therefore recommended that another term be added to the regular course of study in the Normal Schools,— thus requiring an attendance of two years in order to obtain a diploma. This went into effect in all the Normal Schools in March, 1865.

The course of study since 1864 has been conformed to the course adopted by the Board in 1866, as given on page 19. The extension of the course to two years, with the admission of a new class at the beginning of each term, made four regular classes in the shorter course, which were designated respectively, beginning with the entering class, the Junior, Ex-Junior, Sub-Senior, and Senior Classes. The Board, in adopting the course given on page 19, provided that, "The *order* of the studies in the course may be varied in special cases, with the approval of the Visitors."

The order, distribution, and range of studies, June, 1876. The figure after the name of the study indicates the number of lessons a week in that study. The sessions of the School are held each week day, except Saturday, from nine and one-fourth o'clock to twelve and one-fourth, and from two o'clock to four and one-half o'clock. The last twenty minutes of the afternoon session are spent in gymnastic exercises, and the session closes with singing.

The Devotional Exercises, occupying ten minutes, at the opening of the morning session, include Reading of Scripture, Singing, Prayer, and Chanting of the Lord's Prayer by the School. A General Exercise, for twenty minutes, follows, in which a great variety of topics are considered. The last quarter of the term the General Exercise is devoted to singing by the School.

Junior Class. Geometry, 5. Including:—Definitions. Divisions of Geometry. Properties and Relations:—of Lines; of Angles; of Surfaces; of Volumes. Demonstration of Propositions concerning,—Lines and Angles; Triangles; Quadrilaterals; Ratios and Proportions; Relations of Rectilinear Figures; Circles. Physiology and Hygeine. 4. Including:—The Structure of the Human Body, its different Systems, their Functions, and the Conditions of Health. Chemistry. 5. Including:—Chemical Physics and Inorganic Chemistry, with Laboratory practice by each pupil. Vocal Music. 4. Including:—The Reading of Music in all the keys at sight. Methods of Teaching, and the Teaching; Practice in Chorus Singing. Drawing. 4. Including:—Freehand, Memory and Dictation, Design. Model and Object, Geometrical, Perspective. Mineralogy. 2. (Fall Term.) Including:—Study of minerals and rocks from specimens, for the qualities, distribution, and uses, each pupil having the specimen in hand. Zoology. 2. (Spring Term.) Including:—Elementary Course, and classification of Animal Kingdom; Studying the specimens for the appearance, structure, habits, uses. Composition. 1.

Ex-Junior Class. Arithmetic, 4. Including:—Elementary Course. Written Arithmetic—its principles, including Numbers; Expression of Numbers; Combinations of Numbers; Relations of Numbers. Algebra, 5. Including:—Notation, Numerical Processes. Use of Processes in Equations, Simple and Quadratic. Geography, 5. Including:—The Earth as a Sphere; Distribution of Light and Heat; Parts of the Earth's Surface; The Sea; The Atmosphere; Life of the Continents; The Study of each Continent. Grammar, 4. Including:—Definitions; Words in a Proposition, or Parts of Speech; Union of Propositions in Sentences. Mineralogy, 2. (Fall Term.) Including the same work as with Junior class. Zoology, 2, (Spring Term). Including, the same work as with Junior class. Vocal Culture and Reading. 2. Composition, 1.

Sub-Senior Class. Arithmetic, 4. Including:—Applications of Numbers; Mercantile Papers; Mensuration. Physics, 4. Including:—Matter and its Properties; General Relations of Force and Motion; Gravitation; Principles of Machines; Steam Engine; Telegraph. Rhetoric, 4. Including:—Definitions; Principles of Description, embracing Perception; Memory; Imagination; Sensibilities; Emotions and their Expression; Expressions, Literal and Figurative; Use of Expressions; Style and its Qualities; Written Composition. English Literature, 4. Including:—Historical Study of the English Language; Poetry,—Ballads, Ancient and Modern; Idyls of the King; Paradise Lost; Deserted Village. Prose,—Essays of Bacon, Addison, Lamb, Macaulay. In all, characteristics of thought and diction, with Biography of Authors and collateral reading. Drawing, 4. Including the extension of the subjects of Junior course. Vocal Culture and Reading; 4. Geology, 2. (Fall Term) Including:—Structure of the Earth and the History of the Structure. Botany, 2. (Spring Term). Including:—Elementary Course; Study of the Plant itself, each pupil having specimen in hand; and Secondary Course,—Study of the plant with the book, for Analysis. Composition, 1.

Senior Class. Astronomy. 4. Including:—Phenomena of the Heavenly Bodies, their form, size, location, motions, and effects of their motions, and the causes of the phenomena. Civil Government. 4. Including:—Principles of Civil Government; Civil Government of the States before their Independence; The Constitutional Government of Massachusetts; The Constitutional Government of the United States. Book Keeping. 2. Including:—Exchange of Property, Mercantile Papers, Accounts, four Forms, embracing Single and Double Entry. Vocal Culture and Reading. 4. School Laws of Massachusetts, 1. Geology, 2. (Fall Term). Including the same work as with Sub-Senior class. Botany, 2. (Spring Term.) Including the same work as with Sub-Senior class. Education. 8. Including:—Study of Man as Body and Mind; The different Systems of the Body, their Functions, and the Conditions of Health. Psychology,—Definitions; the Intellectual Powers,—Reason, the Presentative, Representative, Reflective; the Sensibilities,—the Appetites, Instincts, Desires, Affections; the Will and the Moral Nature. Principles of Education; Art of Teaching; Courses of Study; School Organization; School Government.

The Advanced Course.—Hon. Joseph White, the Secretary of the Board of Education, than whom, the Normal Schools have had no truer friend nor stronger supporter, in his report for 1867, says, "It cannot have escaped the notice of any who are conversant with the conditions and wants of our public schools, that, within a few years, a demand has arisen for a class of teachers, both male and female, who have a thorough normal training, added to a higher education than our Normal Schools now give. This demand is rapidly increasing, and it appears to me that it has now become so general and urgent, that the proper measures for supplying ought to be devised without further delay." To accomplish this object, Mr. White recommended that " all of the existing Normal Schools be supplied with such additional teachers and apparatus as shall enable them to furnish, in connection with the present course of study, instruction in the higher branches of learning." In accordance with these recommendations the Board of Education, on February 3, 1869, voted, "that a supplemental course of study, occupying two years, be introduced into each of the four Normal Schools, which shall comprise the Latin, French, Higher Mathematics, Ethics, Natural Sciences, and English Literature."

The first regular class under this Advanced Course was formed in September, 1870. The studies are so arranged that graduates from the shorter course may take the two additional years' work. Or pupils who, on entering the school, have in view the completion of this higher course, may take a part of its studies in connection with a part of the branches in the shorter course, and in this way, at the end of four years, be prepared to graduate from both courses simultaneously. The latter arrangement gives the students the benefit of the study of the languages in connection with the study of the other branches of the course.

The Advanced Course now includes the following branches: German and French; the object aimed at in their study being to understand, to speak, to write, and to teach the language. Latin, the ultimate object being to have the pupil get such a command of the language that he can read, and understand, and teach it with ease. Greek is taken in the same way by those sufficiently advanced to take this in addition to the studies of this course. Advanced Algebra and Geometry, Trigonometry, and Surveying. Advanced Physics, Chemistry with laboratory practice, Botany and Drawing, Ancient and Modern History, Advanced English Literature, and an extension of the course on Education, including the preparation of topics on various subjects, the History of Education and essays on Educational topics.

Aims and Methods of the School. — The ultimate end of School work is the education of the child. The ultimate object of the Normal School is to make the Normal pupil a *skilled instrument* for the education of children, or, in other words, to make him, as far as possible, an educator.

Education is *training all the powers of the child till he gains the ability and inclination to make the best use of his powers.* The design of education is two-fold, — first, to secure the right action of the mind; second, the acquisition of knowledge.

The processes of education are instruction, teaching and training. Right thinking is secured by the right use of these processes. The product of right thinking is mental power and knowledge.

The "teacher" is an educator. As such he must know *what* the different mental powers are, the *order* of their development, and *how* they are called into right activity. In addition to this knowledge of mind, he must know each pupil as an individual. He must also know the different kinds of knowledge, the order of their acquisition, and the method of their acquisition.

The mind has three different modes of acting — knowing, feeling, choosing. We feel because we know, and we choose because of knowledge and feeling. The activity of the sensibilities and the will are conditioned upon the action of the intellect, hence the cultivation of the intellect is of primary importance.

The intellectual faculties hold the relation of dependence upon one another. The first activity of the mind is in perceiving the qualities of external objects through the different senses. All ideas of external objects come to the mind through the senses. The idea can be gained only when the object is present to the mind.

The memory reproduces and recognizes the ideas gained by the perceptive faculty; hence the first exercise of the memory depends on the action of the perceptive faculty.

The imagination combines thoughts of parts of different objects, which have been perceived and which memory holds in mind, to form its ideal object; hence, the action of the imagination is conditioned upon the activity of the perceptive faculty and the memory.

The power of generalization in forming the idea, which consists of the qualities common to all the objects of a kind, must use the qualities which the mind has perceived and remembered. The power of generalization, then, depends upon the possession of the facts furnished by the perceptive faculty and memory.

The ideas of classes of objects must be known and remembered, that the reasoning power may judge of their relations; hence, the reasoning power depends upon all the other intellectual faculties.

The mind is one, not divided, but having distinct modes of activity. Skill in the use of any faculty is acquired only by the right use of that faculty. The right action of one power will not give strength to another power that is not used. The exercise of each faculty should be guided by its relation to the other faculties.

The sensibilities are to be called into normal action, and the right purpose is to be formed and followed; right *habits* of observation, of thought, of feeling, of action, are to be established.

A course of study is required for the training of the mind. The course needed for this purpose is a series of objects and subjects for study arranged according to the order of mental development. This course of study, from the nature of the mind, must be in two divisions, an elementary course for training the perceptive faculties, memory and imagination, in gaining a knowledge of facts about individual objects; and a scientific course, for training the reflective faculty in acquiring general ideas and truths, and knowledge systematically arranged. The elementary course must be so conducted as to prepare the mind for the scientific course.

Methods.—The principles of education are derived from the study of the mind. The methods of teaching and training are determined by these principles. Having a knowledge of the mental powers, and of the objects and subjects to be taught there must be a selection from these of what the pupil can understand and most needs to know. Ideas and thoughts are to be gained from the objects of thought. The right arrangement of ideas must be observed. All lessons are conducted upon the topical plan. The same method is employed with both subjects and objects. Each is considered first as a whole, and then in its parts. A subject is presented as a whole by clearly defining it to show what it includes. It is then analyzed into its main divisions, and each division is outlined in topics logically arranged. The topics for the study of an object are arranged in the natural order.

The lessons thus analytically arranged are assigned to the class, showing them what to study, and in what order, and each topic is taught to the class *at the time the lesson is assigned so far as is necessary to teach them how to study it* so as to be able to teach or present it to the class. Oral teaching by question and answer is employed. Preliminary questioning to ascertain precisely what the pupil knows, and to show him what he needs to know, is the first step; then instructive questioning, to lead the pupil to discover for himself the ideas he is to gain, and to aid him to a correct expression of them; with so much of direct statement as is necessary to set before the class in a connected form the results of the teaching and study. All definitions are carefully worked out by explaining or illustrating the ideas included in them. Nothing is to be done for the pupil which he can do for himself.

After preparation, the class are thoroughly examined upon the lesson. The outline of topics is first stated to present the lesson as a whole. The topics are then taught to the class by different pupils, the class and the teacher criticizing the teaching. Or, the pupil presents the topic to the class, other pupils and the teacher make additions, and the class and teacher criticize the presentation. After the teaching, or presenting, the teacher thoroughly questions the class on all the important points of the lesson.

Each day a review of the preceding lesson is made, in its outline and main points, to fix the facts in the mind by repetition, and to connect the topics with the lesson of the day. Each main division of a subject is reviewed, in its outline and main topics, to teach the relation of the topics. The subject as a whole is reviewed before leaving it, in its outline and main points, to teach all the parts in their relations. By the topical mode of arranging and teaching the lessons, the teacher knows what he is to teach, in what order, and how he is to teach. The pupil knows what he is to study, in what order, and how he is to study. In class work both teacher and pupils know what points are to be made, and in what order, and the work moves on promptly. This method aids the pupil to understand and remember, accustoms him to think in a logical manner, and gives him real knowledge.

The teaching of the topics by the pupils secures the most thorough preparation of the lesson, for the pupil must know the subject, the logical arrangement of it, and how to teach it, or fail. It gives the pupil command of himself, makes him self-reliant, develops his individuality.

All the class exercises, from the beginning of the course, are conducted upon the principles and by the methods that have been indicated. After the pupils have been trained in this way, to teach philosophically, in as full a measure as the time will allow, they come in the last term of the course to the study of psychology, and there learn the philosophy of their work by finding in the study of the mind, the principles which underlie the methods they have learned to use.

Text-books are used as books of reference in the preparation of lessons. Statements of important principles and definitions are required to be memorized verbatim. The committing of text-books to memory is avoided, the students being trained to depend upon objects of thought rather than upon words.

The aim of this school is to give the pupil a definite idea of the true object, the principles, and the methods of education; a thorough knowledge of the objects and subjects he will need to teach, with such a degree of facility and skill in the application of these principles and this knowledge, as will enable him to organize and control his own school, and to educate his pupils.

Students are expected to govern themselves; to do without compulsion what is required, and to refrain voluntarily from all improprieties of conduct. Those who are unwilling to conform cheerfully to the known wishes of the Principal and his Assistants, are presumed to be unfit to become teachers.

It is not deemed necessary to awaken a feeling of emulation, in order to induce the scholars to perform their duties faithfully. Faithful attention to duty is encouraged for its own sake, and not for the purpose of obtaining certain marks of credit.

Examinations, both oral and written, are made each term in every study, and the result in each must be satisfactory to enable the pupil to advance to the studies next in order. Only those pupils who have satisfactorily passed all the examinations in the prescribed course of study receive the diploma of the Institution. The demand for graduates of both sexes, to fill good positions in the public schools, is greater than the school can at present supply.

Expenses and Pecuniary Aid.— Tuition is free to all who comply with the condition of teaching in the schools of Massachusetts, wherever they may have previously resided. Pupils who fail to comply with this condition are charged a reasonable sum for tuition. A fee of $2.00 is paid by each pupil at the beginning of the term, for incidental expenses.

For the assistance of those students who are unable to meet the expenses of the course of instruction in the school, the State makes an annual appropriation of eight hundred dollars, one-half of which is distributed at the close of each term among pupils from Massachusetts who merit and need the aid, in sums varying according to the distance of their residences from Bridgewater, but not exceeding, in any case, $1.50 a week. This aid is not furnished during the first term of attendance. It is expected that those who do not complete the prescribed course of study, and those who do not teach in the public schools of Massachusetts will refund any amount they have received from the bounty of the State. Applications for this aid are to be made to the Principal in writing.

NOTES BY THE WAY.

The Town of Bridgewater appropriated and paid five hundred dollars to aid in starting the school, and gave the rent of the town hall for its use for the first three years. Citizens of the town, in 1846, subscribed and paid more than two thousand dollars toward the erection of the new school house. Mr. Tillinghast's pupils and some friends of the school paid four hundred dollars for the same purpose.

Mr. Tillinghast records the following facts: "In December, 1842, Mr. George B. Emerson, to whom, in many respects, the school owes so much, placed at my disposal one hundred and sixty-five dollars, for the purpose of purchasing the class books used in the school. In August, 1844, Rev. R. C. Waterston paid over to me one hundred dollars, that had been collected by him for the school. This sum, with twenty-five dollars raised by subscription in the town, was expended for a theodolite. Hon. Seth Sprague, of Duxbury, presented to the school apparatus to the value of one hundred dollars. Hon. John Davis, late Judge of the U. S. District Court, presented a copy of the London Encyclopedia, in twenty-two volumes.

In 1846, Mr. Emerson again manifested his interest in the school by supplying, at his own expense, the furnaces for heating the new building. Dr. Emerson has always been a warm friend of this school, and has shown his regard by frequent visits in which he has delivered to the school many interesting and instructive addresses. During the last administration he has secured and presented large and valuable additions to the library of the school. Mr. Conant, the second Principal, presented a reflecting telescope. Prof. Alpheus Crosby, former Principal of the State Normal School at Salem, presented a copy of Ree's Encyclopedia, in forty-seven volumes.

Several of the late graduating classes, and some individual graduates, have presented to the school pictures, busts, and statuary, for adorning the school-room. A fund for the purchase of a telescope for the use of the school was started by the members of the seventy-sixth class, which now amounts to two hundred dollars. The members of the school for the eighty-sixth term paid for the chandeliers and other gas fixtures in the main school-room. Other graduates have made valuable contributions to the cabinets. The portraits of Mr. Tillinghast and Mr. Conant, which hang in the school-room, were presented by their pupils, respectively.

In the early history of the school it was sometimes difficult for the students in attendance, who wished to go out and teach in the winter, to find any chance to teach. The school was new, was not known, and there was a disposition on the part of many to wait and see what it would become before encouraging its pupils by employment. The young men often spent Saturday afternoons in the fall of the year in visiting the Prudential Committees of the neighboring towns, seeking to engage with them as teachers for the winter term. They were looked upon with some suspicion, the committee "didn't know as he wanted to hire," or in some instances they were told that "the District didn't like Norman teachers."

The pecuniary inducements to engage in teaching in those days were not great. Some of the lady graduates of the first class report that they taught in the country districts for two dollars a week and board, others for four dollars a week, including board. The young men of this period report their wages at twenty-five or thirty dollars a month, including board, and one reports "thirteen dollars a month and board round." Some young men in the early classes, who have made teaching a profession, began with twenty-five dollars a month, and are now receiving $3,200 a year; a few have reached $4,000 a year in the public schools. The highest income reported by any graduate is $7,000 a year; he is teaching a private school. The salaries of the lady graduates, as reported, have increased in about the same proportion. The highest salary for any lady graduate teaching in the public schools, so far as known, is $2,400.

The school has gradually made itself known and felt in the community through its graduates. Some have signally failed, but a large majority have satisfied all reasonable expectations. Many have sustained themselves for a long series of years in some of the most responsible positions in all the grades of the public schools, as may be seen by consulting the Alumni Record.

Mr. Philbrick, in his report of the school for 1870, writes as follows: "The Visitors of this school take pleasure in reporting that its condition is highly satisfactory. There has never been a period in its history when it has not been a school of high excellence. It has justly merited its reputation for imparting solid instruction and thorough training, rather than superficial and showy accomplishments."

In his report of the school for 1872, he says: "It is believed that the school is every year approaching near to the true standard of what a Normal School should be. While it aims to impart knowledge with thoroughness, it places a greater value upon *right training*. It tries to send out teachers who shall love and respect their profession, and who shall be capable of independent thought and action, and capable of judiciously adapting their plans and efforts to the varying circumstances in which they may be placed.

Mr. White, the Secretary of the Board, in his report for 1870, says: "It is but just to remark that the Normal Schools are better schools to-day than they were ten years ago. Their drill is more thorough, and there is a more complete adaptation of the instruction given, and especially of the method employed in giving it, to the true objects of such a school.

"Although the number of graduates is small in comparison with the whole number of teachers in the Commonwealth, still their influence upon the public schools is everywhere manifest. Furnishing better models, they have raised the standard and improved the methods of teaching. By their professional enthusiasm and devotion to their calling, they have inspired the great body of teachers with a like spirit, and aroused them to earnest efforts for improvement in their work. In this way,— through the example and influence of their graduates,— the Normal Schools have performed a service of the highest value to the public schools, but which cannot be measured by tables of statistics."

In his report for 1872, he says: "Every year's observation of their working has served to deepen my conviction that the Normal Schools are destined to play a far more important part in our school system, and to perform a more signal service for it in the future than they have hitherto done. Hence my strong belief, that no outlay of thought, of labor or of money necessary to give them the highest degree of efficiency, and to add to their number so fast as new schools shall be demanded, can be deemed an unwise expenditure."

The Board of Education, and especially the Visitors of the school, including the Secretaries of the Board, ought ever to be held in grateful remembrance by all the alumni and friends of the school for their disinterested labors to secure for it the means and conditions of success in its work. They have taken broad, generous views of education, and have earnestly sought to promote the highest prosperity of the school. Hon. Joeseph White, the present Secretary of the Board, has been a Visitor of the school for the last sixteen years. Hon. John D. Philbrick was a Visitor for nine years, and during six of these years was Chairman of the Visitors. Gardiner G. Hubbard, Esq., the present chairman, has been a Visitor of the school the last eight years. These gentlemen, by their wise counsel and efficient action, have been instrumental in securing the means for erecting the boarding hall, and enlarging the school building, for extending the course of study and furnishing better appliances for school work, and by their constant encouragement have strengthened the teachers and stimulated the pupils to higher endeavors.

INSTRUCTORS.

ALBERT G. BOYDEN, PRINCIPAL. Appointed August, 1860.
Graduated from the Bridgewater State Normal School, July 3, 1849. Spent the next term in the School upon advanced studies. Taught Grammar School in Hingham six months. Assistant Teacher in the Bridgewater State Normal School, with Mr. Tillinghast from August, 1850 to July, 1853, and during the next term with Mr. Conant. Principal of the Bowditch English High School for boys in Salem, from November, 1853 to March, 1856. Associate Principal in the Classical and English High School, Salem, from March to September, 1856. Sub-Master in the Chapman Grammar School, Boston, from September, 1856, to September, 1857. First Assistant Teacher in the Bridgewater State Normal School, from September, 1857, to August, 1860.

ASSISTANTS.

ELIZA B. WOODWARD, appointed September, 1857.
Graduated from this School, July 28, 1857. Assistant in Bridgewater Normal School with Mr. Conant three years. Has been teaching in this School nineteen years.

CHARLES F. DEXTER, appointed March, 1860. Resigned May, 1863. Merchant in Chicago.

JAMES H. SCHNEIDER, A. B. appointed September, 1860. Resigned September, 1863. Mr. Schneider was the son of Rev. Benjamin Schneider, D. D., Missionary at Aintab, Turkey. Graduated from Yale College in June, 1860. First Assistant in this Normal School three years, when he was drafted into the service of his country. He regarded the draft as the call of duty, and resigned his position in the School. The Visitors of the school, in speaking of his resignation in their report, say: "His ardent and increasing love for his work, with his habits of thorough and exact study, and his aptness to teach, made his services exceedingly valuable, and his resignation is greatly to be regretted." He entered the army, was examined before General Casey's board, and appointed Second Lieutenant. He was attached to the 2d U. S. Colored Regiment encamped at Arlington Heights, and was soon offered the choice between the adjutancy and the chaplaincy of the regiment. He chose to be Chaplain, because he could do more good in this office; came to Bridgewater, was ordained October 27, 1863; returned to his duty with his regiment, which was soon ordered to Ship Island, Mississippi Sound. After two months' stay here the regiment was ordered to Key West, Florida, where, at the end of another two months, Mr. Schneider died of "yellow fever" April 26, 1864, at 25 years of age. He was greatly beloved by all who knew him, an able scholar and teacher, a noble, Christain patriot.

AUSTIN SANFORD, appointed June, 1863. Resigned July, 1864.
Graduated from this school July 24, 1860. Taught Grammar School in Quincy. Assistant in Bridgewater Normal School one year. Graduated from Dartmouth College. Now teaching in Robinson Academy for Young Ladies, Albany, N. Y.

SOLON F. WHITNEY, A. M., appointed September, 1863. Resigned March, 1866.
Graduate of Brown University. First Assistant in this school two and one-half years. Principal of High School in Watertown. Now teacher in High School, Cambridge.

CHARLOTTE A. COMSTOCK, appointed May, 1864. Resigned July, 1866.
Graduated from this school February 19, 1862. Taught Grammar Schools in Attleborough and West Newton. Assistant in Bridgewater Normal School two years; in Connecticut State Normal School one year. Now Mrs. Charles Tomlinson, Elmira, N. Y.

GEORGE H. MARTIN, appointed September, 1864.
Graduated from this school July 29, 1863. Taught Grammar Schools in Peabody and Quincy one year. Has taught in the Bridgewater State Normal School the last twelve years. Has been First Assistant eight years.

ELLEN G. BROWN, appointed March, 1866. Resigned December, 1866.
Graduated from this School February 14, 1866. Taught in this Normal School nine months. Now Mrs. Nelson D. Pratt, 159 Putnam Street, Cleveland, O.

EMMELINE F. FISHER, appointed March, 1866. Resigned February, 1867.
Graduated from this School July 26, 1865. Taught in English and Classical School, West Newton. Taught in Bridgewater Normal School one year. Now Mrs. Francis C. Tucker, Natick.

ELISHA H. BARLOW, A. B., appointed September, 1866. Resigned January, 1868.
Graduate of Amherst College. Taught in this school one and one half years. Now Professor of Rhetoric and Oratory in Lafayette College, Easton, Penn.

EDWARD W. STEPHENSON,* appointed April, 1867. Resigned November, 1867.
Graduated from this School February 14, 1866. Taught in this school six months, when, after a brief illness, he died November, 1867.

ALICE RICHARDS, appointed December, 1867. Resigned September, 1871.
Graduated from this school July 16, 1867. Taught in Grammar School, Lewiston, Me., three months. Assistant in Bridgewater Normal School three years nine months. Married James S. Allen, E. Bridgewater, October 16, 1871.

ALBERT E. WINSHIP, appointed February, 1868. Resigned July, 1871.
Graduated from this school July 27, 1864. Taught Ungraded School in Gorham, Me., one term. Principal of Grammar School, Newton, three years. Assistant in Bridgewater State Normal School, three and one half years. Now Clergyman. Pastor of Congregational Church, Somerville.

MARY H. LEONARD, appointed April, 1868.
Graduated from this school February 5, 1867. Taught High and Grammar School in Long Meadow, one year. Has been Assistant in Bridgewater Normal School the last eight and one half years. Spent the year 1874 in Europe.

MARY A. CURRIER, appointed February, 1869. Resigned July, 1875.
Teacher of Elocution in this school six and one half years. Now Professor of Elocution in Wellesley College, Wellesley.

FRANCIS H. KIRMAYER, appointed October, 1870.
Graduate of University at Munich, Bavaria. Has been teacher of Latin, Greek, French and German in this school the last six years.

BARRETT B. RUSSELL, appointed September, 1871.
Graduated from this school January 26, 1869. Principal of Grammar Schools in Randolph and Dedham two and one half years. Has been Assistant Teacher in Bridgewater Normal School the last five years.

CLARA A. ARMES, appointed September, 1871.
Graduated from this school January 26, 1869. First Assistant in Grammar School, Newtonville, two years. Has been Assistant in Bridgewater Normal School the last five years.

ISABELLA S. HORNE, appointed September, 1875.
Graduate of School of Oratory, Boston University. Teacher of Vocal Culture in Bridgewater Normal School.

EDITH LEONARD, appointed December, 1875.
Graduated from the Advanced Course in this school January 26, 1875. Assistant in Gaston Grammar School, Boston, nine months. Assistant in Bridgewater Normal School.

Special Teachers.

MR. S. P. THACHER, Teacher of Music, 1854.
E. RIPLEY BLANCHARD, Teacher of Music, 1855 to 1860.
MR. O. B. BROWN, " " " 1860 to 1864.
HOSEA E. HOLT, " " " 1864 to 1868.
PROF. WILLIAM RUSSELL, Teacher of Elocution, 1863 to 1865.
E. THORE, Teacher of French, 1869.

# ALUMNI RECORD.

Class 56. September 9, 1860.

SAMUEL P. ALLEN,* E. Bridgewater. T. three years. Died Sept. 17, 1874. Elmwood.
NATHANIEL E. CARVER, Cape Vincent, N. Y. Taught nine years. Principal, Public School, Sextonville, Wis.
S. NELSON GROSVENOR,* Worcester. 2. Killed at Petersburg, Va., June 17, 1864.
ISAAC K. HARRIS, No. Bridgewater. Taught two years. Civil Engineer. 20 W. Green Street, Lynn.
HORACE W. HOWARD, So. Easton. Taught two terms. Farmer. Cochesett.
NOADIAH P. JOHNSON, Fall River. Not heard from.
FRANK W. KELLY, Frankfort, Me. 2. Did not teach. Lawyer. Winterport, Me.
EDWIN N. TUPPER, Monson. 1. Taught six years. Retired Gentleman. Wales.
GEO. A. WHITE, Winterport, Me. Not heard from.
  Total of teaching for six, twenty-one years. Average, three and one-half years.
CHARLOTTE A. COMSTOCK, Swanton, Vt. Taught four years in Grammar and Normal Schools. Mrs. Charles Tomlinson, Elmira, N. Y.
SARAH J. HASWELL, Acushnet. Taught seven years. Mrs. I. V. Braley, Long Plain.
HARRIET G. JOSSELYN, Bridgewater. T. five yrs. Mrs. Rev. H. G. Harris, Guilford, Vt.
ALMEDA C. LORD, Biddeford, Me. Not heard from.
FRANCES A. MASON, Swansea. Taught one year. Mrs. J. P. Barstow, 144 Willow St., Brooklyn, N. Y.
SARAH J. TAFT, Upton. Taught four years. Mrs. D. F. Batchelor, W. Upton.
  Total of teaching for five, twenty-one years. Average, four years.

Class 57. March 20, 1861.

JACOB P. ALMY,* New Bedford. Did not teach. Killed at San Carlos, Arizona, May 27, 1873.
CHARLES B. CUSHING, Winterport, Me. 1. Did not teach.
LUMAN B. FAIRBANKS, N. Reading. 2. Not heard from.
WARREN T. HILLMAN, Chilmark. Taught seven years. Physician. 2723 Washington St., St. Louis, Mo.
HENRY F. HOWARD, W. Bridgewater. T. fourteen years. Grammar School. W. Somerville.
OLIVER HOWARD, S. Easton. T. ten years. Supt. of Schools, Weld Co., Greely, Col.
THOMAS S. HOWLAND, N. Dartmouth. Did not teach. Civil Engineer. Burlington, Iowa.
FRANK W. KELLEY, Frankfort, Me. 1. Did not teach. Lawyer. Winterport, Me.
HOWARD W. KELLEY,* Frankfort, Me. 1. Did not teach. Lost at sea several years since.
J. HERBERT LEONARD, Norton. Taught two years. Farmer. Easton.
D. SWANSON LEWIS, Rochester. Taught two terms. Assistant in Chem. Lab., Bussey Insitute, Jamaica Plain.
JOSEPH L. LOCKE, Manchester, N. H. Did not teach. Book-keeper. 181 Jackson St., Chicago, Ill.
WILLIAM H. MARSHALL, E. Douglass. Taught one year. Bootmaker. St. Joseph, Mo.
LUNAS MENDELL, Rochester. 3. Did not teach. Clerk. 432 Herkimer St., Brooklyn, N. Y.
WEBSTER K. PIERCE, Frankfort, Me. 1. Did not teach. Clergyman. Brimfield.
HENRY L. REED,* No. Easton. Taught four years. Died Dec. 25, 1868.
JEREMIAH SWASEY, E. Douglas. Not heard from.
JOSHUA TREAT, Frankfort, Me. 3. Did not teach. Supt. of Factory, Winterport, Me.

MR. BOYDEN'S ADMINISTRATION.

HIRAM N. WALKER,* Southbridge. 1. Died at Newbern, N. C., Jan. 18, 1863.
CHARLES H. W. WOOD, Campello. Taught three years. Civil Engineer. 9 Bainbridge Street, Boston.
 Total of teaching for eighteen, forty-two years. Average, two years.
VICTORIA R. BLANCHARD, Uxbridge. 2. T. six years. Mrs. Chas. W. Scott, Uxbridge.
LUCETTE M. BROWNING, Richmond, Vt. Taught two terms. Richmond, Vt.
LUCY M. COBB, Rochester. Taught nine years. Berlin Cross Roads, Ohio.
MARY F. CUTLER, Bedford, N. H. Taught four years. Bedford, N. H.
SIBEL EDSON, West Bridgewater. Taught four years. Mrs. Zeno Benson, Bridgewater.
MARY D. FORBES, West Bridgewater. 4. Taught four terms. W. Bridgewater.
MARY A. FOSTER,* Quincy. Taught two years. Mrs. O. Wilber. Died, 1874.
CLIMENA A. GROVER, W. Bethel, Me. T. five years. Mrs. Oliver Howard, Greely, Col.
MELITA A. HOLBROOK,* Upton. Taught five years. Died June 6, 1867.
CAROLINE HOWARD, W. Bridgewater. Taught twelve years. Mrs. Bradford Copeland, Campello.
MARY E. KELLEY, Acushnet. 2. Not heard from.
ROSALIE S. PERKINS, Bridgewater. 3. Did not teach.
MARY WHITMAN, E. Bridgewater. Taught three years. Mrs. C. H. W. Wood, Boston.
 Total of teaching for twelve, fifty-two years. Average, four years.

CLASS 58. SEPTEMBER 18, 1861.

LEROY T. CRAM,* Deerfield, N. H. Did not teach. Died May 3, 1872.
GEO. T. FORD, E. Bridgewater. Taught six months. Machinist. Seattle, W. T.
GRANVILLE H. GOULD, Bridgewater. 1. Did not teach. 102 High Street, Boston.
LATHLEY L. HALEY, Winterport, Me. 1. Did not teach. In business. Winterport, Me.
WALTER HALEY, Winterport, Me. 1. Did not teach. In business. Winterport, Me.
JOHN W. HOBART. Boston, Not heard from.
CYRUS D. HUNT, E. Weymouth. T. one term. Manager of Ames Tack Co., Fairhaven.
THOMAS S. KINGMAN, N. Bridgewater. 1. Did not teach. Clerk. A. T. Stewart's, N. Y.
CHARLES RECCORD, Berkley. 1. Taught one year. Trader. Phelps, Ontario Co., N. Y.
EDWIN L. SARGENT, Lynn. Taught eight years, Lynn High School.
 Total of teaching for five, ten years. Average, two years.
LOUISA L. BALLOU, Keene. N. H. 1. Not heard from.
EMILY M. BLANCHARD, Millville. 1. Has not taught.
ABBIE F. BOYD, Roxbury. Not heard from.
ANNIE E. BOYD, Roxbury. Not heard from.
FANNIE C. BROWNELL, N. Fairhaven. Taught eleven years. Mrs. L. D. Stevens, Concord, N. H.
EMILY C. CHEEVER, Wrentham. Taught two years. Mrs. L. F. Mendell, 432 Herkimer St., Brooklyn, N. Y.
MARY F. CLARK, New Bedford. Taught six years. Mrs. J. P. Wild, 17 Chestnut St., New Bedford.
CAROLINE D. FULLER, S. Freedom, Me. 1. Taught twelve years. Teacher of Elocution Fort Wayne, Ind.
LUCY P. HATHAWAY, N. Dartmouth. Taught five years. New Bedford.
LUCIA HOOPER, Bridgewater. 1. Did not teach. Mrs. Henry T. Pratt, Bridgewater.
MARY S. MENDELL, N. Fairhaven. Taught fourteen years. High School. New Bedford. 187 Middle St.
HANNAH B. MILLER, Rockville. Not heard from. Mrs. Charles Beckwith, Hartford, Ct.
ANGELINE M. QUINCY, Quincy. Taught eleven years. Grammar School. N. Attleboro.
SOPHIA REED, E. Abington. Taught one term. Mrs. Edw. Peabody, Rockland.
ISABEL M. REID, New Bedford. T. ten years. Fifth St. Grammar School. New Bedford.
MARY E. SAWYER, Dover, N. H. 4. Did not teach. Address, Dover, N. H.
CLARA SEABURY, Orleans. Taught one term. Teacher of Music. Orleans.
EDNA M. SHAW, Sudbury. Taught three terms. Mrs. E. M. Stearns, Mansfield.

HEPSIBAH F. STEARNS, Mansfield. 2. Taught one year. Address, Mansfield.
ADELAIDE W. TINKHAM, Acushnet. 1. T. one year. Mrs. J. H. Ricketson, Acushnet.
MARIA A. WITHERELL, N. Adams. 1. Did not teach. Mrs. N. C. Mason, Williamstown.
Total of teaching for seventeen, seventy-five years. Average, four and one-half years.

Class 59. March 19, 1862.

EDWARD K. ALLEN,* Walpole. Did not teach. Lawyer. Died at Washington, D. C.
BRADFORD COPELAND, W. Bridgewater. 4. Did not teach. Farmer. Campello.
HEMAN COPELAND, W. Bridgewater. 4. T. two years. Market Gardener. Campello.
SIMEON J. DUNBAR, W. Bridgewater. T. eleven years. Grammar School. Arlington
EBEN W. FULLER,* Montville, Me. 1. Died in Chesapeake Hospital, Va., Dec. 13, 1862.
GORHAM P. GOULD, North Hanson, Me. 1. Not heard from.
D. W. GUERNSEY, Boston. 1. Not heard from.
J. MILTON HALL, Windham, Me. Taught thirteen years. Principal, Grammar School. Providence, R. I.
GEORGE F. HAYWARD, East Bridgewater. 3. T. ten years. Salesman. E. Bridgewater.
BERIAH T. HILLMAN, Chilmark. Taught seven years. Trader. West Tisbury.
MARCELLUS G. HOWARD, Bridgewater. 1. Did not teach. Butcher. Bridgewater.
WILLIAM H. JOHNSON, Bridgewater. 1. Not heard from.
GEO. H. MARTIN, Lynn. Taught thirteen years. State Normal School. Bridgewater.
EDWARD H. PEABODY, Salem. Taught five years. Editor. Lawrence.
CHARLES L. RUSSELL, N. Fairhaven. 3. Not heard from.
HENRY W. SHAW,* East Bridgewater. 3. Died November, 1866.
JOHN J. SHAW, East Bridgewater. Physician. Plymouth.
EZRA N. SMITH, Wareham. Taught five years. Clergyman. Solon, Maine.
NATHAN T. SOULE, Duxbury. 3. T. thirteen years. Prin. Grammar School. Brockton.
CHARLES F. STUART,* Hampden, Me. 1. Died in Finley Hospital, Washington, D. C., April 23, 1863.
W. R. SWAN, Stoughton. 2. Dry Goods Dealer. Stoughton.
LEMUEL T. TERRY, N. Fairhaven. Book-keeper. New Bedford.
ANDREW J. WATERS, West Sutton. Taught six years. Grammar School. Webster.
TYLER R. WASGATT, JR., Hampden Corner, Me. 1. Did not teach. Steamboat Agent. Hampden, Maine.
Total of teaching for eighteen, eighty-five years. Average, five years.

MARY F. BLISS, Wrentham. Not heard from.
MARY A. BOWMAN, New Bedford. Taught one year. New Bedford.
HELEN B. COFFIN, Harrington, Me. Taught twelve years. Mrs. Beede, Farmington, Me.
KATE C. CROSSMAN, W. Bridgewater. Did not teach. Mrs. Maurice Pechin, Washington, D. C.
IMOGENE L. CUTTER, Bridgewater. 1. Taught five years. Mrs. F. F. Stone, Bridgewater.
MARTHA A. GREENE, Allentown, R. I. 3. Not heard from.
MARY E. HUGHES, N. Bridgewater. 1. T. two years. Music Teacher. Pittsburg, Pa.
FANNIE E. KILBURN, Holden. T. eight years. Mrs. Rev. G. H. French, Johnson, Vt.
SOPHRONIA LANE, Woburn. Taught four years. Mrs. F. A. Gardner, Weymouth.
SARAH E. LEONARD, E. Marshfield. T. twelve years. Harvard School. Charlestown.
ELLA D. PULSIFER, Ellsworth, Me. T. ten years. Mrs. Frederic Matthews, Yarmouthport.
MARY E. ROBINSON, Winterport, Me. Taught eleven years. Mrs. Rev. Theophilus Beaizley, Hydesville, Humboldt Co., California.
ELIZABETH THOMAS, Danville, Vt. 1. Not heard from.
JOSEPHINE UNDERWOOD, E. Bridgewater. Taught five years. Mrs. L. W. Chapman S. Hanover.
MARY E. WOOD, Bridgewater. Taught six years. Mrs. W. B. Thayer, Randolph.
Total of teaching for twelve, seventy-six years. Average, six years.

Class 60. September 17, 1862.

EDWARD E. PERRY,* Mansfield. 4. Taught one year. Physician. Died Sept. 14, 1875
EMMA A. BRYANT,* Groton. Taught seven years. Died Nov., 1871, in Kalamazoo, Mich.
CAROLINE R. BROWN, E. Machias, Me. Taught seven years. E. Machias, Me.
LIZZIE P. BRIGGS, New Bedford. Taught twelve years. High School, New Bedford.
CELIA L. HAYWARD, Bridgewater. Mrs. Wales Hayward, N. Middleboro'.
ANTOINETTE F. HOWARD, W. Bridgewater. Taught five years. Book-keeper. W. Bridgewater.
ADDIE L. LUCE, Mattapoisett. 1. Taught one year. Mrs. J. W. Holmes, Mattapoisett.
SUSAN B. MILLETT, Bridgewater. T. two years. Mrs. Frank Dunphe, E. Bridgewater.
CARRIE MUNROE, S. Seekonk. No information.
SARAH S. MUNROE, S. Seekonk. Taught twelve years. Grammar School. Lincoln, R. I.
JULIA A. PACKARD, N. Bridgewater. Taught twelve years. Ungraded School. S. Easton.
MARTHA J. PACKARD, N. Bridgewater. T. two years. Mrs. George Farwell, Brockton.
CARRIE M. PARKER, Mattapoisett. T. two years. Mrs. Heman Copeland, Campello.
ELIZA B. PETTIS, Somerset. 2. Did not teach. Mrs. Rev. W. S Urmy, Vallejo, Cal.
MARGARET B. PERKINS, Bridgewater. 1. Did not teach.
BETSEY H. PIERCE, Freetown. 2. Taught one year. Address, Assonet.
NANCY M. RICHARDSON, Mattapoisett. T. three years. Mrs. E. G. Caswell, Mattapoisett.
Total of teaching for fourteen, sixty-five years. Average, five years.

Class 61. March 11, 1863.

JOSEPH S. BERRY, N. Wayne, Me. 1. Did not teach. Grocer. Wayne, Me.
WM. W. BREWSTER, Industry, Me. Taught five years. Inventor. Revere.
MELZAR W. CHADBOURNE, Waterford, Me. 1. Not heard from.
FRANK DOLAND, Milford. 1. Not heard from.
FRANK M. LAWRENCE, Castine, Me. Taught one year. Iron Business. Bangor, Me.
JOHN T. PRINCE, Kingston. Taught twelve years. Grammar School. Waltham.
EZRA W. SAMPSON, Lakeville. Taught twelve years. High School. Newtonville.
JAMES M. SAWIN, Brookline, N. H. T. twelve years. Grammar School, Providence, R. I.
HENRY C. SAWIN, Brookline, N. H. Taught twelve years. Grammar School. Newton.
GEO. S. TURNER, Foxborough. 3. Taught ten years. Watertown.
ALBERT E. WINSHIP, Cochesett. Taught seven years. Grammar and Normal Schools. Congregational Clergyman. Somerville.
Total of teaching for nine, seventy-one years. Average, eight years.

ABBIE S. ALMY,* New Bedford. T. three years. Mrs. J. M. Sawin. Died Oct. 17, 1867
KATIE L. W. BARKER, N Dartmouth. Taught twelve years. Grammar School. Brookline.
MARY E. BARKER, N. Dartmouth. Taught ten years. Primary School. Brookline.
HELEN M. HATHAWAY, Assonet. 3. Taught one term. Mrs. A. B. Irons, Providence, R. I.
ANNA A. HAZARD, N. Dartmouth. 3. Not heard from.
MARY A. HOLLIS, N. Bridgewater. Taught four years. Brockton.
MARCIA E. JACKSON,* Plymouth. 1. Did not teach. Mrs. J. P. Gates. Died Jan, 20, 1873.
MARY E. NASH, Addison, Me. Taught two years. Mrs. V. C. Plummer, Addison, Me.
SARAH B. PACKARD, Marshfield. Taught eight years. Mrs. S. F. Cole, Brockton.
ABBIE B. PIERCE, Woonsocket, R. I. T. three years. Mrs. B. T. Hillman, W. Tisbury.
PHEBE H. POPE, Acushnet. 3. Did not teach. Mrs. G. C. Pierce, Ashland.
PHILENA H. ROUNSEVILLE, Rochester. T. twelve years. Dearborn School. Boston Highlands.
MARIA S. RICKETSON, New Bedford. 4. Not heard from.
ESTHER M. SIMMONS, N. Bridgewater. T. five years. Mrs. T. H. Baxondale, Brockton.
MARGARET F. SMALL, Barnstable. Taught four years. Mrs. D. Smith, Putnam, Conn
C. LIZZIE STEPHENSON, Boston. 2. Not heard from.
SARAH S. SWEENEY, Cherryfield, Me. 1. Not heard from.
CLARA A. WHITE, New Bedford. 2. Did not teach. Mrs. G. S. Turner, Watertown.

142   BRIDGEWATER STATE NORMAL SCHOOL.

LUCRETIA A. WILLIAMS, Woonsocket, R. I. Not heard from.
HARRIET P. WINN, Nantucket. Taught two terms Mrs. G. H. Butler, Hyde Park.
SUSAN S. WILBAR, Bridgewater. 1 Not heard from.
    Total of teaching for fifteen, sixty-four years. Average, four years.

Class 62. September 16, 1863.

CYRUS A. COLE, E. Boston. Taught eleven years. Principal High School. Reading.
GIDEON L. DAVIS, Annisquam. 2. Taught five years. Address, Annisquam.
SILAS H. HASKELL, Minneapolis, Minn. Taught nine years. Address, Richmond, Va.
EDWARD T. McMANUS,* Boston. Taught one year. Deceased.
CHARLES T. PICKARD, Hampden, Me. 1. Not heard from.
RICHARD W. SMITH, E. Bridgewater. 2. Not heard from.
    Total of teaching for four, twenty-six years. Average, six and one-half years.
MARY J. BASSETT, Bridgewater. 4. Taught six years. Mrs. Wm. F. Dean, Taunton.
AMY CROSBY, Milton. Taught eight years. Married Rev. Mr. Bygrave, Hudson.
ANNIE T. CLARKE, Blackstone. 2. Not heard from.
ISABEL L. CUSHING. Taught two years. Mrs. G. N. Dresser, Holliston.
L. ARVILLA DEAN, Easton. 3. Taught seven years. Address, Easton.
ABBIE M. DOTON, Pomfret, Vt. Taught seven years. Mrs. J. K. P. Chamberlain, Woodstock, Vermont.
MARTHA A. DOWSE, Sherborn. Taught one term.
ANNIE E. HASKELL, Minneapolis, Minn. 2. Not heard from.
SUSAN B. HOLMES, Kingston. T. eight years. Grammar. 9 Kinnaird St., Cambridgeport.
SARAH HOXIE, Easton. 1. Not heard from.
LUCIA A. KINGMAN, N. Bridgewater. 4. Taught ten years. Teaching Grammar School. Booneville, Mo.
EMMA F. LEONARD, Bridgewater. Taught four terms. Address, Scotland.
ELIZABETH M. LEONARD, Bridgewater. Taught eight years. Mrs. Rev. T. D. Childs Scotland.
ABBY J. MOSHER,* Milton. Taught three years. Died June 6, 1869.
DORA NICKERSON,* S. Harwich. 1. Taught ten years. Died April 24, 1876.
PHILENA R. PERKINS, Pomfret, Vt. T. two years. Mrs. H. B. Parkhurst, Barnard, Vt.
JOSEPHINE P. RAYMOND, E. Bridgewater. T. seven years. Mrs. Alson Poole, Malden.
ADELAIDE REED, Kingston. Taught eleven years. Grammar School. Newton.
HARRIET V. RICHARDSON, Dracut. Taught four years. Mrs. W. Hammond, Nebraska City, Neb.
MARY B. RICHARDSON, Dracut. 3. T. five years. Mrs. C. D. Barrows, New York City.
EARLMIRA M. G. SANBORN, Quincy. T. one term. Mrs. C. M. Leonard, Bridgewater.
ANNIE F. STANLEY, No. Attleboro'. Taught eight years. Mrs. W. W. Pratt, Wollaston, Quincy.
ABBIE D. WHITNEY, New Bedford. Taught eight years. Primary School. New Bedford.
    Total of teaching for twenty, one hundred and sixteen years. Average, six years.

Class 63. March 9, 1864.

ISAAC F. HALL, Dennis. Taught nine years. Principal Washington Grammar School. Quincy, Pt.
FREDERICK KNOWLTON,* Worcester. 3. Did not teach. Killed by the fall of an Elevator, in 1873.
WILLIAM P. A. LAWRENCE, Westport. 1. Taught one year. New Bedford.
EDWARD W. STEPHENSON,* Hingham. Taught six months in Normal School, Bridgewater. Died November, 1867.
    Total of teaching for four, ten years. Average, three years.
MARY E. BATES, Bridgewater. Not heard from.
ELLEN G. BROWN, E. Greenwich, R. I. Taught three years. Mrs. Nelson D. Pratt, 159 Putnam St., Cleveland, O.

ELIZABETH COBB, Somerville. 2. T. eleven years, Grammar School. Boston Highlands.
CORA L. R. DAGGETT, Attleboro' Falls. T. three years. Address, Attleboro' Falls.
GEORGIANA DECKER, Newton. Taught four years. Mrs. Geo. E. Wales, Newton Centre.
MINERVA FARNUM, Millville. Taught five years. Address, Millville.
EMELINE F. FISHER, Southboro.' Taught two years. Mrs. Francis C. Tucker, Natick.
HATTIE W. FREELEY, Pomfret, Vt. T. three years. Mrs. H. W. Chase, W. Randolph, Vt.
MARY C. HALL, Cohassett. Not Heard from.
FLORENCE A. JENKINS, E. Bridgewater. Taught seven years. Mrs. H. A. Foster, M. D., Buffalo, N. Y.
LEORA B. KEITH, Bridgewater. Taught five years. Mrs. Geo. D. Davis, Marlboro'.
PAULINE S. KENNEY,* Orleans. Taught two years. Died Sept. 21, 1870.
KATIE MITCHELL, Bridgewater. Taught five years. Primary School. Bridgewater.
MARY F. REED, E. Bridgewater. Taught ten years. Intermediate School. S. Abington.
ALICE A. THAYER, Mendon. 1. Taught nine years. Mrs. H. H. Holbrook, Mendon.
ABBIE F. TILLSON,* Bridgewater. Did not teach. Died March, 1866.
LUCY WASHBURN, Bridgewater. Taught five years: Mrs. Geo. Eaton, 92 Lippett St., Providence, R. I.
SUSAN C. WILLEY, W. Northwood, N. H. 1. Taught nine years. Coffeyville, Montgomery County, Kansas.
MARIA E. WILLIAMS, New Bedford. 1. Not heard from.
Total of teaching for sixteen, eighty-three years. Average, five years.

Class 64. September 21, 1864.

SAMUEL T. BOWTHORPE, Jamaica Plain. 3. Taught one term. Dentist. 384 Broadway, South Boston.
GEO. D. DAVIS, W. Newton. 1. Did not teach. Sales Agent. London, England.
WILLIAM H. LANE, Raymond, N. H. Lay Preacher. Raymond, N. H.
EMERY G. WETHERBEE, Northboro'. 2. Did not teach. Life Insurance. 153 Tremont Street, Boston.
Total of teaching for four, one term.
ELVIRA M. CLARK, Stow. Taught seven years. Mrs. Dr. Geo. P. Lee, Merced City, Cal.
ELLEN I. COWLS, Milton. Not heard from.
ABBIE M. DEXTER, New Bedford. Taught one year. Mrs. Capt. E. E. Hicks. At Sea.
EUNICE D. HEDGE,* Plymouth. T. two years. Mrs. F. E. Damon. Died July 7, 1870.
HARRIET A. HOLBROOK, Joppa Village. T. five years. Bookkeeper. E. Bridgewater.
MARY A. HOLMES, Putnam, Conn. 1. Not heard from.
FANNIE HOWLAND,* Bridgewater. T. three years. Mrs. D. Hadley. Died Feb. 8. 1872.
MARTHA A. KINGMAN, Bridgewater. Taught nine years. Primary School. Taunton.
ANNA LORD, Ellsworth, Me. 1. Not heard from.
Total of teaching for six, twenty-seven years. Average, four years.

Class 65. March 8, 1865.

C. IRVING FISHER, Canton. 3. Taught two years. Physician. Brookline.
EDWARD L. HERSEY, Cochesett. T. nine years. Prin. Grammar School. Taunton.
THOMAS S. HOLMES, W. Bridgewater. 2. Canal and Gate Keeper. 9 Broadway, Lawrence.
E. F. LOCKE, Rochester, N. H. 1. Taught eight years. High and Grammar School. New Castle, N. H.
EUGENE SANFORD, E. Bridgewater. T. five years. Bookkeeper. Pawtucket, R. I.
W. CLIFTON SPRING, Sandwich. 1. Taught seven years. High School. Wellfleet.
Total of teaching for six, thirty-one years. Average, five years.
ANNIE L. ARNOLD, S. Braintree. 1. Taught eight years. Grammar School. Peabody.
ELLA A. BRETT, E. Stoughton. 3. Taught two terms. Mrs J. P. Beal. Holbrook.
MARY I. BURGESS, Grafton, Vt. 2. Taught three years. Grafton, Vermont.
LOUISA F. COPELAND, W. Bridgewater. T. five years. Mrs. A. S. Lyon. Bridgewater.

144 BRIDGEWATER STATE NORMAL SCHOOL.

HATTIE W. DAVIDSON,* Easton. 3. Taught one year. Died January 31, 1875.
NELLIE C. DAVIS, E. Falmouth. 1. T. two years. Mrs. Wm. S. Baker. E. Falmouth.
LUCINA DUNBAR, W. Bridgewater. Taught ten years. Grammar School. Hyde Park.
ESTHER EMERSON, Reading. Taught five years. Primary School. Medfield.
ISABELLA J. FULLER, Kingston. 1. Not heard from.
C. FANNIE GOULD,* Falmouth. 2. Did not teach. Died April 1, 1869.
SARAH J. KEITH, Middleborough. 3. Not heard from.
AMANDA F. KING, Tiverton, R. I. T. nine years. Grammar School. Fall River.
MARY H. LEONARD, Bridgewater- T. ten years. State Normal School. Bridgewater.
HANNAH O. NOYES, Elmwood. Taught nine years. Mrs. Lucien Eaton, 1621 Olive St., St. Louis.
MARY E. H. OTTWELL, New Bedford. T. nine years. Lawrence Gram. School. Boston.
ENNA M. PACKARD, W. Bridgewater. T. five years. Mrs. J. D. Packard, Brockton.
HANNAH M. RICHMOND,* W. Bridgewater. 3. Taught four years. Died June 24, 1873
SARAH A. SPAULDING, Easton. 3. Taught four years. Mrs. Wm. B. Howard, Taunton.
FLORA C. SWIFT. Bridgewater. Taught ten years. Grammar School. Bridgewater.
OLENA A. WAKEFIELD, Reading. Taught ten years. Primary School. Brockton.
ALLA F. YOUNG, Bridgewater. Taught ten years. High School. Gloucester.
 Total of teaching for nineteen, one-hundred and fifteen years. Average, six years.

CLASS 66. SEPTEMBER 20, 1865.

LEICESTER F. BENTON, Vergennes, Vt. Taught ten years. Bristol Academy. Bristol, Vt.
JOHN D. BILLINGS, Canton. Taught nine years. Principal, Webster Grammar School. Cambridgeport.
JOSEPH E. BOWERS, Kellysville, Pa. T. six years. Dry Goods dealer. Kellysville, Pa.
DARIUS HADLEY, Chicopee Falls. Taught nine years. Sub Master, Harvard Grammar School. Charlestown.
CHARLES M. HAFEY, Cincinnati, O. Not heard from.
JOHN E. PILLING, Clifton, Pa. Did not teach. Millwright. Clifton, Pa.
WILLIAM C. RAYMOND, W. Weymouth. 2 Not heard from.
ALBERT F. RING, Worcester. Taught nine years. Master, Hillside Grammar School. Jamaica Plain, Boston.
 Total of teaching for six, forty-three years. Average, seven years.

JOSEPHINE L. AUSTIN, Norton. Taught six years. Mrs. Rev. H. C. Crane, Franklin.
ELLA R. AVERILL, Quincy. 1. Not heard from.
MARY E. BALDWIN, Foxborough. Taught two terms. Mrs. J. D. Nesbitt, Foxborough.
RUTH F. BOURNE, W. Wareham. 5. Taught nine years. Mixed School. W. Wareham.
JULIA E. BRYANT, S. Groton. 2. Not heard from.
LOTTIE E. BURSE, Plymouth. 4. Taught eight years. Intermediate School. Plymouth.
HATTIE A. COBB, E. Bridgewater. Taught eight years. Intermediate. E. Bridgewater.
ISABELLA F. CRAPO, Bridgewater. Taught nine years. Grammar School. Bridgewater.
HELEN L. FULLERTON, S. Abington. 1. Did not teach. Mrs. Helen L. Alden, S. Abington.
ELLEN E. GOWARD, N. Easton. 1. Taught six years. Mrs. Everett R. Leonard, Norton.
ELLEN HAYWARD, Plympton. Not heard from.
MARIA McCARTER,* E. Bridgewater. 3. Did not teach. Died April 30, 1868.
ALICE RICHARDS, W. Bridgewater. Taught four years. Mrs. J. S. Allen, E. Bridgewater.
LIZZIE S. RIDDELL, Nantucket. Taught nine years. Private School. Nantucket.
ALICE SANDERS, Fall River. Taught eight years. Mrs. Albert Pitts, Fall River.
LUCIE M. WASHBURN, E. Freetown. 2. Not heard from.
MARY P. C. WHITNEY, Southborough. T. three years. Mrs. J. D. Billings, Cambridgeport.
SARAH W. WITTET, Marion. 1. Taught two years. Mrs. J. M. Davis, Fall River.
LIZZIE A. WINWARD, Fall River. Taught nine years. Master's Assistant, Andrew School. S. Boston.
MARY A. YOUNG, Lawrence. Not heard from.
 Total of teaching for fifteen, eighty-four years. Average, five years.

Class 67. March 14, 1866.

WILLIAM B. ATWOOD, Middleborough. Taught nine years. Sub-Master, Winthrop Grammar School. Charlestown.
EDWARD CROWNINSHIELD, 2D, Marblehead. 2. Did not teach. Clergyman. W. Dedham.
HORACE A. FREEMAN, Provincetown. T. eight years. Grammar School. Provincetown.
ALONZO MESERVE, N. Abington. Taught nine years. Sub-Master, Prescott Grammar School. Charlestown.
HENRY PERKINS, Bridgewater. 1. Not heard from.
WILLIAM H. RUSSELL, Dartmouth. Taught eight years. Academy. Burnet, Texas.
JOHN SUTCLIFFE, Fall River. 2. Not heard from.
BRAINARD P. TRASK,* Fitchburg. 3. Taught four years. Died Sept. 29, 1870.

Total of teaching for seven, thirty-eight years. Average, five and one-half years.

ELLA M. ARMES, Barrington, N. H. Taught seven years. Primary School. Brockton.
HARRIET A. CHASE, Nantucket. Not heard from.
GEORGIANA DUCKWORTH, Bridgewater. Taught two years. Bridgewater.
HARRIET L. FISKE, Templeton. T. two years. Mrs. James Price, Warehouse Pt., Conn.
SARAH F. HARRIS,* Catskill, N. Y. Died, August, 1867. No information.
LAURA N. HOWLAND, Fairhaven. 3. Taught Private School. Mrs. S. H. Dudley, 17 Dunster St., Fairhaven.
HARRIET M. HOWLAND, Fairhaven. 2. Taught four years. Teaching in High School. Fairhaven.
IMOGENE A. LAWRENCE, Bridgewater. T. one year. Mrs. E. S. Knapp, Bridgewater.
ELLA F. PEABODY, Newport, R. I. Taught nine years. Grammar School. Newport, R. I.
MARY L. PRESCOTT, Randolph. Taught five years. Address, Randolph.
EMMA A. PRESCOTT, Reading. Taught two terms. Reading.
EMMA J. PRICE, Warehouse Point, Ct. 1. Taught six years. Denver, Col.
MARTHA B. SAWYER, Campello. 1. Not heard from.
EDNA C. TILLEY, Newport, R. I. 1. T. seven years. Mrs. J. F. Chase, 111 Broadway, N. Y.
HELEN E. WILLIAMS, Middleborough. 1. Not heard from.

Total of teaching for eleven, forty-four years. Average, four years.

Class 68. September 11, 1866.

SAMUEL J. BULLOCK, Salem. Taught eight years. Master, Bunker Hill Grammar School. Charlestown.
JAMES A. FRANCIS, Westport. Taught three years. Carpenter. Westport.
EDWARD A. GROSSMAN, Newtonville. 2. Not heard from.
NOAH HATHAWAY, Freetown. Taught one term. Pattern maker. Vallejo, Cal.
WALTER HOXIE, Newburyport. 4. T. seven years. Grammar School. Newburyport.
MOSES W. D. HURD, Boston. Taught eight years. Farm School, Boston. Address care of F. A. Sproul, Esq., Allston.
CHARLES H. KEITH, Campello. T. five years. Grammar School. Norwich, Conn.
WILLIAM A. SYMMES, Beverly. 3. T. eight years. Principal, Academy. Belvidere, N. C.

Total of teaching for seven, thirty-nine years. Average, six years.

EDDIE A. AVERY, East Machias, Maine. 1. Not heard from.
ISABELLA J. DUNHAM. S. Carver. 1. Taught nine years. Dearborn School. Boston. Address, Beverly.
ELLA A. ELLIOTT, Manchester,* N. H. 2. Taught two years. Died February, 1876.
SUSAN W. KIRBY, Fall River. Taught seven years. Factory School. Fall River.
LAURA A. LEONARD, S. Middleborough. T. eight years. Grammar School. Malden.
CLARA F. LEONARD, Bridgewater. Taught six years. Mrs. Dr. C. I. Fisher, Brookline.
FLORA McFARLAND,* Fall River. Died June 7, 1869.
MARY E. MINTER, Plymouth. T. eight years. Prin., Grammar School. Newton Centre.
MARY C. PEABODY, Cambridge. 2. T. six years. Private Kindergarten. New Bedford.

146 BRIDGEWATER STATE NORMAL SCHOOL.

ROSA C. SHAW, Carver. Taught five years. Mrs. Rev. H. H. Hayden, S. Carver.
SARAH R. WALKER, Dighton. Taught seven years. Mrs. Jos. E. Sears, Dighton.
CORA I. YOUNG, Boston. Taught five years. Primary School. Quincy.
    Total of teaching for eleven, sixty-three years. Average, six years.

Class 69. February. 19, 1867.

MERRICK J. FAY, Worcester. Taught two terms. Photographer. Worcester.
MELVIN C. FRENCH, Berkley. Did not teach. Tack Factory. S. Abington.
PHILANDER A. GAY, Rockville. Taught seven years. Grammar School. Milton.
HIRAM L. HUTCHINSON, S. Danvers. 3. Taught three years. Teaching. W. Peabody.
NATHANIEL S. KEAY, Rockville. Taught one year. Clerk. Bridgewater.
BARRETT B. RUSSELL, Dartmouth. T. seven years. State Normal School. Bridgewater.
THOMAS H. TREADWAY, Bridgewater. Taught four years. Grammar School. Harvard.
    Total of teaching for seven, twenty-three years. Average, three years.
CLARA A. ARMES, Barrington, N. H. T. seven years. State Normal School. Bridgewater.
MARY C. BABCOCK, Natick. Taught two years. Mrs. Rev. A. E. Reynolds, Natick.
MARY A. DAVIS, Fairhaven. 1. Not heard from.
OLIVIA S. HOLMES, W. Bridgewater. 4. Taught two years. Address, N. Bridgewater.
CLARA KENRICK, S. Orleans. Taught seven years. High School. Cotuit Port.
SARAH A. LEWIS, Fall River. Taught two years. Mrs. Edw. A. Williams, 36 Washington St., Fall River.
LUCIA MILLETT, Bridgewater. Taught five years. Teaching. East Bridgewater.
LUCRETIA G. OSBORNE, E. Bridgewater. Taught seven years. Teaching Mixed School. Brockton.
HELEN L. PENNIMAN,* S. Braintree. 2. Did not teach. Died August 30, 1870.
SARAH L. PORTER, S. Braintree. 3. T. three years. Mrs. A. R. French. S. Braintree.
SARAH E. PRATT, Reading. Taught seven years. Primary School. Newton.
BETSY P. SIMMONS, W. Duxbury. 1. Taught two years. Address, W. Duxbury.
ABBIE SMITH, E. Bridgewater. T. two years. Mrs. Isaac N. Clements, Cazenovia, N. Y.
CORNELIA SMITH, Easton. 2. Not heard from.
MELORA A. WHITCOMB, Templeton. T. five years. Mrs. A. E. Bragg. Taunton.
    Total of teaching for thirteen, fifty-one years. Average, four years.

Class 70. September 10, 1867.

HENRY J. CLARKE, Southbridge. Taught three years. Attorney at Law. Oxford.
JAMES E. LEACH, Scotland. 1. Taught one year. Student of Law. Boston.
JAMES N. PARKER, Marblehead. Taught seven years. Grammar School. W. Dedham.
HENRY W. SMITH, Russell's Mills. 1. Not heard from.
CHARLES R. COFFIN, Auburn, Me. Taught six years. Instructor in Greek. University Pittsburg, Pa.
    Total of teaching for four, seventeen years. Average, four years.
EVANTIA F. CHESLEY, Fall River. Not heard from.
ELLA F. CHURCHILL, W. Bridgewater. Not heard from.
MARY C. COON, Cotuit Port. 3. Taught one year. Mrs. Wm. H. Crocker. Watertown.
ETTIE CROUCHER, Newport, R. I. 1. Taught three terms. Newport, R. I.
IDA G. DECKER, Newton Centre. 3. Taught six years. Mixed School. Foxborough.
EMMA C. EDSON, Elmwood. T. seven years. Teaching Intermediate School. Fall River.
ELLEN G. FISHER, Yarmouth Port. T. four years. Mrs. E. P. Adams. Honolulu, S. I.
SARAH F. GARDNER, Newport, R. I. T. two years. 22 Washington Place, N. Y. City.
CHARLOTTE E. HAMMOND, Carver. T. five years. Mrs. A. R. Eames. N. Carver.
SUSAN V. JAMES, Fall River. 2. Not heard from.
SUSAN M. LEACH, Scotland. Taught two years. Mrs. H. J. Clarke. Oxford.
CARRIE W. LEACH, Scotland. Taught six years. Mrs. H. K. Braley. Fall River.
IDA A. NOYES, Elmwood. T. seven years. Teaching a Kindergarten. Wilmington, Del.
EMMA W. PECKHAM, Middletown, R. I. 1. T. five years. Newport, R. I. Box 152.

LAURA B. PECKHAM, Middletown, R. I. 1. Taught three terms. Mrs. L. B. Barney, Newport, R. I.
LYDIA A. RYDER, W. Bridgewater. Taught three years. Mrs. H. H. Harlow, W. Bridgewater.
MARTHA R. SMITH,* Assonet. 1. Died, Jan. 27, 1868.
LAURA A. THOMAS, S. Carver. Taught six years. Grammar Schools. Address, S. Carver.
MARY G. WESTGATE, Fairhaven. Taught six years. Mrs. R. H. Whitelaw, 617 N. Second St., St. Louis, Mo.
LUCRETIA F. WYER*, Nantucket. Taught three years. Mrs. S. F. Hatch, N. Marshfield. Died Feb. 6, 1876.

Total of teaching for sixteen, sixty-seven years. Average, four years.

Class 71. February 22, 1868.

JOSIAH G. BASSETT, Bridgewater. Graduated from advanced course. Taught four years. Usher, Bigelow School, Boston.
ALFRED H. CAMPBELL, Litchfield, N. H. Taught five years. Academy. Kingston, N. H.
WILLIAM H. CROCKER, Barnstable. Taught six years. Grammar School. Watertown.
JOSHUA M. DILL, Wellfleet. Graduated from advanced course. Taught four years. Sub-Master, Andrew School. S. Boston.
LORENZO B. GRIGSON, Marston's Mills. Taught four years. Grammar School. W. Somerville.
JOHN N. PIERCE, Edgartown. Not heard from.
ALPHONSO H. POWERS, Hollis, N. H. Taught six years. Grammar School. Address, Hollis, N. H.

·Total of teaching for six, twenty-nine years. Average, five years.

CLARA BARTLEY, Windham, N. H. T. six years. Mrs. C. Whittemore, St George, Me.
EMILY E. BOUTELLE, Leominster. 1. Mrs. H. C. Fuller. Leominster.
CYNTHIA P. BOUTELLE, Leominster. 1. T. three years. Intermediate School. Leominster.
MARIA F. BRAY, Yarmouth Port. T. fiye years. Intermediate School. Yarmouth Port.
ELLEN F. CROCKER, W. Barnstable. Taught six years. Grammar School. Hyannis.
ELLEN M. GIFFORD, Westport. Taught five years. Mrs. L. E. Leland, Newton L. Falls.
HATTIE E. GREENFIELD, Plympton. Taught two terms. North Plympton.
FANNIE HALL, Marshfield. T. six years. Grammar School. Revere.
SARAH M. HAMBLY, Fall River. Taught six years. Primary School. Fall River.
ABBIE M. MAY, Randolph. Taught one year. Mrs. Alonzo Meserve. Charlestown.
CHLOE G. MOORE, Falmouth. T. three terms. Mrs. B. S. Bowerman. W. Falmouth.
HANNAH S. MOORE, Falmouth. Taught six years. Grammar School. Falmouth.
DELIA T. MUNROE, Attleborough. T. five years. Mrs. Henry J. Smith. Central Falls, R. I.
LOELLA R. PARKER, Reading. 3. T. one year. Mrs. A. E. Winship, Somerville.
MARY F. PAULL, Myricksville. 1. Not heard from.
CORNELIA J. F. PIERCE, Fall River. Did not teach.
SUSAN R. REED, Fall River. Taught six years. Grammar School. Fall River.
ELIZA RICHARDS, E. Bridgewater. Taught three years. Teaching in E. Bridgewater.
EMELINE L. ROGERS, Orleans. Taught five years. Grammar School. Malden.
MAGGIE L. SHEA, Newton Centre. T. five years. Mrs. Michael Driscoll. Brookline.
MARY A. A. SHEA, Newton Centre. Taught two years.
LIZZIE S. TENNEY, Antrim, N. H. Taught one year. S. Antrim, N. H.
SUSAN O. THOMAS, Middleborough. 4. T. three years. Mrs. S. L. Goodspeed, Osterville.
LIZZIE O. TISDALE, Leominster. Taught two years. Mrs. O. A. Andrews. E. Milton.
HATTIE E. WINCHESTER, Westport. Taught six years. Westport.

Total of teaching for twenty four, eighty-eight years. Average, four years.

Class 72. September 8, 1868.

ALFRED A. BENNETT, Milford, N. H. 3. Taught three years. Student, Mich. Un., Ann Arbor, Mich.

CLARENCE BOYLSTON, Duxbury. Taught one year. Graduated from Advanced Course.
• Principal, Grammar School. Milton.
JOSHUA A. CROCKER, Provincetown. Taught two years. Trader. Provincetown.
EDGAR J. DUNBAR, Cochesett. Not heard from.
REVERDY HALL, Baltimore, M. D. Did not teach. Physician. 266 South Sharp St. Baltimore, Md.
SUMNER A. IVES, Holyoke. 1. Taught three years. Baptist Clergyman. Alfred, Me.
FRANCIS G. PRATT, E. Middleboro'. Salesman with Lee & Shepard. Boston.
DANIEL D. SMITH, Rutland. Taught five years. Address, Rutland.
JAMES E. T. TONER, Boston.
WILLIAM E. J. VARNEY, Lawrence. T. five years. Grammar School. W. Brookfield.

Total of Teaching for eight, nineteen years. Average, three years.

ANNA L. ADAMS, W. Medway. Taught six years. Primary School. Brockton.
EMMA BAKER, Standish, Me. 1. Taught three years. 47 Tobey St. Providence, R. I.
LEMIRA BENSON, Bridgewater. Taught six years. Mixed School. Bridgewater.
EMILY A. BOSWORTH, Quincy. Taught six years. Primary School. Quincy Point.
LUCY S. BRECK, Bridgewater. Taught five years. High school. Bridgewater.
MATILDA J. BUMP, Lakeville. Taught three years. Mixed School. Lakeville.
MARY E. CAMPBELL,* Bath, Me. 3 Died February 24, 1871.
KATIE H. COOK, So. Boston. Taught three years. Address, So. Boston.
SALLIE B. CRAYTON, Dadeville, Ala. 2. Not heard from.
LUCIE E. CURTIS, Campello. Taught five years. Grammar School. Campello.
JENNIE E. DAVIS, Natick. 1. Not heard from.
MARY E. EATON, Quincy. 2. Not heard from.
MARY E. ELDREDGE, Foxborough. 1. Not heard from.
SOPHIA W. FRENCH, Quincy. 1. T. seven years. Minot School. Walnut St., Dorchester.
ALICE HAMMETT, Newport. R. I. Taught six years. Primary School. Newport, R. I.
LIZZIE HAMMETT, Newport, R. I. Taught six years. Grammar School. Newport, R .I.
ESTHER HAMILTON, Newport, R. I. Taught six years. Grammar School. Newport, R. I.
MARY C. HARDEN, Bridgewater. T. five years. Mrs. Rev. Wm. P. Elsdon, Hyannis.
HELEN HARLOW, S. Middleborough. T. five years. Mixed School. Rock. Middleboro'.
HANNAH HOWES,* E. Dennis. Taught one term. Died September 25, 1872.
MARIA J. KAVANAGH, Newport, R. I. T. six years. Grammar School. Newport, R. I.
SARAH J. KEITH, W. Bridgewater. T. four years. Mrs. R. G. Holmes, Beaufort, S. C.
AFFIE H. MACURDA, S. Boston. 3. Not heard from.
MARY F. PATCH, Lynn. 2. Taught seven years. Principal, Grammar School. Nahant.
ELLEN W. PETERSON, W. Duxbury. Taught four years. Auburndale.
MARTHA M. RING, Milford. T. five years. Mrs. Bateman, 1073 Washington St., Boston
FLORENCE A. SMITH, Boston. 1. T. three years. Address, 13 Warren Ave., Boston.
HANNAH A. SMITH, Rutland. T. five years. Grammar School. Boston Highlands.
HANNAH W. SMITH, Newport. Did not teach. Mrs. D. D. Smith. Westport.
MARTHA E. SMITH,* Rutland 2. Died December 4, 1869.
MARY M. SMITH, Lynn. 2. Not heard from.
ANGENETTE F. TINKHAM, Bridgewater. T. six years. Grammar School. Newton.

Total for teaching for twenty-three, one hundred and twelve years. Average, five years.

Class 73. February, 23, 1869.

CHARLES F. ADAMS, E. Brookfield. Taught four years. Assistant Teacher. State Normal School. Worcester, 31 Laurel St.
GEORGE B. CARR, N. Bridgewater. 1. Did not teach. Lawyer. 210 S. Seventh St. Philadelphia, Pa.
CHARLES HAMMOND, S. Harwich. T. five and one half years. Teaching. Grammar School, Ipswich.
GEORGE T. HUNT, Randolph. Dry Goods and Grocery Dealer. Stoughton.

JAMES H. LEONARD, Scotland. Taught two and one half years. Student. Oberlin College, Ohio.
EDWARD B. MAGLATHLIN, E. Boston. Taught two years. Student in Harvard Theological School. E. Boston.
JAMES POWELL, Haverhill. T. five and one half years. High School. Keene, N. H.
JAMES J. PRENTISS, N. Weymouth. T. five years. Principal Grammar School. Revere.
WILLIAM M. SAWIN, Manchester, N. H. T. one year. Clerk. 146 Oliver St., Boston.

Total of teaching for nine, twenty-six years. Average, three years.

ABBIE J. ADAMS, E. Brookfield. Taught five years. Teacher in Bigelow School. S. Boston.
SARAH P. ALDRICH, E. Bridgewater. 3. Did not teach. Mrs. Rev. Geo. W. Christie, Kittery Pt. Me.
ANNETTA F. ARMES, Campello. Taught four and one half years. Assistant in Comins School. Boston.
ELLEN M. BUTTOMER, W. Bridgewater. Taught five and one half years. Teaching. E. Bridgewater.
MARY E. CHASE, Chilmark. Not heard from.
CARRIE A. COPELAND, W. Bridgewater. T. two years. Mrs. E. T. Ripley, Plymouth.
SUSAN A. CRAPO. Fall River. 1. Taught six years. Teaching in Fall River.
MARY C. CROSBY, E. Orleans. Taught two years. Address, E. Orleans.
CAROLINE A. DUGAN, Brewster. 2. Has not taught.
FANNIE GIFFORD, New Bedford. 1. Not heard from.
ANNIE J. HANDY, Barnstable. T. five and one-half years. Primary School. Fall River.
SARAH A. HATHAWAY, Somerset. 2. Taught six and one-half years. Somerset.
HELEN E. HOOD, New Ipswich, N. H. 2. Not heard from.
GRACE F. HOWES, Bridgewater. Has not taught. Barnstable.
FLORA LEONARD, Bridgewater. Taught two and one-half years. Bridgewater.
LIZZIE E. MORSE, Quincy. 1. Taught seven years. Primary School. Quincy.
CARRIE M. NICHOLS, Berkley. 2. Taught five years. Mrs. A. J. Alden. Providence, R. I.
ABBIE H. PACKARD, W. Bridgewater. 1. Not heard from.
MARY A. PARKER, Bridgewater. 2. Did not teach. Mrs. Barnes, Bridgewater.
ANNIE L. PERRY, Fall River. 1. Not heard from.
LOTTIE F. PRATT, Nantucket. 1. Did not teach. Mrs. L. F. Church, Taunton.
CORINNA E. PURINTON, Somerset 2. Taught six and one-half years. Somerset.
EMMA A. RANDALL, N. Abington. Taught five years. N. Abington.
SYLVIA N. STACKPOLE,* W. Bridgewater. T. two and a half years. Died Nov. 20, 1873.
LIZZIE M. STUBBERT, Deerfield, N. H. 1. Not heard from.
MARY F. TAGGART, Peterboro, N. H. 1. Taught six and one haff years. Hanesville, Md.
ANNIE S. WILLIAMS,* Townsend Centre. 3. Taught two years. Died May 20, 1875.
SARAH C. WINN, Nantucket. Taught five and one-half years. Gaston School. Boston.
BESSIE M. YOUNG, W. Chatham. Taught six and one-half years. Barrington, R. I.

Total of teaching for twenty-two eighty-six years. Average, four years.

Class 74. September 7, 1869.

BENJAMIN S. ANDREW, Danvers. Taught four and one half years. Principal, Grammar School. Watertown.
ORRIN A. ANDREWS, Essex. Taught five years. Prin. Grammar School. E. Milton.
ARTHUR C. BOYDEN, Bridgewater. Taught one year in High School. Graduated at Amherst College, 1876.
GEORGE M. CONANT, Bridgewater. 3. Did not teach. Clerk. Bridgewater.
JAMES E. COTTER, Marlborough. 4. Did not teach, Att'y at Law. 22 Old State House, Boston.
THOMAS F. DESMOND, N. Braintree. 1. Did not teach. Lawyer. Braintree.
WILLIAM F. HAYWARD, Watertown. T. four years. French's Business College. Boston.
FRED MERRILL, S. Randolph. 3. Has not taught. Grocer. Brookville.

150   BRIDGEWATER STATE NORMAL SCHOOL.

FRANKLIN H. PIERCE, Edgartown. 3. Student. Yale College, New Haven, Conn.
WILLIAM A. SANDERSON, Newton Centre. T. one year. Farmer. Newton Centre.
ELI S. SANDERSON, Newton Centre. Taught one year. Graduated from Advanced Course. Manufacturer. Bridgewater.
JAMES C. WOOD, Bridgewater. 2. Boxmaker. Bridgewater.
SOLOMON W. YOUNG, Pittsfield, N. H. 1. Did not teach. Physician. Pittsfield, N. H.
  Total of teaching for thirteen, sixteen years. Average, one and one half years.
LAURA E. BAKER, E. Brewster. 1. Taught six years. Teaching in Brewster.
MARIA S. BANCROFT, Reading, Taught five years. Teaching in Bedford.
CARRIE M. BARROWS, Searsport, Me. Taught five years. Grammar School. Revere.
ELLEN F. BRALEY, Middleborough. Taught four years. Teaching in Dighton.
HARRIET E. BROWN, Randolph. 1. Did not teach. Mrs. Thomas Hall. Campello.
JULIA A. COBB, Marion. Taught three years. Reading.
MARY J. COOK, Brookbury, C. E. 1. Taught one term. Brookbury, P. Q.
JOSEPHINE DODGE, S. Boston. 1. Not heard from.
EMILY J. GALLAGHER, W. Bridgewater. 3. Did not teach.
SARAH A. GOSS, Rye, N. H. 2. Taught five years. Teaching in Rye, N. H.
ANNA R. HALEY, Baltimore, Md. 1. Taught six years. Principal, Colored Academy. Lake City. Forida.
CLARA J. HANDY, W. Barnstable. 2. Not heard from.
ELLA F. HANDY, Barnstable. Taught four years. Teaching in Barnstable.
HELEN M. HILLS. Manchester, N. H. Taught five years. Everett School. Dorchester.
ABBIE M. HINCKLEY, Centreville. Taught five years. Teaching in Osterville.
JULIA B. HODGES, Norton. 3. Taught five years. Teaching in Norton.
HARRIET A. LOTHROP, E. Stoughton. 2. Taught one year. E. Stoughton.
CHARLOTTE McDANIELS, Lowell. 2. Taught five years. Teaching. Newton Centre.
EDITH McLEOD, Middleborough. Taught five years. Teaching in Pierce Academy. Middleborough.
HARRIET H. MORSE, Quincy. Taught five years. Principal, Grammar School. Quincy.
ELLEN R. PAGE, Peterborough, N. H. T. five years. Mrs. A. S. Hodge, E. Templeton.
CHARLOTTE A. PIERCE, Edgartown. Taught two terms. Edgartown.
SARAH A. C. PRAY, New Bedford. Taught five years. Teaching in New Bedford.
EMILY W. STANLEY, Attleboro' Falls. 4. Taught four years. Teaching in Attleboro'.
GEORGIANA TILDEN, N. Marshfield. 1. Taught five years. Teaching. Scituate Harbor.
EMMA F. VEAZIE, Randolph. T. five years. Assistant, Grammar School. Cambridge.
FANNIE H. WALDRON, Rochester. 1. Not heard from.
SARAH M. WOOD, Sandwich. 1. Taught six years. Teaching. Sandwich.
  Total of teaching for twenty-four, ninety-nine years. Average, four years.

CLASS 75.   FEBRUARY 23, 1870.

GEORGE A. ARNOLD, Swansea. 3. Not heard from.
HORACE T. ATWOOD, Middleborough. Taught four and one half years. Principal, Grammar School. Norwood.
FRANK B. DAVIS. Tyngsboro'. T. three years. Principal High School. Longmont, Col.
EDWARD O. DYER, S. Abington. T. one year. Student. Amherst College.
JOHN A. ELLIS, Southbridge. 1. Has not taught. Mechanic. Globe Village.
EDWARD P. FITTS, Medfield. Taught four and one half years. Prin. Grammar School. N. Woburn.
JOSEPH E. FOX, Tuftonboro', N. H. 1. Taught two years. Farmer. Wolfborough, N. H.
DAVID H. GIBBS. Bridgewater. T. four and one half years. Prin. Gram. School. Plymouth.
JOHN B. GIFFORD, Westport. T. two years. Graduated from Advanced Course. Principal, High School. Ayer.
BENJAMIN F. HIGGINS, Eastham. Not heard from.
  Total of teaching for eight, twenty-two years. Average, three years.

IOLINE L. BACON, E. Attleborough. 1. Has not taught. Attleborough.

MR. BOYDEN'S ADMINISTRATION. 151

ELLA F. BAKER, Dennis Port. 1. Has not taught. Dennis Port.
EMMA BARNES, Boston. 2. Not heard from.
ELLA J. BASSETT,* Reading. T. two years. Mrs. E. E. Fox. Died May 21, 1876.
MARY E. BENNETT, Milford, N. H. 1. Did not teach. Mrs. J. F. Gillis. Bedford, N. H
KATIE R. BORDEN, New Bedford. 2. Not heard from.
SARAH A. BURT, Taunton. Taught four years. Teaching. Weir Village, Taunton.
MARY L. B. CAPEN, Stoughton. Taught four and one-half years. Laboratory Assistant, Girls' High School. Boston.
EMILY F. CARPENTER, Brookfield. Taught four and one-half years. Dwight School, Boston.
ANNA B. CARTER, Sturbridge. T. four and one-half years. Sherwin School. Boston.
LUCY H. B. COPELAND, Bridgewater. Taught one year. Mrs. F. C. Davis, Fall River.
ELLA H. COREY, Woonsocket, R. I. 1. Not heard from.
ELVIRA E. CUSHMAN. Middleborough. 3. Has not taught.
ARDELLE J. CUTTER,* Provincetown. 1. Did not teach. Died July 1, 1873.
MARY A. DAVIS, Lake Village, N. H. 1. T. five years. Teaching. Lake Village, N. H.
CELIA L. DEAN, Monroe, Ohio. 2. Not heard from.
ANNIE H. DELANO, Fairhaven. T. four years. Teaching in High School. Fairhaven.
MARY L. DORGAN, W. Bridgewater. 5. T. three years. Teaching in Burlington, Iowa.
MARY A. DYER, S. Braintree. 1. Taught one term. Mrs. G. H. Lakin, S. Braintree.
ANNIE E. FISHER, Yarmouth Port. T. three years. Student in Medical College. Boston.
MARION E. FITTON, N. Easton. 3. Taught four years. Teaching in N. Easton.
LIZZIE J. FRENCH, Randolph. Taught four years. Mrs. E. O. Leach, Randolph.
MARY E. FRENCH. E. Randolph. 1. Taught one year. Copyist. Holbrook.
ELIZABETH D. GIFFORD, Westport. 2. Not heard from.
ELZADA M. GOSS, Rye, N. H. Taught five years. Teaching in Rye, N. H.
EMILY B. HODGES, Attleborough. 1. Has not taught. Attleborough.
L. CARRIE JACKMAN, Medway. 3. Taught four years. Teaching in Medway.
EVANGELINE B. JONES, E. Stoughton. Taught three years. W. Scituate.
MARY J. KEITH, Bridgewater. 1. Mrs. A. W. Alden, Norwood.
HARRIETTE L. KING, Bridgewater. 3. T. two years. Mrs. W. K. Goward, N. Easton.
VIOLA F. LITTLEFIELD, Stoughton. T. four and one half years. Teaching. Newton.
SUSAN E. LONGLEY, Fall River. 1. Not heard from.
FANNIE E. LOTHROP, W. Bridgewater. 1. Not heard from.
MARY L. MILLS, N. Bridgewater. 3. T. three years. Mrs. Charles S. French, N. Easton.
EMMA C. NICHOLS, Berkley. 3. T. four years. Teaching Kindergarten. Milwaukee, Wis.
MATTIE E. NYE, Fairhaven. 1. Mrs. J. Stoddard. Petrolia City, Penn.
JANETTE SNELL, E. Randolph. 2. T. two years. Mrs. J. Southworth. Holbrook.
LUCY A. S. SNOW, E. Orleans. 2. Taught three years. E. Orleans.
JENNIE L. WHITE, Holbrook. 1. Taught two years. Holbrook.
ANN M. WILDE, Holbrook. 2. T. five and one-half years. High School. Charlestown.
HELEN A. WILLIAMS, S. Braintree. T. four and one-half years. Teaching. S. Braintree.
   Total of teaching for thirty-four, eighty-seven years. Average, two and one-half years.

CLASS 76. SEPTEMBER 6, 1870.

LOUIS H. DECKER, Newton Centre. Taught three years.
GEORGE M. POWERS, Leominster. Not heard from.
JAMES ROCHE, Bridgewater. 2. Has not taught.
HENRY L. SAWYER, Hopkinton. Taught four years. Usher. Dwight School, Boston.
HENRY J. SEELYE, Carbondale, Ill. 1. Not heard from.
   Total of teaching for three, seven years. Average, two and one-half years.
HANNAH E. ALDEN, Scotland. T. two years. Mrs. Dr. Ira B. Cushing, Brookline.
SYLVIA B. ALMY, New Bedford. T. one year. Mrs. H. M. Knowlton, New Bedford.
MARY E. BARKER, S. Hanson. Taught four years. Teaching in Fall River.
ELIZA A. BARROWS,* Freetown. Taught one year. Died Nov. 7, 1874.

SARAH A. BARROWS, Freetown. Taught two years. Freetown.
LUCINA A. BARTLETT, Newport, N. H. 1. T. three years. Teaching in Newport, N. H.
MERCIE K. BARTLETT, New Bedford. 1. Taught four years. Teaching, New Bedford.
JOSEPHINE BARTLEY, Windham, N. H. Taught three years. Teaching in S. Adams.
ABBY M. BUFFINTON,* Fall River. Taught one term. Died Sept. 9, 1874.
LIZZIE C. CAPEN, Stoughton. T. four years. Teaching. Sargent School, Cambridgeport.
ELIZABETH R. CASE, Swansea. Did not teach. Mrs. F. S. Stevens. Swansea.
MARY D. CHAMBERLAIN, Sturbridge. Taught four years. Teaching in Lewis School. Boston.
MARY F. CLARKE, Royalston. Taught four years. Teaching in North Adams.
KATHARINE W. CUSHING, Cambridge. Graduated from Advanced Course. Assistant in High School. Hingham.
SARAH B. CUSHMAN, New Bedford. 1. Not heard from.
FLORA J. DYER, S. Braintree. 1. Not heard from.
HARRIET R. GARDNER, W. Scituate. 1. Taught four years. Teaching in Hingham.
E. EMMA GROVER, Foxborough. Taught four years. Teaching in Clarke Institution. Northampton.
GERTRUDE E. HALE, Peterborough, N. H. Graduated from Advanced Course. Master's Assistant, Grammar School. Cambridgeport.
MARY E. HAYDEN, Bridgewater. 3. Did not teach. Mrs. Seth Crocker. E. Stoughton.
FANNIE W. HEMPHILL, Northfield. Taught one year. Mrs. Joseph Talbot. Georgetown, Texas.
ALMIRA M. HOLMES, Yarmouth Port. Taught three years. Teaching in Norton.
MATTIE HOWE, Holden. Taught three years. Teaching in S. Adams.
JULIA P. HUMPHREY, Sutherland Falls, Vt. Taught four years. Teaching. Sutherland Falls, Vermont.
MARIETTA K. JOHNSON, E. Bridgewater. Taught four years. Mrs. Frank Kingman, Wareham.
LORA L. LINCOLN, N. Easton. Taught two years.
HARRIET McCONNELL, Brandon, Vt. 2. T. four years. Teaching in Sutter Creek, Cal.
CARRIE E. MILLER, Swansea. 1. Taught one term. Mrs. ——— Weeden, Swansea.
LUCY D. MORTON, Randolph. 2. Taught four years. Teaching in S. Walpole.
IDA A. OMEY. Acushnet. Taught four years. Teaching in Acushnet.
GEORGIE PALMER, Stoneham. T. four years. Head Ass't, Bennett School. Brighton.
CHARLOTTE L. PERKINS, Bridgewater. 3. Did not teach.
LAURA H. PICKENS, Middleborough. 4. Not heard from.
CLARA C. PRINCE, Chelsea. Graduated from Advanced Course. Taught two years. Teaching in Andrew School, S. Boston.
ELOISE A. SEARS, So. Yarmouth. Taught two years. Teaching in Wesleyan Academy, Wilbraham.
IDA M. SEARS, E. Dennis. Taught four years. Teaching in Fall River.
MIRANDA STEELE, Gloucester. T. three years. Ass't, High School. Lewiston, Me.
MARY E. STONE. Lowell. 3. Taught four years. Ass't., Grammar School. Lowell.
FANNY M. TALBOT, Georgetown, Texas. T. three years. Teaching in S. Chelmsford.
ABBY M. VINAL, W. Scituate. Taught five years. Mrs. Wm. H. Howe, S. Weymouth.
HELEN F. WARD, Carver. Taught four years. Teaching in Plymouth.
EMILY B. WATSON, Narragansett, R. I. 1. Not heard from.
MARY E. WEFER, E. Dennis. 2. Not heard from.
ISABEL G. WESTON, Duxbury. Taught three years. Teaching in Duxbury.
ELLA WOOD, Swansea. 1. Has not taught.

CLASS 77. FEBRUARY 21, 1871.

JOHN BRODRICK, Chelsea. 1. Not heard from.
GEORGE G. EDWARDS, N. Middleboro'. Graduated from Advanced Course, July, 1875.

LEVI W. FOGG, N. Hampton, N. H. Taught three and one half years. Principal Grammar School. Waltham.
ELI E. FOX, Tyngsborough, N. H. Taught three and one half years. Prin. High School. Weston.
WALTER S. GOODNOUGH, S. Boston. Taught three years. State Normal School, Salem; and Normal and High School, Columbus, Ohio.
CHARLES F. KENDALL, Tyngsborough. Taught three and one-half years. High School. Scituate.
EDGAR K. MORRISON, Hancock, N. H. Taught three years. Teaching in Alstead Centre, N. H.
EGBERT N. MUNROE, Cornwallis, N. S. 4. Not heard from.
WILLARD B. NORTHORP, Stoughton. T. three and one-half years. Principal, Public Schools. Hancock, Mich.
FRED. H. RIPLEY, W. Bridgewater. Taught three and one-half years. Grammar School. Natick.
WILLIAM J. SANBORN, Rockport. 2. Never taught.
HENRY S. SPAULDING, Peterboro', N. H. 3. Has not taught. Editor. Napa City, Cal.

Total of teaching for ten, twenty-four years. Average, two and one-half years.

CLARA F. ALLEN, Rockland, Me. Taught three and one-half years. Assistant, Normal School. Farmington, Me.
MARIA S. BRIGGS, N. Dighton. 3. Taught four years. Teaching. N. Dighton.
GEORGIE BROWN, Swansea. 1. Taught one and one-half years.
JULIA BROWN, Swansea. 1. Taught three years. Swansea.
HARRIETTE A. BURRAGE, S. Royalston. 1. Taught one year. Student in Normal Art School. Boston.
REBECCA A. BUSH, Provincetown. T. one year. Mrs. C. E. Wheeler. Rockland.
EVELINA J. CHAMBERLAIN, N. Bridgewater. Taught one term. Died Dec. 27, 1873.
CARRIE A. DAVIS, Westport Point. Taught one term. Westport.
MARY A. DEWYER, Cochesett. Taught three years. Teaching. W. Bridgewater.
SUSAN G. DRAPER, S. Natick. Taught three and a half-years. S. Natick.
SARAH C. FALES, Rockland, Me. Taught three and one half years. Assistant, Dwight School. Boston.
ELIZABETH S. FREE, Plymouth. Taught two years. Mrs. E. S. McHenry, Plymouth.
EMMA J. HALE, S. Royalston. Taught one year. Mrs. F. O. Ellis, S. Boston.
EDITH LEONARD, Scotland. Graduated from Advanced Course. Taught two years. Assistant in Normal School. Bridgewater.
ELVIRA M. LINCOLN, N. Bridgewater. 2. Taught four years. Mrs. Geo. W. Barnefield, Pawtucket, R, I.
MAUDE McWILLIAMS, Boston. Taught two and one-half years. Master's Assistant, Grammar School. Natick.
ABBIE E. MOREY, N. Bridgewater. T. three and one half years. Teaching in Brockton.
HELEN L. MORRIS, Abington. 1. Taught one year. Mrs. C. W. Reed, Abington.
RHODA F. RICE, W. Bridgewater. 1. Has not taught. Mrs. Rhoda Wilbur, W. Bridgewater.
Mrs. ELIZA M. ROBINSON, Petersham. Taught three and a half years. Prin. Grammar School. Chelmsford.
BETSEY W. SHERMAN, Plympton. Taught two and one-half years. Plympton.
MARY E. STOWELL, Petersham. Taught three years. Grammar School. Erving.
CLARA O. WEBB, Northfield. Taught two terms. Northfield.
EDITH WHEELER, W. Bridgewater. T. three and one-half years. Teaching. Dighton.
EMMA J. WINSLOW,* Abington. 1. Did not teach. Died Feb., 1874.
EMMA WRIGHT, E. Abington. 3. Has not taught. Rockland.
CHARLOTTE B. YOUNG, Rockland, Me. Taught two and one-half years. Mrs. W. S. Goodnough, Columbus, O.

Total of teaching for twenty-five, fifty-six years. Average, two years.

Class 78. September 12, 1871.

JOHN J. BURKE, E. Weymouth. Has taught two terms. N. Weymouth.
GEORGE T. KEECH, Lower Merion, Pa. T. two years. Teaching in Lower Merion, Pa.
HERBERT O. McCRILLIS, Middleboro'. T. one year. Clerk, Tack manuf'y. Taunton.
CLARENCE E. WHEELER, E. Abington. 3. T. three years. Grammar School. Rockland.
Total of teaching for four, seven years. Average, two years.
KATIE BASSETT, Bridgewater. Graduated from Advanced Course July, 1875.
ABBIE S. BROWN, Westminster. Taught two years. Westminster.
KATIE P. BROWN,* Westminster. 2. Died May 11, 1874.
CLARA M. CHASE, Hanover. Taught two years. Mrs. Freeman. Taunton.
ANN CHURCH,* S. Scituate. 2. Taught one year. Died June, 1876.
ELLEN L. CUSHMAN,* Fairhaven. 2. Taught one term. Died May, 1876.
EMMA M. CUTTER, Jaffrey, N. H. Graduated from Advanced Course. Taught two years. Assistant in Normal School. Nashville, Tenn.
LUCY E. DAVIS, W. Newton. T. three and one-half years. Private Kindergarten. Boston.
CLARA P. DUNBAR, N. Bridgewater. 4. Has not taught. Brockton.
SARAH E. DUNHAM. Fairhaven. 4. T. three and one-half years. Teaching. Fairhaven.
MARY A. DUPEE, Westminster. 2. Taught four years. Teaching in Princeton.
FLORENCE EDDY, Middleborough. 3. T. two years. Pratt Free School. N. Middleboro'.
MARY E. FAIRCHILD, Fairhaven. 1. Taught three years. Primary School. Fairhaven.
ANNIE J. FAIRCHILD, Fairhaven. Graduated from Advanced Course. Taught one year. High School. Fairhaven.
MELISSA C. GAY, Medway. Taught three years. Grammar School. Fall River.
MARY E. HAMMONS, Haverhill. Taught three years. Teaching in Middletown, R. I.
ASENATH C. HOLMES, Kingston. 2. Mrs. Wm. L. Jones, Buffalo, N. Y.
ELLA F. KEYES. Pelham, N. H. Taught three years. Teaching in Fall River.
MARY L. LINCOLN, Hingham. T. three years. Prin. Grammar School. W. Bridgewater.
AGNES I. LUZARDER, E. Bridgewater. T. three years. Teaching in Elmwood.
OPHELIA McCONNELL, Brandon, Vt. 1. T. two years. Teaching. Sutter Creek, Cal.
EMILY W. NEWCOMB, Kingston. 2. Has not taught. Westborough.
GRACE M. PHELPS, Jaffrey, N. H. Taught three years. Teaching. Billerica.
CHARLOTTE K. RICHARDS, W. Bridgewater. 1. T. four and one half years. Teaching N. Raynham.
ELIZABETH SAVILLE, Quincy. 1. Has not taught. Quincy.
MARTHA H. SEARS, W. Dennis. Not heard from.
MARIA L. SOUTHWICK, Millville. Taught three years. Teaching. Fall River.
CAROLINE L. SPARROW, Middleboro'. 3. T. three years. Mrs. H. W. Aldrich. N. Middleborough.
REBECCA L. H. TABER, Fairhaven. 1. Has not taught.
HANNAH H. TAFT, E. Bridgewater. Taught three years. Teaching. Raynham.
ELLEN A. WALKER, Bridgewater. Taught two years. Private School. Harrisburg, Penn.
SOPHIA A. WALKER, Bridgewater. 1. Teaching Drawing in Normal School. Trenton, N. J.
JOSEPHINE WHITE, Bridgewater. Taught two years. Bridgewater.
Total of teaching for twenty-two, sixty-three years. Average, three years.

Class 79. February 18, 1872.

FREEMAN A. ARNOLD, S. Braintree. 1. Has taught four years. Teaching. Grammar School. S. Braintree.
WILLIAM BASSETT, Bridgewater. 4. Has not taught. Farmer.
MAURICE CONDON, Bridgewater. Did not teach.
GEORGE W. DELAND, Brookfield, N. H. 1. T. three years. Prin. High School. Alton, N. H.
GEORGE EVANS, Freetown. Taught two terms. Freetown.
ARTHUR J. FRENCH, Boston. 3. Not heard from.
HAMILTON L. GIBBS, Bridgewater. 1. Did not teach.

FRANK M. KING, Bridgewater. T. one year. Teaching. Gram. School. Bridgewater.
FREDERICK E. MARSHALL, Tyngsboro'. 1. Has not taught. Marketman. Dover, N. H.
GEORGE F. MUNSEY, Barnstead. 1. Not heard from.
WALDO WASHBURN, Kingston. Taught one term. Salesman. Kingston.
  Total of teaching for nine, nine years. Average, one year.
KATIE C. ALLEN, New Bedford. T. two years. Teaching in Clarke Institute, Northampton.
MARY C. ALLEN Randolph. 1. Not heard from.
CORA H. ALGER, W. Bridgewater. Taught two years. Teaching. Carver.
LUCY S. ATWOOD, Chatham. T. two and one half years. Grammar School. Chatham.
GERTRUDE E. BALL, Warwick. 2. Has taught three years. Teaching. Holyoke.
MARTHA A. BRALEY, Middleborough. Taught one term. Middleborough.
VIRGINIA G. BRAMAN, Bridgewater. Taught two years. Teaching. Brockton.
ELIZABETH A. CHACE, Freetown. Not heard from.
ADA M. CRAPO, Bridgewater. 3. Mrs. A. M. Howland. Bridgewater.
ISABELLA G. DRISCOLL, Randolph. T. two and one half years. Teaching. Randolph.
LYDIA E. ELDRIDGE, S. Chatham. 1. Has not taught.
LOUISE L. FLAGG, W. Bridgewater. 3. Has not taught. Mrs. H. L. Kingman, Cochesett.
SARAH L. HARRIS, Wilmington. Taught two and one-half years. Teaching. E. Dedham.
ELLA F. IVERS, New Bedford. Has not taught. New Bedford.
ELLA F. JAMES, Deerfield, N. H. T. two years. Teaching. Grammar School. Fall River.
LOIS E. JENKINS, S. Braintree. 3. Not heard from.
EUDORA LAWRENCE, Freetown. 1. Taught three years. Teaching. Dartmouth.
EUDORA MOREY, Malden. Taught two and one-half years. Teaching, High School. Malden.
EMILY H. PHINNEY, Barnstable. Taught two and one-half years. Assistant, Webster Grammar School. Cambridgeport.
EMILY J. REED, Pembroke. 1. Not heard from.
EMILY C. ROBINSON, Bridgewater. 3. Mrs. Geo. Peterson, Bridgewater.
JULIA H. J. SOMES, Revere. 1. Taught two years. Revere.
FRANCES M. TALBOTT, Bridgewater. Taught two years. Teaching. Westford.
ANNIE H. TAYLOR, New Bedford. Mrs. J. G. Bassett, Bridgewater.
ANNA R. THATCHER, Wareham. 2. Has not taught.
ABBIE G. WALLACE, Epsom, N. H. Taught two and one-half years. Ass't, Grammar School, Chicago. 48 Ruble St.
ANNIE M. WILDE, Randolph. 3. Taught three years. Teaching in Randolph.
  Total of teaching for twenty-three, thirty-six years. Average, two years.

Class 80. September 3, 1872.

DANIEL J. BAKIE, Kingston, N. H. T. two years. Principal, Academy. Kingston, N. H.
LAWRENCE M. GOULD, S. Boston. 1. Not heard from.
HERBERT L. MORSE, Sherborn. T. two years. Prin. Grammar School. Shirley Village.
L. ELIOT PACKARD, N. Bridgewater. Has taught.
GEORGE W. PRATT, E. Middleboro'. Has not taught. Member of Harvard College.
WARREN C. TYRRELL, Fisherville, N. H. 1. Not heard from.
GEORGE E. WALES, N. Abington. Taught two years.
  Total of teaching for five, six years.
AMY F. ALLEN, Scituate. 2. T. one year. Mrs. Charles W. Frye. Grand Rapids, Mich.
NELLIE W. ALLEN, Scituate. T. two years. Teaching, Andrew Grammar School. Boston.
MARTHA F. AMES, Bridgewater. Taught two years. Teaching. Bridgewater.
MARY E. AUSTIN, New Bedford. T. two years. Teaching. High School, New Bedford.
SERENA BAILEY, Haverhill. Taught one year. Teaching. S. Attleborough.
CATHARINE W. BOWEN, Rehoboth. 2. T. one and one-half years. Mrs. J. F. Earle, Rehoboth.
ELLA L. BUSH, Provincetown. Taught two years. Teaching. Raynham.

156   BRIDGEWATER STATE NORMAL SCHOOL.

MARY J. COLLINGWOOD, Plymouth. Taught two years. Teaching. Grammar School. Brookline.
ANNIE E. DAMON, W. Scituate. Took one year of advanced course. Mrs. Geo. P. Rich.
ALICE C. DICKERMAN, Randolph. 2. Taught two years. Randolph.
ELIZA L. DOULL, New Bedford. T. one and one half years. Teaching. Westport.
JULIA M. DREW, Bridgewater. Taught one year.
EVA M. ELLIOTT, Randolph. 2. Teaching.
LUCY V. EVANS, Tiverton, R. I. Married.
ESTHER HALL, Quincy. 3. T. two and one half years. Primary School. Quincy.
LIZZIE L. HATCH, Sandwich. 2. Not heard from.
MYRA C. HATHAWAY, Assonet. 1. Not heard from.
MARY A. HIGGINBOTTOM, N. Easton. T. two years. Intermediate School. N. Easton.
SARAH H. HINCHEY, Somerset. 3. Not heard from.
EMELINE F. JACOBS, W. Scituate. 3. Not heard from.
ALICE L. LANMAN, Plymouth. T. two years. Teaching. Grammar School. Westboro'.
MINNIE F. LEWIS, E. Falmouth. Teaching.
SARAH D. LYON, E. Bridgewater. 4. Has not taught.
ADDIE S. MITCHELL, Provincetown. T. one year. Teaching. High School. Provincetown.
ANNA L. NOYES, Abington. Taught two years. E. Weymouth.
NELLIE E. PAIGE, Taunton. 2. Not heard from.
ABBIE M. PARKER, Reading. 2. Has not taught
MARY B. PICKENS, Middleboro'. 2. Not heard from.
LOTTIE E. PHELPS,* E. Abington. 2. Died in 1873.
ELLA F. REGAN, Attleboro'. Taught one year. Teaching. Attleboro'.
MARY B. RICHARDSON, E. Medway. Taught two years. Teaching.
LUCRETIA N. SMITH, New Bedford. T. two years. Grammar School. New Bedford.
MERCENA SMITH, W. Chatham. 1. Has not taught. Seamstress. W. Chatham.
S. LOUISA STOWELL, Petersham. 1. Taught one year. Address, Worcester.
JERUSHA B. THOMAS, Plymouth. Has taken three terms on the Advanced Course.
M. A. THOMPSON, Barrington, N. H. 3. Not heard from.
ABBIE M. WISWALL, Newton Centre. Taken one year of Advanced Course. Teaching.
Total of teaching for twenty-nine, thirty-one years.

Class 81. February 18 1873.

CHARDES F. COLE, Wellfleet. Taught one year. Teaching.
SETH S. CROCKER. S. Yarmouth. 2. Taught two and one-half years. Grammar School. Quincy.
BRADFORD W. DRAKE, Stoughton. Taught one and one-half years. Teaching. Grammar School. Mendon.
JUNIUS B. GOULD, S. Boston. 1. Not teaching.
HENRY HARLOW, Bridgewater. 1. Not teaching.
YAHBAH, Bassein, Birmah. 2. Not heard from.

EUDORA M. ALLEN, Berkley. Taught one and one-half years. Teaching. Raynham.
IDA E. ANDREWS, Brockton. 4. Not teaching.
ELLEN W. BASSETT, Bridgewater. 2. Has not taught.
JULIA BURT, Berkley. Teaching. Berkley.
LUCY C. CARRUTH, Petersham. Teaching.
FANNIE A. COMSTOCK, Milford. Assistant, State Normal School. Castine, Me.
CLARA J. CONNELL, Fall River. 2. Not heard from.
ALETTA F. DEAN, Mansfield. Teaching.
MARY C. FISHER, Walpole, N. H. 3. Teaching.
PERSIS S. FOSTER, W. Brewster. 1 Not heard from.
LUCY E. GASSETT, Bridgewater. Teaching.
ALICE GRAY, Stoughton. Assistant, Webster Grammar School. Cambridgeport.
MARY A. GREGORY, Sandwich. 3. Not heard from.

LUCY B. HASKELL, Westminster. 1. Not heard from.
LILLIE A. HICKS, E. Bridgewater. Assistant, High School. E. Bridgewater.
ELIZABETH M. HOSMER, Camden, Me. 1. Not heard from.
MARY M. M. LEONARD, Bridgewater. Taught one year. Teaching. Bridgewater.
LIVA A. LITTLE, Littleton, N. H. 1. Not heard from.
EMMA F. MANSON, Scituate. Teaching.
ABBIE L. MARBLE, Somerset. Taught one year.
MARY E. PECKHAM, Petersham. Teaching.
ELLA J. REED, Freetown. 1. Has taught one term. Bryantville.
HARRIET P. RICH, Wellfleet. 1. Not heard from.
MARY F. THOMPSON, S. Abington. 2. Teaching.
EMMA J. VOSE, Boston. 2. Not heard from.
MARY A. WADSWORTH, Bridgewater. Teaching. Brockton.
MARY WALTON, Livermore, Me. 3. Teaching.
ABBIE J. WHEELER, Fitchburg. Taught one year. Mrs. A. J. Adams. Dublin, N. H.
SOPHIA A. WILBUR, Plympton. Teaching. Taunton.
HELEN W. WINSLOW, Freetown. 2. Has taught one year.

Class 82. September 2, 1873.

ZEMIRA BAKER, W. Dennis. Teaching.
GEORGE W. CLAPP, Quincy. 1.
EUGENE H. DIBBLE, Camden, S. C. 2. In business.
NELSON FREEMAN, Milton, N. S. Has taught one year.
HORATIO D. NEWTON, Chatham. Teaching. High School. Westport.
LOUIS A. PRATT, N. Abington. Teaching. Grammar School. Abington.
CHARLES L. PRINCE, Chelsea. In business.
GEORGE O. SMITH, Randolph. Teaching.
ARTHUR C. WADSWORTH, Bridgewater. Teaching. Grammar School. Woburn.
CHARLES E. WALDRON, E. Taunton. 1. Not heard from.
HENRY R. WHIDDEN, Concord, N. H. Student in Advanced Course.
CLARA B. ALDEN, Fairhaven. 3. Teaching.
MARY E. ANDERSON, Ackworth, N. H. Teaching.
ELVA W. ANDREW, Danvers. 2. Teaching.
ELVIRA F. ATKINSON, Rochester. Teaching. N. Easton.
CARRIE J. BARBER, E. Windsor, Ct. 1. Not heard from.
ANNA F. BASS, Boston. 3. Teaching.
CARRIE C. M. BENEDICT, Wilton, N. H. 1. Not heard from.
ANNA S. BENSON, Bridgewater. Teaching.
CAROLINE E. BROWN, New Bedford. Teaching.
AUGUSTA BUNKER, Nantucket. Taking the Advanced Course.
EMELINE L. CARY, Medway. 2. Not heard from.
CARRIE D. CUSHMAN, Acushnet. 1.
CLARA E. DELANO, New Bedford.
GEORGIE M. DIKE, Stoneham. Teaching.
FLORA L. ELLIS, Weston. 1.
CLARA A. EMERTON, Moscow, Me. Graduates June, 1876.
EMMA L. FARRINGTON, Everett. Teaching.
MATILDA O. GAMANS, E. Falmouth. Teaching.
ALINE E. GARDNER, Boston. Teaching.
CINDA M. GARDNER, W. Scituate. 1. Teaching.
SARAH C. GARDNER, W. Scituate. 2. Teaching.
HATTIE E. GOVE, Washington, D C. Teaching. Newton.
MELVINIA J. HAMMOND, Lewiston, Me.
AMELIA HEARSEY, Charlestown. Graduates June, 1876.
MARY L. HOLMES, S. Plymouth. 3. Teaching.
ELIZA C. HOWLAND,* S. Fairhaven. 3. Died May 24, 1876.

CAROLINE E. MORSE, Quincy. 2. Teaching.
MARY E. REED,* Middleboro'. Died March 12, 1876.
CAROLINE E. SQUIRES, Lewiston, Me. 1. Teaching.
LYDIA H. TAPPAN, Fairhaven. 3.
SUSAN A. WALKER, Grantville. Teaching.
ANNA D. WICKES, New Bedford. Taught one year.
EDITH E. WILLIAMS, No. Easton. 3. Teaching.

Class 83. February 24, 1874.

WALTER KEYES, E. Princeton. 2. Not heard from.
HORACE PACKARD, W. Bridgewater. Teaching. Brockton.
WARREN A. RODMAN, Wellfleet. Teaching. S. Hanson.
ROGER SHERMAN, Middletown, R. I. 1. Not heard from.
EDWARD P. SHUTE, Windham Depot, N. H. Teaching. Groton.
CALEB SLADE, Acushnet. 3. Teaching.
JULIUS H. TUTTLE, W. Acton. Teaching. Grammar School. Freetown,
ELLA F. BALL, Hollis, N. H. In the School.
ANNIE M. BARNEY, N. Swansea. 1. Not heard from.
LILLIAN BRYANT, E. Bridgewater. Teaching. Kindergarten.
GEORGIANNA BULLENE, Hingham. 3. Married.
EDITH S. COPELAND, W. Bridgewater. In the advanced Course.
ELIZABETH H. COLTING, Meredith, N. H. Graduates June, 1876.
JULIA F. CUTLER, Pelham, N. H. Teaching. E. Dennis.
CYNTHIA B. DRAPER, E. Brookfield. 3. Teaching.
CARRIE E. ELLIS, Vineland, N. J. 1. Teaching.
FLORA B. GOODWIN, Mowray, N. H. 2. Mrs. Josiah P. Higgins. Norway, Maine.
HATTIE D. HALL, Yarmouth. Teaching.
ESTHER T. HAMBLIN, W. Falmouth. Graduates June, 1876.
MYRA C. HARDING, S. Chatham. 2. Not heard from.
EMILY J. HERRICK, Stoughton. Teaching.
MARY E. HEWETT, Auburn. 2.
ANNIE D. JOHNSON, Worcester. 1.
MARY H. KELLEY, Nantucket.
ELLEN M. LOVERING, Medfield. Teaching.
CLARA I. METCALF, Norfolk. Graduates June, 1876.
CLARA L. OYLER, Black Hawk, Col. Graduates June, 1876.
EMMA J. PURDY, Stoughton. Teaching.
IDA H. SANBORN, Quincy. 2.
ABBIE C. THAYER, Weymouth. 1.
ANNA WHEELER, W. Bridgewater. 3. Teaching.
LUCY M. WILBER, Milford. Teaching.

CLASSES IN THE SCHOOL JUNE, 1876.

Class 84. September 8, 1874.

HENRY D. ALDEN, Bridgewater.
GEORGE BENEDICT. Jr., Dedham.
FRED W. CRAIG, Farmington, Me.
JAMES W. DECKER, Newton Center.
WALTER R. HUSSEY, Nantucket.
WILLARD E. JONES, Rockville.
TILSON A. MEAD, Hingham.
CALVIN F. STANLEY, Kingfield, Me.
CHARLES O. TURNER, Wiscasset, Me.
FRANK M. WEIS, Boston.

MARIA S. BANCROFT, Peabody.
CORA A. BARKER, Mount Auburn. 1.
MARY E. BARNES, Hardwick.
EUNICE P. BARRETT, Chelsea.
CORA I. BATES, Braintree.
ALICE E. BODFISH, West Barnstable.
MABEL BRYANT, East Bridgewater.
MARY A. BURNHAM, Andover. 2.
ANNIE B. CARROLL, Dedham.
JENNIE C. CARROLL, Dedham.

LILLIE M. CHAPIN, Lawrence.
HANNAH M. COSTIGAN, Fall River.
MARY L. CUSHING, Cambridge.
CORA G. DAGGETT, Somerville.
SARAH R. DAMON, North Scituate.
LIZZIE A. DAVIDSON, Stowe.
CARRIE B. DAVIS, East Falmouth.
MARTHA DONAGHY, New Bedford.
JENNIE S. EDSON, East Bridgewater.
HATTIE A. FRENCH, Peterboro', N. H.
KATHERINE GAFFREY, W. Bridgewa'r.
JULIA L. HARDING, Truro.
MARY B. HATHAWAY, Fall River.
JESSIE K. HILL, Norwood.
ELSIE M. KELLEY, E. Dennis.
JENNIE E. KENDALL, Lancaster.
ETTA KILBRETH, Livermore Falls, Me.
ISABELLE C. KINGMAN, Stoneham.

ELLEN G. McDONNELL, Quincy.
C. ADELAIDE MASON, Medfield.
EDITH PAINE, E. Bridgewater.
ESTELLE REDINGTON, Perry, Me.
HATTIE B. RICE, Newton, Lower Falls.
ELNORA F. SAWTELLE, Nantucket.
CAROLINE M. SAYER, New Bedford.
FANNIE H. SEARS, E. Dennis.
OLIVE M. SIMMONS, Kingston.
CORA E. STURTEVANT, W. Bridgewater.
SUSAN TRUE, Salisbury.
CLARA S. VINCENT, New Bedford.
SALOME A. WAITE, Stamford, Conn.
EMMA F. WHEELOCK, Norwood.
LUCINDA W. WHORF, Provincetown.
MARY B. A. WIGHT, Medfield.
MARY F. WOODBRIDGE, Andover.

Class 85. February 23, 1875.

HENRY L. ARMES, Woodstock, Conn.
HENRY M. COLE, Bridgewater.
GEORGE A. CONANT, Littleton.
MAYNARD B. COPELAND, Norton.
LAWRENCE COPELAND, Norton.
HAMMOND T. FLETCHER, Littleton.
ARTEMAS H. HOBART, Bridgewater.
JOHN C. LYETH, Martinsburg, W. Va.
CHARLES W. ROBINSON, E. Sandwich.
HENRY B. WORTH, Nantucket.
MARY C. ALLEN. New Bedford.
ELIZABETH C. BAKER, Yarmouth Port.
MIRRIE S. BARBER, Brockton.
IRENE C. CHIPMAN, Rehoboth.
LIZZIE T. CLARKE, Holbrook.
MYRA E. CLARKE, Holbrook.
ANNIE L. CLEARE, Bridgewater.
HATTIE A. CORTHELL. So. Abington.
SUSAN E. CRANE, Hanover.
FLORENCE L. CROCKER, Bridgewater.
HELEN A. DAVIS, Fall River.
JOSEPHINE C. FLAGG, Dover, N. H.

JANE M. HART, N. Dartmouth.
GERTRUDE H. HATCHMAN, Boston.
AMELIA A. KEITH, Easton.
MARY K. LEONARD, W. Bridgewater.
EMMA V. LEVI, New Bedford.
ELIZABETH E. MACY, Nantucket.
ADDIE I. MEARS, Woburn.
CLARA PERKINS, Bridgewater.
ELLEN O. B. PERRY, E. Bridgewater.
ALICE C. PHINNEY, Barnstable.
MARY L. RIDER, N. Dartmouth.
ELIZABETH A. SAVAGE, Bridgewater.
EMMA J. SHARPE, S. Abington.
ALICE L. SMITH, S. Weare, N. H.
CAROLINE E. SOUTHWICK, Grantville.
CLARA B. SPRINGER, New Bedford.
LIZZIE THOMAS, Nantucket.
MARY E. THOMPSON, Fall River.
SALLIE C. WASHBURN, Bridgewater.
LOTTIE H. WEEKS, S. Royalston.
SARA E. WILBUR, Bridgewater.

Class 86. September 7, 1875.

WILLIAM H. ALDEN, Bridgewater.
MARCELLUS D. BARNES, Lee, Me.
CHAS. N. BENTLEY, Upper Stewiacke, N. S.
WILLIAM H. BURNES, Lowell.
HERBERT I. CONANT, Bridgewater.
FRANCIS A. GRAY, Danversport.
OSCAR L. GURNEY, S. Abington.
ALBERT D. HANDY, South Boston.
SHUJE ISAWA, Tokei, Japan.

MELVIN W. JEFTS, Ashby.
FRANK F. MURDOCK, Charlestown.
WILLIAM F. NICHOLS, Reading.
WEBSTER E. POTTER, Waltham.
CHARLES H. SEARS, W. Brewster.
BENJAMIN SMITH, Reading.
WALDO H. STONE, Brockton.
GEORGE SYMONDS, Wolfboro', N. H.
MOUNG TWAY, Bassein, Burmah.
MABELLE S. ALMY, Somerville.

160   BRIDGEWATER STATE NORMAL SCHOOL.

HELEN K. ANDREWS, Bridgewater.
SARAH J. AUSTIN, New Bedford.
MARY E. BALCOM, Freetown.
CORNELIA BANCROFT, Reading.
IDA M. BLAIKIE, Somerville.
CARRIE P. BURSLEY, W. Barnstable.
LUCY W. CAIN, Hingham.
L. ROBERTA CAPEN, Stoughton.
IDA M. CLEMENT, Great Falls, N. H.
MARY CROWE, Hingham.
ADAH M. DANIELS, Charlestown.
LAURA E. FELT, Sharon.
ADDIE J. GOODHUE, Hyde Park.
OLIVE A. GOSS, Rye, N. H.
ANNIE C. HART, New Bedford.
SARAH E. HOLBROOK, Stoughton.
CARRIE E. HOWES, N. Dennis.
ANNA V. HUNT, Farmington, Me.
ANNIE L. KENDALL, Brockton.
HELEN M. KIMBALL, New Portland, Me.
CLARA C. LEONARD, Middleborough.
MARY M. MACY, New Bedford.
AMANDA L. MARTIN, Newton Centre.
ORPAH L. MAXIM, N. Rochester.
KATIE L. MORSE, Norwood.
HELEN M. PACKARD, Brockton.
CHARLOTTE E. PAGE, Stoughton.
ANNIE M. PIERCE, Stoughton.
ELIZABETH A. RAUSCH, Brookline.
ESTELLE REDINGTON, Perry, Me.
ELIZA M. REED, Stowe.
LIZZIE C. RICHARDSON, Winchester.
MARY L. STINCHFIELD, Reading.
CAROLINE B. THACHER, Bridgewater.
EMMA L. THOMAS, S. Carver.
ADDIE L. THOMPSON, Stoneham.
RACHEL J. UPHAM, Stoughton.
SARA J. WALKER, Bridgewater.
ALICE F. WILBUR, Bridgewater.
EVELYN S. WORDELL, N. Dartmouth.

CLASS 87.   FEBRUARY 15, 1876.

JOSEPH BELCHER, 2D, Holbrook.
WALLACE C. BOYDEN, Bridgewater.
CYRUS B. COLLINS, Rockland.
A. FRANK CONWELL, Provincetown.
WILLIAM CRONELLY, Bridgewater.
SAMUEL DYER, JR., Truro.
DAVID G. ELDRIDGE, JR.,Yarmouth Port.
GEORGE H. HASTINGS, Lunenburg.
ALBERT E. HEARD, Weston.
WILLIAM D. JACKSON, Bridgewater.
EDWIN F. KIMBALL, Winchester.
HOLDEN T. MOORE, Raynham.
FRED H. MORTON, Reading.
LOUIS D. WASHBURN, N. Perry. Me.
MARIA L. ANDERSON, W. Windham, N. H.
SARAH L. ARNOLD, N. Abington.
MARY T. ASHLEY, New Bedford.
CARRIE C. BALLOU, Stoughton.
ANNIE E. CARNES, Attleborough.
ANGIE C. DAMON, Marshfield.
ALICE A. DEARING, Denmark, Me.
FANNIE J. DELANO, Fairhaven.
SARAH E. DREW, Bridgewater.
EDITH M. GIBBS, Brighton.
FLORENCE W. HARRIS, E. Bridgewater.
MARGARET LANE, Brewster.
FLORENCE H. LUND, Bridgewater.
ABBIE A. MILLS, Brockton.
LUCY B. MILLS, Lawrence.
MARY V. MORSE, Quincy.
HATTIE E. NOYES, Hampstead, N. H.
ANNIE E. OGLEVEE, Springfield, Ohio.
MARIETTA SHERMAN, Dartmouth.
CARRIE F. SPEER, Quincy.
MARY N. TAYLOR, Germantown, Pa.
MARY B. TITCOMB, W. Windham, N. H.

ROLL OF HONOR.

Officers.

Teacher. REV. JAMES H. SCHNEIDER.* Chaplain, 2d U. S. Colored Regiment. Eight months. Died of yellow fever at Key West, Florida, April 26, 1864.

Class.

3. JOSEPH UNDERWOOD, M. D. Assistant Surgeon. Volunteer. Fifteen months.
11. JONATHAN CASS, M. D. First Ass't Surgeon, 40th Regt. Mass. Volunteers, one year. Chief Surgeon of Hospitals, Alexandria, Va., two years.
11. NAHUM LEONARD. Private to Captain and Judge Advocate, 2d division Ninth Army Corps. Three Years.
11. BENJAMIN F. STURBRIDGE. Corporal, Infantry. Nine months' service.
14. GEORGE D. WILLIAMS. Captain, Infantry. Four years four months.
17. GEORGE L. ANDREWS. Staff Officer from Lieut. Colonel to Brigadier General, and Major General by brevet.
17. HIRAM A. OAKMAN. First Lieut. and Captain in 7th Regt. Mass. Volunteers. Lieut. Colonel 30th Regt. U. S. Colored Troops. Four years.
18. SIDNEY C. BANCROFT. Captain.
19. LEWIS G. LOWE. Acting Medical Cadet. 2d Lieutenant. Three months.
19. CARLTON A. STAPLES. Chaplain, Infantry, One year.
21. JOHN W. ATWOOD. Sergt. Company E, 43d Reg't. Mass. "Nine month's troops." In service eleven months.
23. EDWIN H. KEITH. Acting Assistant Engineer in Navy. Four years.
23. ALBERT J. MANCHESTER. Sergeant, 10th Regiment R. I. Volunteers. One hundred days.
23. HENRY MITCHELL. Officer of the Coast Survey, under orders of Gen. McClellan.
24. WILLIAM J. POTTER. Chaplain, detailed for special service in prisons and hospitals in Washington and vicinity. One year.
27. IRA MOORE. Captain, Co. G., 33d Ill. Regiment. In Vicksburg campaign. Three years.
28. JOSEPH B. READ. Sergeant, Co. F., 58th Regiment Mass. Infantry. One and one-half years.
29. SAMUEL W. CLAPP. Lieutenant, Co. A., 81st Regiment from Platte Co., Missouri.
29. LEWIS WHITING, M. D. Surgeon's Steward. West Gulf Squadron. Two years.
30. WILLIAM H. WARD. Sergeant, Co. K., 45th Regt. Mass. Vols. Nine months.
31. EDWIN MAY, M. D. Surgeon, with rank of Major, in 99th Regt. Illinois Infantry. Four years.
31. WILLIAM A. WEBSTER, M. D. Surgeon 9th Regt. N. H. Vols. Surgeon-in- Chief, 2d Div. 9th Army Corps, Army of Potomac. Major and Brevet Lieut.Col. U. S. Vols. Three years.
32. JABEZ M. LYLE. Lieutenant and Captain. In Quartermaster's Dept. and Commissary. One year.
33. WALTER GALE. Captain, 15th Regt. Mass. Vols. Three years.
38. FRANKLIN JACOBS. Sergeant-Major, 4th Mass. Regt.
38. JAIRUS LINCOLN, Jr. Sergeant, 5th Regt. Mass. Vol. Militia. Nine months.
38. ALBERT WOOD, M. D. Assistant Surgeon and Surgeon, 29th Regt. Mass. Vols., and 1st Mass. Cavalry. Rank, Major. Six months Acting Staff Surgeon, U. S. A. Three years.
41. LEANDER WATERMAN. Private to Captain, 25th Regt. Conn. Vols. One year.
42. ELBRIDGE P. BOYDEN. Corporal, 43d Regt. Mass. Vol. Militia. One year.
43. J. FRANCIS TOURTELOTTE, M. D. Surgeon in Navy. Three years.

44. O. BALFOUR DARLING. Nine months in 45th Regt. Mass. Volunteers. Captain, 12th United States Colored Heavy Artillery. Four years.
44. G. MELVILLE SMITH. Captain and Aid de Camp on Staff of Major-General Canby, Military Division of West Mississippi. Three years.
45. BENJAMIN T. CROOKER, M. D. Assistant Surgeon, United States Army, rank First Lieutenant. In charge of Hospitals most of the time, for four and one-half years.
45. E. F. SPAULDING, M. D. Asst. Surgeon, 7th Regt. Wisconsin Vols. Three years.
46. SAMUEL P. GATES. Sergeant in general service, United States Army. Stationed at Washington, D. C.
46. HENRY R. LYLE. Captain, 101st Regiment New York Volunteers, Heintzleman's Corps, Kearney Division, Army of the Potomac. Two years.
46. HOWARD MORTON. Private to Captain, Infantry. Three years, nine months.
46. WALLACE A. PUTMAM.* Entered service as 2d Lieut. in Company from Hampden Co., 10th Regt. Mass. Vols. Promoted to First Lieut. Discharged Jan. 1863. Raised a Company and was commissioned Captain in 46th Mass. Regt. In the Seven Battles of the Wilderness acted as Field Officer, leading his regiment, "the bravest of the brave," May 34, 1864, near the banks of the North Anna, was wounded in head, came home for "thirty days." Died from this wound June 20, 1864. Commissioned Major, May 7, 1864.
48. NATHANIEL B. HODSDON. First Lieut. of Company in 87th Regt. Illinois Vols. Three years.
48. FREDERIC C. SMITH.* Adjutant, 73d Regt. Ohio Vols. Was very active in raising the Regt. in Oct. 1869. Died in service, of typhoid fever, at Weston, West Virginia, April 18, 1862.
48. LEWIS H. SWEET,* Sergeant, wounded in the arm in the attack on Port Hudson June 14, 1863, and died the next day. Nine months in the service.
49. EDMUND COTTLE. Second Lieutenant Co. D., 4th Reg't Mass. Vol.
49. A. JUDSON GRAY, M. D., from acting Assistant Surgeon, to Surgeon-in-Chief and Inspector of Military District. Three years.
49. THOMAS GURNEY. Lieutenant. In service two years, nine months.
50. A. SUMNER DEAN, M. D. Acting Assistant Surgeon in the Navy. Two years.
50. ISAAC F. KINGSBURY. From Sergeant in Co. K., 32d Reg't Mass. Vols. Infantry, to Acting Assistant Adj. General. In all the great battles of the Army of Potomac, from Antietam to Petersburg. Three years.
50. VIRGIL D. STOCKBRIDGE. First Lieutenant in Infantry. Three years.
51. GEORGE L. SMALLEY, M. D. Surgeon. Died from excessive efforts in saving men after battle of Antietam.
51. WILLIAM B. GROVER. Medical Cadet U. S. Army. Rank, 2d Lieutenant. Two years, six months.
52. EDMUND W. NUTTER, Corporal, Co. D. 38th Reg't. Mass. Vol's. Infantry. One year.
53. WILLIAM R. CROSBY. Lieutenant.
53. JOSEPH W. HAYWOOD, M. D. From Medical Cadet, U. S. A., to Assistant Surgeon and Brevet Major U. S. Vol's. Two years, seven months.
53. BENJAMIN W. PARSONS.* 1st Lieut. 3d Reg't Mass. Cavalry. Died of Disease contracted in the Army, at Lynnfield, August 14, 1864.
53. HENRY MANLEY. Corporal, 3d Reg't Mass. Vols. Nine months.
53. ALBERT E. SMITH. Brev't Lieut. Col. 3d Regular Artillery. U. S. Army.
53. ELISHA M. WHITE, M. D. From Private to Surgeon. 37th Reg't Mass. Vol's. Infantry. Three years.
54. WILMON W. BLACKMER. Enlisted as private and passed through all grades to Captain, and was mustered out as Capt. and Provost Marshall, 3d Brigade, 3d Division Sheridan's Cavalry. Three years.
54. PETER C. SEARS. Captain, 33d Regt. Mass. Vols. Infantry. Three years.
55. THOMAS CONANT, JR. Second Lieut. 29th Regt. Mass. Vols. Infantry. Three years.
55. EDWARD SOUTHWORTH. From private to Quartermaster. In 2d U. S. Regiment Colored Troops, Infantry. Three years two months.

ROLL OF HONOR.

56. SILAS N. GROSVENOR. 1st Sergeant, Company C, 29th Regt. Mass. Vols. Infantry. Killed at Petersburg, Va., while carrying the colors of his regiment, June 17th, 1874. Three years.
57. JACOB P. ALMY.* Corporal, 33d Regt. Mass. Vols. nine months. Entered U. S. Military Academy at West Point. Graduated in 1867. Commissioned Second Lieut. 5th Cavalry. Stationed in South Carolina, Nebraska, Arizona. Promoted to 1st Lieut. 1873. Met his death by treachery of Indians at Don Carlos, May 27, 1873.
57. WARREN T. HILLMAN. Corporal. One year.
57. THOMAS S. HOWLAND. Private to 2d Lieutenant. 33d Regt. Mass. Vols. Infantry. Three years.
57. JOSEPH L. LOCKE. First Lieut. 33d Regt. Mass. Vols. Infantry. Three years.
59. BERIAH T. HILLMAN. Private to 2d Lieutenant. 43d and 60th Regts. Mass. Vols. Infantry. One year.
67. BRAINARD P. TRASK. Ensign in Navy during the war.
68. SAMUEL J. BULLOCK. Private and Sergeant. "Army of Potomac." One year in active service under McClellan, Burnside, Hooper and Meade. Lost a leg at Gettysburg. In hospital one year.

Total of officers, sixty-nine.

PRIVATES.

1. GUSTAVUS D. BATES. Co. D., 38th Regt. Mass. Vol. Infantry. One year.
13. GEORGE W. DEAN. Assistant in U. S. Coast Survey Army service. During the war.
17. H. CARLTON CHEEVER. Musician. Band of the 18th Regt. Mass. Vols. Infantry.
18. J. S. P. WHEELER. U. S. Engineer Corps, Co. C. Three years.
38. EDWARD L. HILL. Co. A., 44th Regt. Mass. Vols. One year.
38. BERNARD PAINE. Relief Agent, Sanitary Commission. Five months.
39. JOSIAH R. FLETCHER. In 6th Regt. Mass. Vols. Infantry. Nine months.
46. JOHN HUMPHREY.* In the Navy, on the U. S. Ship "Cumberland," in the fight with the "Merrimac" in Hampton Roads; was fatally wounded by the bursting of a shell, and sank with his ship, March 8, 1862.
46. LUTHER RUGG. Co. K., 53d Regt. Mass. Vols. Infantry. One year.
46. SIMSON S. SANBORN. In Quartermaster's Dept., Nashville. Seven Months.
49. AUGUSTUS REMICK. Co. A., 84th Regt. Ill. Vols. Infantry. In Medical Purveyor's Department most of the time. Three years.
51. FRED. O. ELLIS. 45th Regt. Mass. Vols. Infantry. Ten months.
51. GEORGE B. HANNA. Mass. Vols. Infantry. Eight months.
51. ELLIS V. LYON.* Co. I., 1st Mass. Cavalry. Died at Petersburg, Sept. 24, 1864.
53. FRANCIS T. CRAFTS. In 3d Regt. Mass. Vols. Nine months.
53. JOHN E. BRYANT. Detailed as P. O. Clerk at Fortress Monroe, then at Newbern, N. C. The only one of nine in charge who remained at his post during the raging of the yellow fever at Newbern, of which he died Oct. 1, 1864. "Faithful to the end."
53. ABRAHAM G. R. HALE. In 45th Regt. Mass. Vols. Infantry. Ten Months.
53. HENRY C. HOUGHTON. Gen. Agent U. S. Christian Commission in the South, two and one-half years.
53. CHARLES W. McMAHON. In service of Christian Commission seven months.
53. WILLIAM R. OSBORNE. Co. C. 28th Regt. Mass. Vols. Infantry. Twenty months. In six battles, wounded and disabled for life.
53. JOHN W. PRENTISS. In Maj. Gen. Banks Division at New Orleans and Port Hudson. Twelve months.
53. THEODORE RODMAN. Co. C, 29th Regt. Mass. Volunteers. Infantry.
54. CALVIN PRATT. Acting Medical Cadet, Judiciary Square Hospital, Washington, D. C. Eighteen months.
54. GEORGE A. WHEELER. Co. D, 38th Regt. Mass. Vols. Infantry. Thirty-four months.
55. WILLARD E. CLARK.* 3d Mass. Cavalry, 19th Army Corps. Killed in the battle of Cedar Creek, Va., October 19, 1864.
55. GEORGE T. KEITH. In 3d Mass. Regt. Nine months.

BRIDGEWATER STATE NORMAL SCHOOL.

56. SAMUEL P. ALLEN. Captain's Clerk on ship "Fort Donaldson." Fourteen months.
56. NOAHDIAH P. JOHNSON. In Connecticut Regiment.
57. OLIVER HOWARD. In service 100 days.
57. D SWANSON LEWIS. In Mass. 6th Regiment "100 days" men.
57. WILLIAM A. MARSHALL. In army six months.
57. LUNAS A. MENDELL. In army four months.
57. WEBSTER H. PIERCE. In Christian Commission service.
57. HENRY L. REED. One of the "100 days men."
57. HIRAM N. WALKER.* Co. E., 51st Reg't Mass. Vols. Infantry. Died at Newbern, N. C., January 18, 1863.
57. CHARLES H. W. WOOD. Co. A, 42d Regt. Mass. Vol. Militia. Four months.
58. GRANVILLE H. GOULD. In 29th Regt. M. V. M. Nine months. 56th Regt. N. Y. V. M. Six months. In Navy, U. S. Steamer "Fort Donaldson." Thirteen months.
58. CHARLES RECORD. 3d Regiment, M. V. M. Nine months.
59. CHARLES F. STUART.* 1st Maine Cavalry. Died in Finlay Hospital, Washington, D. C., April 23, 1863.
59. EBEN W. FULLER.* In 26th Regt. Maine Vol. Militia. Died in Chesapeake Hospital, Va., Dec. 13. 1862.
59. MARCELLUS G. HOWARD. Co. K, 3d Regt. M. V. M.
61. ALBERT E. WINSHIP. Mass. Vol. Militia. Five months.
64. EMORY G. WETHERBEE. Drummer. Eighteen months.
66. JOHN D. BILLINGS. 10th Mass. Light Artillery. Thirty-four months.
66. DARIUS HADLEY. Musician, 2d Reg't N. H. V. M. In Navy six months.
66. ALBERT F. RING. 6th Reg't M. V. Militia. Six months.

Total of privates, forty-six. Total in Army and Navy, one hundred fifteen.

SUMMARY.

TABLE 1.—Showing number of gentlemen and ladies admitted at commencement of each term, the number in attendance each term, and the number graduated each term. The figure in the left of the space indicates the number graduated from the advanced course.

CLASS.	ADMITTED.			IN ATTENDANCE.			GRADUATED.		
	Gentlemen.	Ladies.	Total.	Gentlemen.	Ladies.	Total.	Gentlemen.	Ladies.	Total.
1	7	21	28	7	21	28	6	17	23
2	7	7	14	9	26	35	5	5	10
3	9	9	18	21	30	51	7	6	13
4	2	10	12	15	26	41	2	7	9
5	3	8	11	22	30	52	1	2	3
6	3	11	14	8	30	38	2	3	5
7	5	10	15	18	27	45	1	4	5
8	16	9	25	26	17	43	4	4	8
9	9	8	17	11	22	33	3	1	4
10	17	3	20	29	15	44	7	3	10
11	26	7	33	51	20	71	5	2	7
12	8	17	25	11	34	45	1	8	9
13	14	7	21	27	14	41	10	7	17
14	10	10	20	43	24	67	5	6	11
15	7	15	22	19	26	45	4	9	13
16	10	7	17	16	19	35	8	6	14
17	20	18	38	36	43	79	18	16	34
18	9	15	24	26	30	56	7	11	18
19	15	16	31	25	38	63	11	16	27
20	7	18	25			102	6	15	21
21	4	9	13			51	3	7	10
22	2	9	11			64	2	8	10
23	7	6	13			52	7	6	13
24	6	4	10			40	5	3	8
25	6	10	16			48	4	9	13
26	3	7	10			47	2	5	7
27	7	8	15	12	25	37	7	6	13
28	11	14	25	24	28	52	10	11	21
29	7	11	18	27	29	56	7	11	18
30	7	10	17	23	36	59	7	8	15
31	8	23	31	26	45	71	6	18	24
32	12	13	25	33	46	79	9	11	20
33	8	16	24	24	49	73	8	11	19
34	9	23	32	28	58	86	7	15	22
35	4	12	16	30	49	79	3	10	13
36	9	16	25	20	44	64	9	12	21
37	7	20	27	21	50	71	3	14	17
38	15	24	39	38	54	92	10	18	28
39	8	16	24	22	48	70	4	11	15
40	16	17	33	30	34	64	14	12	26
41	2	3	5	23	31	54	2	3	5
42	7	6	13	24	23	47	7	6	13
43	4	4	8	30	21	51	4	4	8
44	8	7	15	20	18	38	7	6	13
45	9	23	32	27	39	66	6	20	26
46	15	21	36	35	54	89	14	16	30

166 BRIDGEWATER STATE NORMAL SCHOOL.

CLASS.	ADMITTED.			IN ATTENDANCE.			GRADUATED.		
	Gentlemen.	Ladies.	Total.	Gentlemen.	Ladies.	Total.	Gentlemen.	Ladies.	Total.
47	7	27	34	28	52	80	6	23	29
48	5	17	22	27	62	89	4	14	18
49	16	19	35	25	61	87	10	14	24
50	10	9	19	23	40	63	7	8	15
51	13	24	37	31	48	79	7	19	26
52	13	28	41	30	61	91	12	24	36
53	22	12	34	43	56	99	18	8	26
54	7	10	17	30	43	82	7	6	13
55	14	22	36	44	40	84	10	19	29
56	9	6	15	29	38	67	6	6	12
57	20	13	33	44	39	83	12	9	21
58	10	21	31	37	50	87	5	13	18
59	24	15	39	50	44	94	10	8	18
60	1	16	17	28	51	79	1	10	11
61	11	21	32	31	54	85	7	12	19
62	6	23	29	23	57	80	3	15	18
63	4	19	23	23	63	86	2	14	16
64	4	9	13	13	51	64	1	7	8
65	6	21	27	19	57	76	2	11	13
66	8	20	28	18	62	80	4	11	15
67	8	15	23	19	59	78	4	9	13
68	8	12	20	22	53	75	5	8	13
69	7	15	22	24	53	77	6	9	15
70	5	20	25	22	56	78	3	13	16
71	7	25	32	21	63	84	2	5	20	27
72	10	32	42	26	83	109	1	4	18	23
73	9	29	38	29	92	121	8	13	21
74	13	28	41	36	94	130	1	5	13	19
75	10	41	51	36	100	136	1	5	12	18
76	5	45	50	36	106	142	3	3	26	32
77	12	27	39	38	96	134	1	7	1	16	25
78	4	26	30	32	107	139	3	3	13	19
79	10	27	37	32	118	150	4	15	19
80	7	37	44	28	111	139	5	20	25
81	6	30	36	28	122	150	2	15	17
82	11	33	44	30	115	145	5	16	21
83	7	25	32	31	109	140	4	12	16
84	8	47	55	33	121	154	2	6	19	27
85	10	33	43	37	114	151			
86	18	41	59	45	115	160			
87	14	22	36	49	118	167			

TABLE 2. — Showing from what towns and counties (in Mass.), and States the School has received pupils, and the number from each.

TOWNS.

Abington.................24
Acton.................... 1
Acushnet.............. 11
Andover................ 4
Ashby................... 9
Athol................... 1
Attleboro'..............23
Auburn................. 2
Ayer.................... 1
Barnstable.............21
Bellingham............. 2
Berkley................14
Berlin.................. 3
Bernardston........... 1
Beverly................. 2
Blackstone............. 3
Bolton.................. 5
Boston.................76
Braintree..............14
Brewster............... 9
Bridgewater..........230

Brighton................ 1
Brimfield............... 1
Brockton...............50
Brookfield............. 9
Brookline.............. 1
Cambridge............. 6
Canton.................20
Carver.................. 7
Charlestown...........10
Charlton................ 4
Chatham...............11
Chelmsford............ 2
Chelsea................. 6
Chicopee............... 1
Chilmark............... 5
Clinton................. 1
Cohasset............... 2
Dancers................ 8
Dartmouth.............30
Dedham................ 8
Dennis.................13

Dighton................. 8
Dorchester............. 4
Douglass............... 2
Dover................... 4
Dracut.................. 4
Duxbury................12
East Bridgewater.....51
Eastham................ 2
Easton.................28
Edgartown............. 2
Essex................... 1
Fairhaven..............24
Fall River.............31
Falmouth..............10
Fitchburg.............. 3
Foxboro'................ 9
Framingham.......... 3
Franklin................ 5
Freetown..............26
Gloucester............. 2
Greenfield............. 1

STATISTICAL SUMMARY.

TOWNS.

Greenwich 1	Montague................. 1	Somerville............... 5
Groton 2	Nantucket 37	Southboro' 3
Halifax 3	Natick 3	Southbridge.............. 4
Hanover.................. 5	Needham................. 7	South Scituate........... 9
Hanson 4	Newbury.................. 1	Springfield 1
Hardwick................. 1	Newburyport............. 2	Sterling 10
Harvard.................. 3	New Bedford............50	Stoneham................12
Harwich.................. 2	Newton 25	Stoughton................35
Haverhill................. 4	North Adams 1	Stow 4
Hingham.................21	Northampton 1	Sturbridge 3
Hinsdale.................. 1	Northboro' 19	Sudbury.................. 4
Holbrook 3	Northbridge.............. 1	Sutton 4
Holden 2	Northfield 2	Swansea 12
Holliston 2	Norton.................... 8	Taunton..................19
Holyoke 1	Norwood 3	Templeton................ 4
Hopkinton................ 1	Orleans................... 8	Tisbury 6
Hyde Park................ 1	Oxford.................... 1	Townsend................ 2
Ipswich 2	Peabody.................. 6	Truro 3
Kingston.................19	Pembroke................11	Tyngsboro'............... 3
Lakeville................. 2	Pepperell................. 2	Upton.................... 2
Lancaster................. 2	Petersham 5	Uxbridge................. 6
Lawrence................. 8	Plymouth................50	Walpole..................10
Leominster............... 4	Plympton................. 7	Waltham................. 5
Lexington................ 4	Princeton................. 2	Wareham 6
Littleton 4	Provincetown............17	Warren 2
Lowell 5	Quincy...................20	Warwick.................. 2
Lunenburg................ 1	Randolph................37	Watertown............... 3
Lynn 8	Raynham................15	Wayland 1
Lynnfield................. 1	Reading 15	Webster 3
Malden................... 2	Rehoboth 7	Wellfleet 6
Mansfield 10	Revere 1	Westboro' 1
Marblehead 7	Rochester................20	Westford 2
Marlboro' 5	Rockland................. 1	Westminster.............. 6
Marshfield 15	Rockport................. 2	Weston 8
Marion................... 4	Roxbury*................12	Westport.................11
Mattapoisett.............. 6	Royalston................ 4	Weymouth 12
Medfield 16	Rutland 3	West Bridgewater........72
Medway..................15	Salem.................... 7	Wilmington.............. 1
Mendon 6	Sandwich 8	Winchester............... 2
Methuen 1	Salisbury................. 2	Woburn..................10
Middleboro'...............57	Scituate..................23	Worcester................ 8
Milbury................... 1	Seekonk 4	Wrentham 23
Milford. 11	Sharon 5	Yarmouth................10
Milton 14	Sherborn................. 6	
Monson 1	Somerset................. 6	

COUNTIES.

Plymouth................702	Barnstable 132	Hampden................. 5
Bristol 381	Suffolk................... 99	Franklin 4
Norfolk 250	Essex 71	Hampshire................ 2
Worcester................170	Nantucket 37	Berkshire................. 3
Middlesex................162	Dukes 14	

STATES.

Massachusetts............2031	Maryland 3	Texas 1
New Hampshire...........100	West Virginia............. 1	California 1
Maine 85	Ohio 3	Canada 1
Rhode Island............. 40	Illinois.................... 2	Nova Scotia............... 3
Vermont 15	Kentucky................. 1	Burmah 2
Connecticut 10	Minnesota 2	Japan..................... 1
New York................ 11	Michigan 1	
Pennsylvania.............. 4	Colorado 1	Total................2324
New Jersey............... 1	South Carolina........... 1	
District of Columbia..... 2	Alabama 1	

The following Tables, 3 and 4, are not entirely correct, since the returns from which they were compiled were incomplete. More than three fourths of all the past members of the School have been heard from, and much pains has been taken to get facts in every case. They may, therefore, serve to show with a good degree of accuracy the character and amount of the work which has been done by our Alumni, together with some of the important facts in their history.

TABLE 3.— Showing the number of persons heard from in each class, the number of graduates heard from in each class, the total number of years of teaching for all those heard from in each class, and the average number of years of teaching for all those heard from in each class. Persons who remained in the School only a short time after their admission have not been counted in the record given in this table.

CLASS.	NUMBER IN THE CLASS.	GENTLEMEN.					LADIES.				
		Not heard from.	Heard from.	Known to have taught.	Total of teaching in years.	Average of teaching in years.	Not heard from.	Heard from.	Known to have taught.	Total of teaching in years.	Average of teaching in years.
1	27	0	7	6	44	6	1	19	15	151	8
2	14	0	7	5	21	3	2	5	5	41	8
3	18	2	7	7	53	7½	3	6	6	34	6
4	11	0	2	1	2	1	2	7	5	67	8¼
5	10	2	1	1	2	2	0	7	7	27	4
6	13	1	2	2	4	2	2	8	8	85	8¼
7	11	1	2	2	7	3½	2	6	5	53	9
8	24	5	10	6	18½	2	2	7	6	26	4
9	18	2	7	5	14	2	2	7	5	36	5
10	19	3	13	11	128	10	1	2	1	1	½
11	33	7	19	18	160	8	1	6	5	15	2½
12	26	2	7	5	33	5	1	16	16	150	9½
13	20	2	11	11	79	7	2	5	5	20	4
14	20	5	5	3	29	6	6	4	4	30	7½
15	19	2	2	2	20	10	4	11	10	80	7
16	16	3	6	6	108	18	3	4	4	26	6½
17	38	1	19	19	251	13	5	13	9	71	5½
18	24	4	5	4	62	12	6	9	7	44	5
19	30	6	8	7	10	1	8	8	7	113	14
20	24	1	6	6	36	6	3	14	11	83	6
21	13	1	3	2	21	7	1	8	7	82	10
22	11	1	1	1	5	5	1	8	7	67	8
23	13	0	7	5	55	8	1	5	5	39	8
24	10	1	5	5	31	6	1	3	2	28	9
25	15	0	4	2	5	1	0	11	10	76	7
26	9	0	3	3	49	16	0	6	5	15	2½
27	14	2	5	5	20	4	1	6	6	30	5
28	23	2	9	7	64	7	4	8	7	46	6
29	18	1	6	6	35	6	1	10	8	55	5½
30	16	1	6	6	72	12	6	3	3	15	5
31	31	2	6	6	72	12	4	10	18	148	8
32	22	2	7	7	62	9	4	9	7	93	10
33	24	2	6	5	62	10	5	11	11	84	8
34	32	1	7	6	81	11½	4	20	16	145	7
35	15	2	1	1	7	7	7	5	5	21	4
36	23	2	7	7	49	7	4	10	10	68	7
37	22	2	4	4	33	8	3	13	13	124	9½
38	32	4	8	7	55	7	5	15	15	145	10
39	20	6	2	2	2	1	3	9	9	87	10
40	32	3	13	11	77	6	3	13	13	91	7
41	5	0	2	2	43	21½	0	3	3	15	5
42	13	1	6	6	69	11½	0	6	5	44	7
43	8	0	4	3	24	6	1	3	3	31	10
44	15	1	7	6	63	9	0	7	6	14	2
45	32	1	8	8	29	4	3	20	20	151	8
46	36	0	15	13	77	5	3	18	18	155	9

STATISTICAL SUMMARY.

CLASS.	NUMBER IN THE CLASS.	GENTLEMEN.					LADIES.				
		Not heard from.	Heard from.	Known to have taught.	Total of teaching in years.	Average of teaching in years.	Not heard from.	Heard from.	Known to have taught.	Total of teaching in years.	Average of teaching in years.
47	34	2	5	4	34	7	3	24	23	177	7
48	22	1	4	4	13	3	3	14	14	104	7
49	35	8	8	8	79	10	5	14	12	52	4
50	19	2	8	5	40	5	1	8	7	24	3
51	37	1	12	9	48	4	4	20	19	120	6
52	40	2	11	11	73	7	4	23	22	134	6
53	34	3	19	19	71	4	2	10	9	49	5
54	17	0	7	6	39	6	3	7	6	49	7
55	36	2	12	8	83	7	4	18	18	99	5½
56	15	3	6	5	21	3½	1	5	5	21	4
57	33	2	18	8	42	2	1	12	11	52	4
58	31	5	5	4	10	2	4	17	13	75	4½
59	39	6	18	10	85	5	3	12	11	76	6
60	17	0	1	1	4	1	2	14	12	65	5
61	32	2	9	8	71	8	6	15	12	64	4
62	29	2	4	4	26	6½	3	20	20	116	6
63	23	0	4	3	10	3	3	16	15	83	5
64	13	0	4	1	0	0	3	6	6	27	4
65	27	0	6	5	31	5	2	19	18	115	6
66	28	2	6	5	43	7	5	15	13	84	5½
67	23	1	7	5	38	5½	3	12	11	44	4
68	29	1	7	7	39	6	1	11	10	63	6
69	22	0	7	6	23	3	2	13	12	51	4
70	25	1	4	4	17	4	3	17	16	67	4
71	32	1	6	6	29	5	1	24	22	112	5
72	42	2	8	6	19	3	8	24	22	112	5
73	38	0	9	7	26	3	7	22	18	86	4
74	41	0	13	6	16	1½	4	24	23	99	4
75	51	2	8	7	22	3	7	34	26	87	2½
76	50	2	3	2	7	2½	5	40	36	105	2½
77	39	2	10	8	23	2½	0	27	23	58	2
78	30	0	4	4	6	1½	2	24	24	60	2½
79	37	2	0	5	9	1	4	23	16	36	2
80	38	2	5	3	6	1	8	29	22	31	1

SUMMARY.

TABLE 4. Showing the total results as gathered from the returns which have been made.

Whole number of Admissions, Gentlemen, 804; Ladies, 1,520; total,	2,324
Whole number of Graduates, Gentlemen, 506; Ladies, 934; total,	1,440
Whole number heard from, Gentlemen, 598; Ladies, 1,105; total,	1,703
Number of those heard from who are known to have taught, Gentlemen, 479; Ladies, 971; total,	1,450
Whole number of years of teaching for eighty classes, Gentlemen, 3,344; Ladies, 5,619; total,	8,963
Number of Alumni deceased, as returned,	249
Number of Ladies married, as returned,	574
Number in the Army and Navy during the late war,	115
Number of Admissions under Mr. Tillinghast, Gentlemen, 344; Ladies, 477; total,	821
Number of Graduates under Mr. Tillinghast, Gentlemen, 213; Ladies, 314; total	527
Number of years of Teaching by pupils of Mr. Tillinghast, Gentlemen, 1,862; Ladies, 2,521; total,	4,383
Average number of years of teaching for all the pupils of Mr. Tillinghast heard from, Gentlemen, 7 2-3 years; Ladies, 7 1-3 years.	
Number of Admissions under Mr. Conant, Gentlemen, 168; Ladies, 249; total,	417
Number of Graduates under Mr. Conant, Gentlemen, 133; Ladies, 207; total,	340
Number of years of Teaching by pupils of Mr. Conant, Gentlemen, 862; Ladies, 1,309; total,	2,171
Average number of years of teaching for all the pupils of Mr. Conant heard from, Gentlemen, 6 years; Ladies, 6 1-3 years.	
Number of Admissions under Mr. Boyden, Gentlemen, 292; Ladies, 794; total,	1,086
Number of Graduates under Mr. Boyden, Gentlemen, 160; Ladies, 413; total,	573
Number of years of Teaching by pupils of Mr. Boyden, Gentlemen, 620; Ladies, 1,789; total,	2,409

BRIDGEWATER NORMAL LYCEUM.

In the autumn of 1839, several of the students of the Bridgewater Academy formed themselves into a society called the "*Bridgewater Speaking Club,,*" having for its object, as its name indicates, the improvement of its members in the exercise of declamation. This society may be considered the germ from which has grown this Lyceum. It consisted originally of ten members, which number was increased in a few weeks to seventeen. Two public exhibitions were given with success. The interest in declamation began to diminish after the stimulus of the exhibition was withdrawn, when it was suggested that occasional debate would be more beneficial. It was soon after voted to spend one-half of the evening in debate. The first question for debate was "Are the works of nature more pleasing to the eye than the works of Art?" The debate was a success. Meetings were held once a week, and were private until September, 1840; after this time spectators were allowed, and their presence greatly increased the interest of the meetings.

In January, 1841, a lecture was delivered before the society by Rev. Mr. Thurston, on the discovery of America by the Northmen, A. D. 1000. This lecture gave so much satisfaction that it was proposed to have occasional lectures from the members of the Club; each in his turn was to favor the Club with his ideas on some familiar subject. The lectures seemed to give a new life and interest to the meetings of the society. About this time some of the students of the Normal School became members of the Club, a new constitution was formed, and the society adopted the name of "The Bridgewater Young Men's Lyceum." The meetings continued to be held regularly and with increasing interest.

In August, 1844, it was thought that some additional rules were necessary for the government of the large number of members that then attended the meetings of the society. A set of By-Laws was adopted, among which was one making Jefferson's Manual the standard by which to decide all disputes on points of order. The Constitution was amended so as to have a standing President and Vice President instead of choosing a President at each meeting. On the sixth ballot, Horace Chapin was elected the first President. The Lyceum had now passed from the Academy into the hands of the Normal students, although open to all the young men. Its meetings were often crowded, a large part of the audience consisting of ladies.

From this time onward the Lyceum continued to hold its meetings on Friday evenings during the terms of the school, until within a few years when it has held them on alternate Friday evenings during the term. For many years ladies have been members, and have taken an active part in the exercises, with the exception of the debate, in which they participate only to a limited extent. The object of the Lyceum is mutual improvement. The present By-Laws provide that the order of exercises shall be as follows: Calling of the Roll; Reading of the Journal; Appointments by the President; Transaction of business; Report of Prudential Committee; Declamations; Reading of Selections, or reading of the "Normal Offering," as the case may be; Debate; Criticism by the President, at his option. Music shall be inserted in the order of exercises, at the discretion of the President. The "Normal Offering" shall be read once in four weeks, by a member appointed for the purpose. On evenings alternating with those on which the Offering is read, there shall be declamations by two gentlemen, appointed four weeks previous. On the same evenings select pieces shall be read by two ladies, appointed four weeks previous. At each regular meeting, the discussion of the question reported at a previous meeting shall be in order, and shall close five minutes before the time of adjournment.

BRIDGEWATER NORMAL ASSOCIATION.

In 1842, the number of persons who had been pupils in the school was one hundred and thirty. "As they were widely scattered, and had few opportunities for perpetuating school friendship, the plan of a Convention was devised, having for its objects the gathering of the Alumni and pupils of the school, thus enabling them to spend a day in social intercourse and *Normal* enjoyment."

"The first convention was held in the school-room at Bridgewater, August 3, 1842. Ninety-nine of the past members of the school were present. Joseph Underwood, Jr., presided. After the transaction of the necessary business, addresses were delivered by Mr. Tillinghast, the Principal of the school, Rev. S. J. May, Hon. Horace Mann, and Dr. Kendall, of Plymouth. At noon the Convention proceeded to the Academy Hall and partook of a collation provided by the Normal students and their friends. From the Academy the company proceeded to the Unitarian Church and listened to a lecture on "Punishment," delivered by Horace Mann. When Mr. Mann had concluded, Rev. S. J. May made some remarks on the duties of parents toward their children, as scholars. The procession then returned to the school-room where a committee, who had previously been chosen for the purpose, reported a series of six resolutions complimentary to the following: The Normal School, the Common School Journal, the Friends and Patrons of the Normal School, the Board of Education and its Secretary, the Teachers of the Normal School, and the people of Bridgewater." The Convention then adjourned for one year.

The Convention continued to be held annually. In 1845, the Convention formed itself into an Association by adopting the following preamble and a Constitution.

PREAMBLE.—The State Normal School at Bridgewater, being now permanently established, it is desirable that the graduates and scholars of the Institution should effect a more perfect organization than has hitherto existed.

It is believed that an Association, embracing the advantages of a "*Corresponding Society,*" a " *Teachers' Institute,*" and a "*Social Gathering,*" of all who have been or may become members of this school would give permanence to the friendship here formed, would strengthen the attachment of its members to the duties of their calling, and in many ways be an important auxiliary to the cause of Common

School education. For the promotion of these objects, we, the graduates and scholars of the Normal School, in Convention assembled, hereby form an Association, and agree to be governed by the following CONSTITUTION:

1. "The Association shall be called the Bridgewater Normal Association."

2. "The Officers shall be a President, three Vice Presidents, two Secretaries, and a Treasurer. And these officers shall constitute an Executive Committee.

3. This Association shall hold a meeting in Bridgewater, Mass., annually, on the third Wednesday of August, for the purpose of transacting business, hearing addresses, and of discussing questions relating to education.

4. "The officers shall be chosen annually, and shall perform the duties usually incumbent on such officers."

5. "All the graduates and scholars of the State Normal School, Bridgewater, shall be considered members of the Association."

6. "The Teachers, past and present, of the State Normal Schools of Massachusetts, shall be Honorary Members of the Association."

7. "In selecting orators to deliver the annual addresses, preference shall be given to members, or honorary members of the Association."

Many amendments to this Constitution have been made, and By-Laws have been adopted; but the main objects and features of the Association have remained substantially the same, except the idea of making the Association a "Corresponding Society." Articles were in the Constitution for the first two years after its adoption, requiring each member of the Association to write a letter annually, in the month of June, to the Executive Committee of the Normal Association, Bridgewater, Mass., giving a full account of himself for the year, with his Post-office address. This plan was soon found impracticable, and abandoned.

The main features of the Association have been a business meeting in the school-room, a public address in one of the churches, a collation, with after-dinner speeches, and a social reunion in the town hall in the evening. Since 1858, the meetings of the Association have been held biennially.

The following is a list of the Presidents and Orators of the Association, at each meeting:

DATE.	PRESIDENTS.	ORATORS.
1842.	Joseph Underwood, Jr.	Horace Mann.
1843.	Alson A. Gilmore.	George B. Emerson.
1844.	Albert Conant.	Wm. B. Fowle.
1845.	James E. Leach.	Rev. Charles Brooks.
1846.	James E. Leach.	Amasa Walker.
1847.	Mertoun C. Bryant.	Rev. H. B. Hooker.
1848.	John A. Goodwin.	James Ritchie.
1849.	Richard Edwards, Jr.	James E. Leach.
1850.	Nathaniel T. Allen.	Christopher A. Greene.
	Horace Chapin.	
1851.	Dana P. Colburn.	Rev. Horace James.
1852.	Thomas Metcalf.	Rev. E. B. Wilson.
1853.	John Kneeland.	Richard Edwards, Jr.
1854.	Albert G. Boyden.	Edw. A. H. Allen.
1855.	Edward A. H. Allen.	Rev. Samuel P. May.
1856.	William P. Hayward.	Richard Edwards, Jr.
1857.	George A. Walton.	William J. Potter.
1858.	William H. Ladd.	John Kneeland.
1860.	Samuel S. Wilson.	John A. Goodwin.
1862.	Joshua Kendall.	Marshall Conant.
1864.	Benjamin F. Clarke.	Thomas Hill, D. D.
1866.	James T. Allen.	Theodore D. Weld.
1868.	Granville B. Putnam.	Lewis B. Monroe (Reading).
1870.	Albert J. Manchester.	Rev. ——— Clark.
1872.	Albert Stetson.	Rev. J. W. Chadwick.
1874.	Thomas H. Barnes.	Albert G. Boyden.
1876.	George H. Martin.	Edwin P. Seaver.

ALPHABETICAL INDEX.

GENTLEMEN.

Class.		Class.		Class.		Class.	
34	Abbot A. B.	51	Blood S. J.	3	Colwell T. B.	17	Dickerman Q. E.
73	Adams C. F.	19	Bogue T. H.	38	Comey C. H.	34	Dickerson E. W.
33	,, J. M.	38	Bolles W. A.	54	Conlins E. I.	38	Dietrich J. B.
11	Aikin W. P.	11	Boomer F. A.	1	Conant A.	71	Dill J. M.
10	Alden A.	38	Bowers A. B.	8	,, C.	18	Dix G. W.
84	,, H. D.	06	,, J. E.	85	,, G. A.	61	Doland F.
8	,, I. F.	64	Bowthorp S. T.	74	,, G. M.	9	Drake B. F.
30	,, J. E.	74	Boyden A. C.	86	,, H. I.	81	,, B. W.
14	,, J. F.	26	,, A. G.	55	,, T.	7	,, J. S.
51	,, W. H.	42	,, E. P.	44	,, W. P.	72	Dunbar E. J.
86	,, W. H.	87	,, W. C.	79	Condon M.	59	,, S. J.
17	Allen E. A. H.	72	Boylston B. C.	87	Conwell A. F.	45	Dunham L. G.
50	,, E. K.	61	Brewster W. W.	53	Cook D. E.	20	Dunn J. L.
33	,, H. F.	28	Briggs F.	32	,, J. T.	75	Dyer E. O.
6	,, H. W.	14	,, S. D.	59	Copeland B.	87	,, S., Jr.
34	,, J. T.	36	Brigham T. R.	59	,, H.		
17	,, N. T.	55	Broad O. J.	28	,, I.	14	Eastland J. D.
50	,, S. P.	50	Brock G. A.	85	,, L.	13	Eaton H. L.
11	,, W. P.	77	Broderick J.	85	,, M. B.	45	,, J. H.
57	Almy J. P.	29	Brown J. F.	15	,, V.	3	Eddy J. M.
10	Ames E. G.	25	,, J. N.	41	,, W. T.	29	Edmands B. B. W.
74	Andrew B. S.	26	,, M. T.	10	Cornish T. O.	77	Edwards G. G.
17	Andrews G. L.	34	,, S. M.	74	Cotter J. E.	45	,, H. R.
74	,, O. A.	48	Bruce W. G.	49	Cottle E.	17	,, R.
85	Armes H. L.	53	Bryant J. E.	53	Crafts F. T.	87	Eldridge D. G.
79	Arnold F. A.	1	,, M. C.	84	Craig F. W.	8	Ellis A.
75	,, G. A.	31	,, O. F.	58	Cram L. T.	51	,, F. O.
12	Atherton N.	47	Buffington G. B.	31	Crane S.	75	,, J. A.
19	Atwood D.	42	Bullard H. C.	45	Crocker B. T.	44	Emery J. A.
75	,, H. T.	37	,, I. H.	30	,, C. F.	79	Evans G.
21	,, J. W.	68	Bullock S. J.	72	,, J. A.	20	Everett H. J.
07	,, W. B.	50	Bunker A.	81	,, S. L.	40	,, J. B.
08	Avery E. A.	8	Burden T. A.	71	,, W. H.	45	,, W. J.
		40	Burditt W. D.	87	Cronelly W.	31	Ewell T. B.
51	Babcock E. A.	39	Burgess N. A.	53	Crosby W. K.		
16	Baker G. M.	78	Burke J. J.	07	Crownlnshield F.	57	Fairbanks L. B.
50	,, J.	80	Burnes W. H.	43	Cummings W. H.	53	,, W. G.
82	,, Z.	28	Burr E. W.	36	Currier S. E. D.	24	Farnsworth A. W.
80	Bakie D. J.	11	Burt B.	57	Cushing C. B.	36	Farwell G.
20	Bailey B. H.	22	,, S.	17	,, M. G.	28	Faunce E.
32	Ballou A. A.			19	Cushman A.	49	Fay L. D.
18	Bancroft S. C.	52	Caldwell A.	19	,, C.	69	,, M. J.
25	Barnard J. F.	71	Campbell A. H.	28	,, C. M.	50	Felt C. W.
86	Barnes M. D.	19	Capen A.	2	,, N. T.	49	Ferguson J. H.
32	,, T. H.	19	,, F.	29	,, S.	65	Fisher C. I.
40	Barrell W. A.	73	Carr G. B.			75	Fitts E. P.
55	Burrows C. M.	56	Carver N. E.	9	Daily H.	30	Fitz C. F.
16	Bartlett F. W.	13	Case J.	47	Damon W.	55	Fletcher G. T.
71	Bassett J. G.	11	Cass J.	36	Dunn J. J.	85	,, H. F.
70	,, W.	61	Chadbourn M. W.	33	Daniels D. H.	30	,, J. R.
1	Bates G. D.	50	Chadwick J. W.	19	,, M. S.	77	Fogg L. W.
54	Baxter J. F.	31	Chamberlain F. H.	16	,, W.	46	Folger A. M.
3	Beal G. W.	11	Chapin H.	42	Darling L. A.	58	Ford G. T.
28	Benis E. H.	17	Cheever H. C.	44	,, O. B.	77	Fox E. E.
32	Beard E. S.	51	Christian C. F.	20	Davis C. D.	73	,, J. E.
20	Belcher A. H.	10	Clapp E.	75	,, F. B.	08	Francis J. A.
18	,, C. W.	82	,, G. W.	64	,, G. D.	40	Freeman D.
87	,, J., 2nd	55	,, H. L.	62	,, G. L.	67	,, H. A.
34	Bell W.	29	,, S. W.	23	Davol W. C.	82	,, N.
84	Benedict G.	44	Clarke B. F.	13	Dean A.	70	French A. J.
72	Bennett A. A.	10	,, E. C.	50	,, A. S.	14	,, E.
1	Benson C.	70	,, H. J.	13	,, G. W.	13	,, E. G.
86	Bentley C. N.	55	,, W. E.	3	,, S.	09	,, M. C.
52	,, D.	30	,, W. N.	84	Decker J. W.	5	,, O.
66	Benton L. F.	27	,, W. P.	76	,, L. H.	8	Fuller B. B.
61	Berry J. D.	17	Cleland W.	79	Deland G. W.	59	,, E.
43	Bigelow G. D.	26	Clough W. A.	30	Delano E. C.	11	,, G. B.
66	Billings J. D.	8	Cobb W. S.	81	Depuy W.	40	,, H. B.
35	Bird S.	37	,, W. S.	74	Desmond T. F.		
53	Bisbce A. W.	70	Coffin C. R.	11	Devens R. M.	49	Gage G. M.
40	,, J. V.	10	Colburn D. P.	52	Dexter C. F.	33	Gale W.
40	Blackman T. B.	02	Cole C. A.	82	Dibble E. H.	9	Gardner F. B.
54	Blackman W. W.	81	,, C. F.	12	Dickerman E. T.	46	Gates S. P.
49	Blackmer G. A.	85	,, H. M.	11	,, G. H.	14	Gault J. H.
40	Blanchard H.	87	Collins C. B.	11	,, L.	9	Gay C.

ALPHABETICAL INDEX. 177

Class.		Class.		Class.		Class.	
40	Gay E., Jr.	53	Houghton H. C.	32	Lovewell S. J.	62	Pickard C. T.
69	P. A.	11	Howard C. H.	19	Lowe L. G.	74	Pierce F. W.
75	Gibbs D. H.	55	H. F.	52	Ludington F. H.	8	H. L.
79	H. L.	57	H. F.	85	Lyeth J. C.	14	J.
75	Gifford J. B.	56	H. W.	46	Lyle H. R.	71	J. N.
2	Gilmore A. A.	59	M.	32	J. R.	57	W. K.
36	Goodale F. W.	57	O.	33	Lynde E. A.	66	Pilling J. E.
78	Goodnough W. S.	57	Howland T. S.	51	Lyon E. V.	55	Pillsbury D. S.
32	Goodrich H. G.	08	Hoxie W.			47	Pope A. A.
12	Goodwin J. A.	46	Humphrey J.	73	Maglathlin E. B.	30	Porter A.
13	Gordon W. R.	58	Hunt C. D.	23	Manchester A. J.	30	Potter H. A.
40	Goss E.	73	G. T.	53	Manley H.	86	W. E.
47	Gould G.	68	Hurd M. W. D.	28	Mann E., 2nd.	24	W. J.
58	G. H.	84	Hussey W. R.	57	Marshall W. H.	73	Powell J.
39	G. P.	69	Hutchinson H. L.	79	F. E.	71	Powers A. H.
81	J. B.			59	Martin G. H.	76	G. M.
80	L. M.	86	Isawa S.	31	May E.	54	Pratt C.
49	Graves H.	72	Ives S. A.	12	E. F.	36	D. H.
49	Gray A. J.			9	Mayhew F.	72	F. G.
40	Green O. H.	87	Jackson W. D.	78	McCrillis H. O.	80	G. W.
18	Greene C. C.	38	Jacobs F.	32	McDonald A.	10	H. A.
71	Grigson L. B.	86	Jefts M. W.	29	McKendry D.	43	H. T.
68	Grossman E.	17	Jenney F.	40	Mc Mahan J. W.	82	L. A.
56	Grosvenor S. N.	46	Jewell D. L.	53	McMahon C. W.	20	M. V.
51	Grover W. B.	84	Jewett F. G.	62	McManus E. T.	6	N. F. C.
59	Guernsey D. W.	84	L.	84	Mead T. A.	73	Prentiss J. J.
42	Gunnison R. W.	40	Johnson C. B.	57	Mendell L.	53	J. W.
4	Gurney L.	56	N. P.	74	Merrill F.	82	Prince C. J.
49	T.	5	S.	67	Meserve A.	61	J. T.
		59	W. H.	19	Messenger G. N.	46	Putnam A. L.
66	Hadley D.	16	Jones H. A.	30	Metcalf R. C.	44	G. B.
66	Hafey C. M.	84	W. E.	23	T.	46	W. A.
2	Hagar J.	49	Josselyn J. W.	13	Miller S., Jr.		
53	Hale A. G. R.			53	Mirick A. K.	47	Rankin W. J.
58	Haley L. L.	32	Kaine J. E.	23	Mitchell H.	1	Raymond S. E.
58	W.	00	Keay N. S.	27	Moore C. C.	66	W. C.
13	Hall C. N.	78	Keech G. T.	87	H. T.	28	Read J. B.
63	I. F.	68	Keith C. H.	27	I.	58	Reccord C.
50	J. M.	23	E. H.	1	Morehead J., Jr.	57	Reed H. L.
72	R.	35	G. T.	77	Morrison E. K.	49	Remick A.
73	Hammond C. H.	45	J. H.	80	Morse H. L.	52	Reynolds J.
86	Handy A. D.	56	Kelley F. W.	45	L. V.	40	Rice J. M.
51	Hanna G. B.	57	H. W.	17	S., Jr.	81	Rich G. P.
42	Hardy A. N.	77	Kendall C. F.	17	Morton C., Jr.	49	Richardson A. I.
1	Harlow A.	16	J.	87	F. H.	31	C. A.
3	E. H.	83	Kent C. C.	46	H.	55	E. B.
22	J.	83	Keyes W.	25	N.	08	Ring A. F.
3	J. E.	87	Kimball E. F.	77	Munroe E. N.	77	Ripley F. H.
8	Harris B. W.	79	King F. M.	79	Munsey G. F.	85	Robinson C. W.
11	C. W.	13	P. C.	86	Murdock F. F.	76	Roche J.
49	G. A.	8	Kingman C. D.			19	Rodman H. A.
50	I. K.	9	J.	53	Newcomb C. A.	53	T.
52	Hartwell H. T.	58	T. S.	17	Newell W.	83	W. A.
02	Haskell S. H.	50	Kingsbury I. F.	15	W. H.	32	Rogers G. W.
50	W.	31	L.	82	Newton H. D.	18	S R.
87	Hastings G. H.	3	Kneeland J.	86	Nichols W. F.	11	W.
53	W. H. H.	63	Knowlton F.	21	Nickerson F., Jr.	38	Root J. H.
45	Haswell A. K.			17	J. G.	32	Rowe L. S.
58	Hathaway N.	16	Ladd W. H.	77	Northup W. B.	46	Rugg L., 2nd.
68	Hawes M. B.	64	Lane W. H.	16	Nourse A.	09	Russell B. B.
53	W.	20	Lathrop J. A.	52	Nutter E. W.	59	C. L.
46	Hayward E. R.	62	Lawrence F. M.	44	Nutting.	65	W. H.
59	G. F.	63	W. P. A.			27	Ryder H. C.
54	J. P.	12	Lawton B. H.	17	Oakman H. A.	52	J. B.
53	J. W.	9	Leach J. E.	10	Oliver O. M.		
74	W. F.	70	J. E.	53	Osborne W. H.	10	Sampson C. E.
11	W. P.	36	Leavitt L.	19	Osgood I. C.	61	E. W.
87	Heard A. E.	53	Leighton W.	14	Otis D. G.	48	Sanborn S. S.
19	Herrick G.	2	Leonard C.			77	W. J.
65	Hersey E. S.	57	J. H.	37	Packard C. W.	74	Sanderson E. S.
34	Hewett E. C.	73	J. H.	83	H.	74	W. A.
11	Hewins H.	11	L.	80	L. E.	52	Sanford A.
75	Higgins B. F.	11	N., Jr.	88	Paine B.	65	E.
38	Hill E. L.	16	P. D.	10	Palmer S.	18	J. B.
59	Hillman B. T.	57	Lewis D. S.	70	Parker J. N.	9	J. E.
57	W. T.	17	Lincoln E. H.	35	S. A. W.	58	Sargent E. L.
85	Hobart A.	38	J., Jr.	12	Parmenter P. G.	38	Savage J. D.
8	E.	11	Littlefield G. T.	53	Parsons B. W.	61	Sawin H. C.
58	J. W.	17	J. D.	14	Paul A. W.	01	J. M.
48	Hodsdon N. B.	17	S.	47	Peabody C. H.	73	W. M.
47	Holbrook T. W. J.	10	Locke D. J.	59	E. H.	76	Sawyer H. L.
11	Holmes A.	65	E. F.	33	S.	10	R.
18	E. H.	19	E. H.	11	Perkins F.	2	Scarborough.
52	F. L.	44	G. W.	67	H.	96	Scars C. H.
27	S.	57	J. L.	7	N. S. C.	54	P. C.
65	T. S.	6	Lathrop C.	15	N. T.	46	Seaver E.
10	Hooper C. L.	2	H. T.	00	Perry E. E.	52	W. H.
46	G. M.	5	T. S.	24	Pervear H. K.	76	Seeley H. J.
		11	Lovering N.				

19

BRIDGEWATER STATE NORMAL SCHOOL.

Class.		Class.		Class.		Class.	
50	Shaw F. W.	17	Stratton J.	80	Tyrrell W. C.	64	Wetherbee E. G.
50	J. J.	11	Strobridge B. F.			78	Wheeler C. E.
17	N. W.	59	Stuart C. F.	3	Underwood J., Jr.	54	G. A.
37	Shearman N.	24	Sturtevant J M.	4	J. M.	18	J. S. P.
83	Shute E. P.	24	Sumner A.	50	Upton T.	82	Whidden H. R.
13	Simons J. E.	28	J.			40	Whitaker G.
80	Slade C.	40	J. H.	72	Varney W. E. J.	51	Whitcomb A. A.
51	Smalley G. L.	67	Sutcliffe J.	30	Vose B. C.	8	White C.
11	Smiley J. V.	23	Swain J. H.			53	E. M.
53	Smith A. E.	59	Swan W. R.	82	Wadsworth A. C.	56	G. A.
86	B.	57	Swasey J.	82	Waldron C. E.	29	Whiting L.
72	D. D.	48	Sweet L. H.	80	Wales G. E.	8	Whitman A. T.
13	D. M.	24	Sweetser S.	8	N.	23	Whitmore J. D.
50	E. N.	2	Sweezy J. C.	57	Walker H. N.	7	Whitney L. L.
14	F. A.	68	Symmes W. A.	13	Walton D. G.	38	Wight O. L.
48	F. C.	86	Symonds G.	10	G. A.	51	Wilcox I. W.
34	G. M.			30	Ward W. H.	15	Willey H.
44	G. M.	30	Taber F.	42	Warren L. F.	12	Williams A. H.
82	G. O.	35	G. A.	50	Wasgatt T. R.	78	D. G.
39	H. F.	10	Talbot A.	33	Washburn A., Jr.	12	G. B.
70	H. W.	59	Terry L. T.	35	C. L.	14	G. D.
62	R. W.	9	Thayer A. D.	28	J. F.	11	V. H.
30	Snow H. C.	8	Thomas C. C.	51	J. P.	34	Willis J. N.
59	Soule N. T.	42	Thompson V.	87	L. D.	46	N. E.
55	Southworth E.	79	Tourr J. E.	30	N.	55	Wilson C. H.
45	Spaulding E. F.	46	Torrey E.	70	W.	17	S. S.
77	H. S.	51	J. A.	11	Waterman D. S.	61	Winship A. E.
65	Spring M. C.	43	Tourtelotte F.	41	L.	18	Wiswall A.
84	Stanley C. F.	67	Trask B. P.	59	Waters A. J.	38	Wood A.
37	Stanyan C. H.	69	Treadway T, H.	33	Watson W.	57	C. H. W.
19	Staples C.	57	Trent J.	31	Webster W. A.	74	J. C.
63	Stephenson E. W.	21	Tripp J. C.	24	Weeden R. G.	11	John.
37	Stetson A.	28	Tucker B.	84	Weis F. M.	85	Worth H. B.
30	Stevens C. J.	56	Tupper E. N.	27	Wellington E.		
21	G. H.	84	Turner C. O.	40	Wentworth D. C.	81	Yahbah.
50	Stockbridge V. D.	61	G. S.	28	D. S.	74	Young S.
49	Stone O. B.	3	P.	40	H. W.		
27	S. W.	83	Tuttle J. H.	55	West T. H.		
86	W. H.	86	Tway M.	25	W. H.		

LADIES.

Class.		Class.		Class.		Class.	
73	Adams A. J.	87	Ashley M. J.	76	Barker M. E.	14	Blackington H.
72	A. L.	47	Athearn S.	75	Barns E.	13	N. M.
55	M. Q.	26	Atkins H. M.	36	F. A.	86	Blaikie I. M.
31	Alden C.	50	R.	84	M. E.	30	Blake H. A.
82	C. B.	89	Atkinson E. T.	38	Barney A.	45	J. M.
51	E. C.	51	J. B.	83	A. M.	58	Blanchard E. M.
76	H. E.	12	Atwood A. M.	84	Barrett E. P.	45	M. R.
17	M.	70	L. S.	74	Barrows C. M.	57	V. R.
25	T.	47	Austin J. F.	76	E. A.	52	Blanding M. H.
73	Aldrich S. P.	66	J. C.	76	S. A.	34	Blish S. S.
79	Alger C. H.	80	M. E.	33	Bartlett E. M.	59	Bliss M. F.
20	Allen A. E.	86	S. J.	12	J. F.	2	Blood S. M.
80	A. F.	66	Averill E. R.	76	L. A.	84	Bodfish A. E.
77	C. F.			76	M. K.	41	Bond M. F.
5	E. A.	31	Babcock E. C.	46	M. W.	45	Borden A. J.
81	E. M.	69	M. C.	38	S. E.	75	K. R.
20	F. W.	20	S. J.	71	Bartley C.	72	Bosworth E. A.
18	H.	27	Bacon E, D.	76	J.	66	Bourne E. F.
70	K. C.	75	I. L.	82	Bass A. F.	71	Bontelle C. P.
36	L. C.	52	Backup E. E.	12	Bassett C.	71	E. E.
79	M. C.	80	Bailey S.	31	C.	80	Bowen C. W.
85	M. C.	53	Baker A. A.	78	K.	10	Bowers M.
80	N. W.	72	E.	75	E. J.	50	Bowman M. A.
24	R. B.	85	E. C.	81	E. W.	58	Boyd A. E.
27	Allyne H. M.	75	E. F.	20	M. C.	58	A. F.
61	Almy A. S.	20	F. A.	62	M. J.	40	Boyden A. L.
86	M.	74	L. E.	14	O. K.	51	E. A.
76	S. B.	44	S. A.	8	S. P.	12	Boynton L. F.
53	Ames A.	34	S. J.	19	Ratchelder S. R.	4	Bradford A. S.
80	M. F.	86	Balcom M. E.	84	Bates C. I.	51	L. A.
82	Anderson M. E.	66	Baldwin M. E.	1	E.	45	M. E.
87	M. L.	54	Balkam E. M.	7	M.	74	Braley E. F.
82	Andrew E. W.	83	Ball E. F.	63	M. E.	79	M. A.
86	Andrews H. R.	70	G. E.	4	Battelle M. E.	78	Braman V. G.
81	I. E.	87	Ballou C. C.	20	Beal A. G. W.	71	Bray M. F.
73	Armes A. F.	58	L. L.	18	Beaumont E. F.	35	Breck A.
60	C. A.	82	O. S.	38	Beauvais A. H.	72	L. S.
67	E. M.	86	Bancroft C.	40	Bemis G. M.	38	S. A.
53	Arnold A.	74	M. J.	75	Bennett M. E.	65	Brett E. A.
65	A. L.	84	M. S.	82	Benson A. S.	47	Briggs E. D.
47	L. A.	82	Barber C. J.	72	L.	60	E. P.
87	S. L.	85	M. S.	11	Bessey J. A.	34	R. M.
31	Ashcroft E. L.	84	Barker C. L.	1	N. C.	77	M. S.
3	Ashley C. A.	61	K. L. W.	38	Bigelow M. J.	33	Brigham A. E.
27	I. B.	61	M. E.				

ALPHABETICAL INDEX. 179

Class.		Class.		Class.		Class.	
40	Brigham M. A.	67	Chase H. A.	85	Crocker F. L.	77	Draper S. G.
47	M. A.	18	H. B.	26	M. R.	18	Drew J. A. W.
8	S. B.	73	M. E.	17	Crooker E. A.	80	J. M.
34	Brooks E.	19	N. G.	7	H. R.	87	S. E.
4	H. E.	31	R. E.	62	Crosby A.	79	Driscoll I. G.
55	M. W.	58	Cheever E. C.	73	M. C.	31	Drown M. H.
55	R. C.	70	Chesley E. F.	59	Crossman K.	67	Duckworth G. M.
78	Brown A. S.	85	Chipman I. C.	70	Croucher E.	73	Dugan C. A.
82	C. E.	17	Christian C. C.	46	Crowell P. S.	78	Dunbar C. P.
14	C. R.	44	L. B.	72	Curtis L. E.	65	L.
63	C. R.	28	S.	12	Cushing H. H.	68	Dunham I. J.
03	E. G.	78	Church A.	62	I. L.	78	S. E.
76	G.	70	Churchill E. F.	76	K. W.	78	Dupee M. A.
74	H. E.	37	Clapp C. M.	41	M.	31	Durfey A. B.
77	G.	31	F. A.	84	M. L.	34	Dwight C.
78	K. P.	9	R. M.	82	Cushman C. D.	14	M. F.
37	L. P.	64	Clark E. M.	30	E. E.	76	Dyer F. J.
52	N. S.	46	E. N.	75	E. E.	75	M. A.
58	Brownell F. C.	46	L.	78	E. L.		
6	H. P.	58	M. F.	70	S. B.	45	Eaton A. M.
57	Browning L. M.	76	M. T.	57	Cutler M. F.	17	C. W.
61	Bryant E. A.	62	Clarke A. F.	84	Cutter A. E.	72	M. E.
47	H. C.	26	I. W.	75	A. J.	34	Eberle M. A. E.
66	J.	42	L. M.	48	C. F.	78	Eddy F.
83	L.	85	L. T.	78	E. M.	11	Edson C. L.
12	L. H.	85	M. E.	50	I. L.	70	E. C.
84	M.	85	Cleare A. L.	83	J. P.	1	J.
76	Buffington A. M.	86	Clement I. M.			84	J. S.
51	M. P.	45	Cloud H.	84	Daggett C. J.	45	M.
48	Bugbee A.	66	Cobb H. A.	63	C. L. R.	57	S.
39	Bullard R.	74	J. A.	35	Daman E. P.	34	Edwards R. W.
83	Bullene G.	57	L. M.	87	Damon A. C.	69	Eldridge L. E.
72	Bump M. J.	50	M. E.	80	A. E.	72	M. E.
51	Bumpers L. A.	63	M. L.	15	E.	68	Elliott E. A.
82	Bunker A.	52	S. E.	84	S. R.	80	E. M.
49	P. W.	50	Coffin H. B.	37	Dana M. M.	49	Ellis A. J.
24	S.	46	J. A.	86	Daniels A. M.	31	C.
40	Burdon A. D.	14	Colby H. S.	34	Durling A. S.	83	C. E.
18	Burgess J. D.	18	Cole L. F.	43	C. H.	82	F. L.
65	M. I.	41	Coleman S. H.	65	Davidson H. W.	49	J. A.
52	S. A.	9	Collamore J.	84	L. A.	33	M. M.
53	Burnap M. A.	80	Collingwood M. J.	42	Davie E.	8	M. W.
84	Burnham M. A.	61	Comstock F. A.	77	Davis C. A.	65	Emerson E.
77	Burrage H. A.	50	L. A.	84	C. B.	7	M.
43	Burrell L.	21	Conant L.	65	C. E.	82	Emerton C. A.
66	Burse L. R.	1	L. M.	85	H. A.	80	Evans L. V.
80	Bursley C. P.	45	P.	72	J. E.	47	Everett E. J.
13	Burt E.	81	Connell C. J.	78	L. E.		
54	J. F.	45	Conner S. W.	60	M. A.	78	Fairchild A. J.
81	J. R.	49	Cook A. O.	75	M. A.	78	M. E.
17	P.	24	H.	46	Day D. P.	77	Fales S. C.
30	R. A.	79	K. H.	48	L. B.	63	Farnum M.
75	S. A.	23	L. R.	81	Dean A. F.	48	Farrington C. E.
80	Bush E. L.	74	M. J.	75	C. L.	31	E. C.
77	R. A.	51	O.	18	E. A.	82	E. L.
73	Buttomer E. M.	70	Coon M. C.	4	H.	47	Faulkner H.
		73	Copeland C. A.	29	H. H.	48	Fay M. A.
86	Cain L. W.	20	E. F.	7	L.	10	Fearing M.
72	Campbell M. E.	22	E. H. W.	62	S. A.	86	Felt L. E.
47	Capen B. T.	23	E. S.	5	Deane J. G.	29	Fish L. A.
12	L. C.	46	L.	54	D'arcy M. E.	51	Field E. W.
76	L. C.	65	L. F.	63	Decker G.	75	Fisher A. E.
86	L. R.	75	L. H. B.	70	I. G.	63	E. F.
75	M. L. B.	28	M.	87	Deering A. A.	70	E. G.
5	Carey M. A.	30	M. H.	6	Delano A.	45	E. H.
87	Carnes A. E.	75	Corey E. F.	75	A. H.	38	J. T.
75	Carpenter E. F.	36	Cornell S. A.	82	C. E.	21	M. A.
31	L. A.	21	Cornish E. D. F.	49	Derby L. W.	39	M. C.
84	Carroll A. B.	18	S. S.	40	Derrick J. J.	81	M. C.
81	J. C.	85	Corthelle H. A.	46	Dewey F. A.	15	M. M.
28	M. A. A.	52	M. B.	46	P. L.	33	P. D.
81	Carruth L. C.	84	Costigan H. M.	43	Dewing C. C.	46	S. E.
75	Carter A. B.	83	Cotting E. I.	77	Dewyer M. A.	84	Fiske A. S.
7	Carver O. S.	18	Covington H.	64	Dexter A. M.	53	C.
82	Cary E. B.	64	Cowls E. I.	80	Dickerman A. C.	67	H. L.
76	Case E. R.	31	Crafts E.	17	M. J.	47	S. B.
19	Caswell M. A.	31	Cragin M. J.	82	Dike G.	75	Fitton M. E.
21	S. H.	30	Crane E.	37	L. S.	85	Flagg J. C.
17	S. K.	47	F. S.	20	Dimick C.	79	L. L.
34	Cathelle P. B.	17	M.	74	Dodge J.	30	Flynn A. L.
3	Chace D.	30	S.	23	L. C.	28	Fogg F. W.
79	E. A.	85	S. E.	84	Donaghy M.	57	Forbes M. D.
38	Chadbourne H. R.	79	Crapo A. M.	75	Dorgan M. L.	57	Foster M. A.
77	Chamberlain E. J.	66	I. F.	62	Doton A. M.	81	P. S.
9	F. M.	18	S. A.	80	Doull E. L.	47	Fowle M. R.
76	M. D.	72	Crayton S. B.	62	Dowse M. A.	47	M. R.
84	Chapin L. M.	1	Crocker C.	55	M. E.	77	Free E. S.
78	Chase C. M.	72	E. F.	83	Draper C. B.	63	Freley H. W.

Class.	Class.	Class.	Class.
34 French C. B.	48 Hanna E. A.	45 Holmes L. D.	44 Keith H. M.
51 C. F.	72 Hurden M. C.	64 M. A.	63 L. B.
33 F. A.	19 Harding E. A.	82 M. L.	51 M.
84 H. A.	12 F. J.	60 O. S.	17 M. E.
75 L. J.	84 J. I.	62 S. B.	75 M. J
75 M. E.	12 M.	1 S. D.	44 P.
51 S. H.	1 Harlow D. S.	25 W.	65 S. J.
40 S. R.	72 H.	48 Hood E. P.	72 S J
72 S. W.	4 L. W.	73 H. E.	84 Kelly E. M.
55 Frye J. M.	39 O. G.	16 Hooper B.	57 M. E.
1 Fuller A.	87 Harris F. W.	1 J. H.	83 M. H.
65 A. J.	07 S. F.	58 L.	86 Kendall A. H.
39 A. M. C.	79 S. L.	4 S. A.	52 E. A.
58 C. D.	80 Hart A. C.	81 Hosmer E. M.	84 J. E.
13 C. J.	85 J. M.	60 Howard A. F.	1 J. P.
22 C. M.	14 P. J.	57 C.	52 M. A. W.
6 H.	3 Hartwell I. N.	14 E.	15 Kennedy E.
66 Fullerton H. L.	02 Haskell A. E.	79 M. S.	63 Kenney P. S.
	81 L. B.	37 Howe C. M.	69 Kenrick E.
84 Gaffney K.	53 Hastings A. S.	37 L. B.	78 Keyes E. F.
15 Gale C. R.	56 Haswell S. J.	76 M.	59 Kilburn F. E.
74 Gallahger E. F.	23 Hatch A. W.	86 Howes C. E.	84 Kilbreth E.
82 Gamans M. E.	16 J. A.	73 G. F.	86 Kimball H. M.
82 Gardner A. E.	80 L. L.	15 H.	38 M. D.
31 C. M.	85 Hatchman G. H.	72 H.	65 King A. F.
82 C. M.	61 Hathaway H. M.	55 M. A.	75 H. L.
38 E.	20 I. S.	54 S. F.	28 M. H.
40 H. A.	18 L. D.	46 Howland A. A.	51 Kingsman A.
70 H. R.	56 L. P.	82 E. C.	50 H. N.
34 M. E.	84 M. B.	64 F.	84 I. C.
82 S. C.	80 M. C.	67 H. M.	64 L. A.
70 S. F.	17 O. D.	3 H. T.	02 L. A.
27 S. M.	73 S. A.	67 L. N.	32 M.
81 Gassett L. E.	17 S. P.	52 M. O.	64 M. A.
78 Gay M. E.	28 Haven M.	52 M. P.	53 Kingsbury H. F.
1 O. C.	40 Hawes E. M.	52 P. F.	68 Kirby S. W.
33 Gerry B.	47 M. E.	02 Hoxie S.	
47 Getchell S. B.	47 Hayden L. J.	9 Hubbard E. A.	48 Lackey M. B.
87 Gibbs E. M.	76 M. E.	59 Hughes M. E.	23 Ladd A. C.
75 Gifford E. D.	60 Hayward C. L.	47 V.	87 Lane M.
71 E. M.	66 E. M.	76 Humphrey J. P.	59 N.
73 F.	28 L.	15 Hunt A. J.	80 Lanman A. L.
37 Gilmore A. S.	45 M. A.	86 A. V.	40 Laselle H. G.
52 J. E.	15 M. K.	34 M. J.	79 Lawrence E.
50 Goodell M. F.	35 M. P.	37 Hurd M. F.	67 I. A.
86 Goodhue A. J.	19 R.	84 Hutchinson E. H.	70 Leach C. W.
83 Goodwin F. B.	61 Hazard A. A.	39 Hyde.	22 E. G.
75 Goss E. M.	82 Hearsey A. L.		20 H. A.
80 O. A.	64 Hedge E. D.	31 Ide A. C.	3 H. H.
74 S. A.	76 Hemphill F. W.	20 Ireson A S.	45 H. M.
65 Gould C. F.	55 Henshaw S. A.	79 Ivers E. F.	55 M. T.
82 Gove H. E.	83 Herrick E. J.		70 N. M.
66 Goward E. E.	35 Hersey M. J.	75 Jackman L. C.	49 Leavitt S. D.
81 Gray A.	53 S. L.	19 Jackson J.	63 Lefler M. E.
59 Greene M. A.	83 Hewett M. E.	01 M. E.	15 Leonard A.
37 P.	81 Hicks L. A.	80 Jacobs E. F.	23 A.
71 Greenfield H. E.	33 Higgins C. M.	2 James A. A.	86 C. C.
81 Gregory M. A.	80 Higginbottom M. A.	79 E. F.	08 C. F.
57 Grover C. A.	34 Hill A. H.	1 H.	5 C. M.
70 E. E.	55 H. E.	70 S. V.	77 E.
51 M. A.	84 J. K.	36 Jenney M. T.	02 E. F.
	20 S. J.	63 Jenkins F. A.	02 E. M.
77 Hale E. J.	74 Hills H. M.	40 L.	1 F.
76 G. E.	80 Hinchey S. H.	79 L. E.	73 F.
74 Haley A. R.	74 Hinckley A. M.	83 Johnson A. D.	17 J. A.
19 Hall A.	30 E.	40 C. L.	08 L. A.
18 B. A.	38 L.	38 E.	6 L. T.
80 E.	26 Hitch E. B.	43 E. F.	9 M.
71 F.	9 Hixon J. M.	28 J.	05 M. H.
62 H. K.	12 Hobart C. H.	23 M. C.	85 M. K.
33 L. E.	47 O. M.	76 M. K.	81 M. M. M.
20 M. A.	31 Hodges A. W.	35 M. R.	59 S. E.
31 M. A.	75 E. B.	34 Jones C. E.	34 Lewis E. B.
51 M. B.	74 J. B.	75 E. B.	37 E. L.
63 M. C.	04 Holdbrook H. A.	31 L. S.	80 M. T.
83 Hamblin E. T.	37 M A.	25 O. C.	60 S.
71 Hambly S. M.	86 S. E.	81 S. A.	85 Levi E. V.
72 Hamilton E.	36 S. W.	16 Josselyn E. M.	12 Lincoln C. R. T.
72 Hammett A.	6 V.	50 H. G.	55 E.
72 L.	8 Holland F. T.		77 E. M.
70 Hammond C.	25 L. P.	32 Kaime M. A.	3 E. W.
55 M. E.	01 Hollis M. A.	72 Kavanagh M. J.	75 L. L.
82 M. J.	78 Holmes A. C.	11 Keith A.	52 M.
49 S. L.	70 A. M.	28 A. A.	81 M. L.
78 Hammons M. E.	3 B. A.	86 A. A.	6 R. P.
73 Handy A. J.	54 E. M.	49 E. A.	12 S. G.
74 C. J.	52 H. E.	47 E. M.	52 Lindsey E. L.
74 E.	7 H. G.	47 H. A.	15 Littlefield C. A.

ALPHABETICAL INDEX. 181

Class.		Class.		Class.		Class.	
75	Littlefield V. F.	87	Morse M. V.	02	Perkins P. R.	40	Rideout E.
75	Longley S. E.	25	P. M.	57	R. S.	38	Ring L. B.
56	Lord A. C.	20	R. A.	73	Perry A. L.	72	M. M.
5	Loring S.	44	S.	85	E. O. B.	42	Robbins I. G.
33	Lothrop E. E.	1	Morton A.	72	Peterson E. W.	42	L. F.
75	F. E.	70	L. D.	48	M. H.	42	L. R.
74	H. A.	02	Mosher A. J.	52	Pettengill R. R.	42	R. D.
32	S. C.	35	Mowry M. A.	60	Pettis E. B.	44	Robinson A. L.
83	Lovering E. M.	60	Munroe C.	29	Pevear M. E.	1	C. E.
47	Loud S. B.	19	D. C.	78	Phelps G. M.	70	E. C.
36	Lowe M. F.	60	S. O.	80	L. E.	77	E. M.
60	Luce A. W.	38	Munyan H. L.	85	Phinney A. C.	25	H.
78	Luzarder A. I.			79	E. H.	55	H. A.
80	Lyon S. D.	61	Nash M. E.	76	Pickens L. H.	29	I. E.
		78	Newcomb E. W.	80	M. B.	59	M. E.
36	Macomber E. M.	50	Newell M. B.	13	Pickett J.	55	Roberts R. A.
19	H. S.	55	S.	61	Pierce A. B.	55	Rodman E.
72	Macurda A. H.	73	Nichols C. M.	30	A. L.	71	Rogers E. L.
85	Macy E. E.	75	E. C.	86	A. M.	79	L. E.
33	E. G.	45	F.	61	B. H.	34	Ross H.
45	E. G.	45	M.	71	C. J. F.	47	Rotch R.
86	M. M.	12	S. O.	50	Pillsbury K. B.	53	Rounseville C.
40	Mahaffey J. C.	02	Nickerson D.	37	Pinkham E. M.	61	P. W.
6	Mann M. A.	49	R. A.	25	Pond S. D.	33	Rowe S. A.
76	M. E.	47	R. H.	45	Poor A. R.	48	Rowland D.
4	M. B.	36	S. S.	16	Pope E.	85	Rugg M. A.
81	Manson E. F.	34	Niles M. E.	61	P. H.	46	S. H.
81	Marble A. L.	54	North F. M.	60	Porter S. L.	19	Russell E. B.
86	Martin A. I.	52	Norton J. G.	18	Potter E.	22	M.
51	Mason A.	14	Nourse M. B.	27	E.	8	Rust M. H.
84	C. A.	80	Noyes A. L.	2	R. H.	70	Ryder L. A.
50	F. A.	87	H. E.	14	Pratt D.	85	M. L.
51	R.	65	H. O.	32	E.	34	R. C.
27	Maxfield S. R.	55	K. M.	73	L. F.		
86	Maxim O. L.	70	L. A.	12	M. C.	20	Salisbury A. M.
34	May A. F.	19	S. G.	21	M. N.	45	Sampson C.
71	A. M.	49	Nye A. E.	55	S. E.	2	E.
66	McCarter M. F.	75	M. E.	69	S. E.	23	E.
76	McConnell H.			74	Pray S. A. C.	45	M. D.
78	O.	87	Oglevee A. E.	67	Prescott E. A.	6	Samson B. J.
74	McDaniels C.	70	Omey I. A.	67	M. L.	02	Sanborn E. M. G.
84	McDonnell E. G.	46	Orchard M. H.	67	Price E. J.	83	I. H.
68	McFarland F.	69	Osborne L.	28	M. S.	66	Sanders A. S.
38	F. P.	47	Osgood M. S.	76	Prince C. C.	36	Sanford S. H.
54	McIntyre M. S.	65	Ottiwell M. E. H.	46	Proctor M.	78	Saville I.
74	McLeod E.	25	S. D.	50	Pulsifer E. D.	84	Sawtelle E. P.
77	McWilliams M.	83	Oyler C. L.	83	Purdy E. J.	56	Sawyer H. E.
37	Meader M. J.			73	Purinton C. E.	67	M. B.
85	Mears A. I.	2	Packard A. A.			58	M. E.
30	Meggett M. J. W.	73	A. H.	58	Quincy A. M.	19	Z.
58	Mendell M. S.	65	E. M.			84	Sayer C. M.
49	Merrill S. F.	86	H. M.	35	Randall C. L.	3	Scarborough C.
83	Metcalf C. I.	60	J. A.	73	E. A.	53	Scofield E. I.
29	H. S.	60	M. J.	52	M. A.	11	Scott A.
35	N. N.	61	S. B.	86	Rausch E. A.	21	C. F.
40	Miller A. F.	80	Page C. E.	19	Raymond A. S.	40	M. E.
76	C. E.	50	E. E.	40	O. H.	58	Seabury C.
58	H. B.	74	E. F.	02	J. P.	76	Sears E. A.
69	Millet L. B.	80	Paige N. E.	1	S. L.	84	F. H.
60	S. B.	84	Paine E.	29	Read E.	76	I. M.
87	Mills A. A.	76	Palmer G.	71	S. R.	52	J. A.
87	L. B.	52	Parish E. F.	84	Redington E.	78	M. H.
75	M. L.	34	E. J.	02	Reed A.	20	Shankland S. E.
08	Minter M. E.	80	Parker A. M.	81	E. J.	30	Shaw A. M.
80	Mitchell A. S.	84	A. P.	87	E. M.	11	C. W.
63	K.	60	C. M.	40	H. M.	58	E. M.
21	P.	18	E.	82	M. E.	8	H. L.
33	S. A.	71	L. R.	03	M. F.	38	L. E.
71	Monroe D. T.	73	M. A.	58	S.	49	M. H.
71	Moore C. G.	15	M. W.	80	Regan E. F.	68	R. C.
71	H. S.	36	Parkman C. A.	58	Reid I. M.	35	S. H.
22	M. E. D.	72	Patch M. F.	84	Rice H. B.	71	Shea M. A. A.
51	R. C.	52	M. J.	54	M. E.	71	M. L.
27	S. H.	71	Paull M. F.	77	R. F.	45	Shedd E. E.
77	Morey A. E.	67	Peabody E. F.	52	S. E.	7	Shepherd S.
79	E.	08	M. F.	81	Rich H. P.	78	Sherman B. W.
77	Morris H. L.	74	Pease C. A.	49	M. M.	32	L. A.
48	Morrison C. E.	29	Peck S. M.	66	Richards A.	87	M.
51	D. C.	70	Peckham E. W.	75	C. K.	6	Shockley A. B.
51	L.	70	L. B.	71	E.	6	M. F.
21	Morse A. M.	81	M. E.	02	Richardson H. V.	9	Shorey H. N.
82	C. E.	51	Penniman A. M.	86	H. C.	69	Simmons B. P.
81	F. C.	09	H. L.	02	M. B.	61	E. M.
74	H. H.	85	Perkins C.	80	M. B.	84	O. M.
86	K. L.	76	C. L.		N. M.	37	Simpson A. A.
45	L. E.	50	H. F.	65	Richmond H. M.	37	F.
73	L. E.	60	M. B.	61	Ricketson M. S.	61	Small M. F.
40	M. E.	44	M. W.	66	Riddell L. S.	09	Smith A.

Class.		Class.		Class.		Class.	
38	Smith A. D.	78	Taber R. L. H.	76	Vinal A. M.	19	White M. B.
38	A. E.	31	Taft A. S.	34	M. E.	8	M. P.
85	A. L.	33	E.	84	Vincent C. S.	32	S. H.
69	C.	78	H. H.	19	Vinton E. O.	51	Whiting A. G.
25	E. G.	36	H. M.	81	Vose E. J.	57	Whitman M.
72	F. A.	36	S. F.	25	M. E.	62	Whitney A. D.
72	H. A.	50	S. J.	22	S. M.	55	A. M.
72	H. W.	73	Taggart M. F.			66	M. P. C.
37	J. B.	76	Talbot F. M.	15	Wadsworth E.	84	Whorf L. W.
51	K.	79	F. M.	81	M. A.	82	Wickes A. D.
80	L. N.	28	Tallant C. L.	84	Wnite S. A.	32	Wight A.
15	M.	82	Tappan L. H.	65	Wakefield O. A.	84	M. B. A.
80	M.	13	M.	74	Waldron F. H.	48	S. H.
35	M. A.	20	Taunt S. J.	8	S. G.	61	Wilbar S. S.
22	M. E.	79	Taylor A. H.	78	Walker E. A.	17	Wilber H.
72	M. E.	5	B. C.	17	L. M.	83	L. M.
31	M. J.	1	C.	45	M. E.	80	Wilbur A. F.
72	M. M.	11	E.	78	S. A.	81	S. A.
70	M. R.	18	L. B.	82	S. A.	83	S. E.
15	N.	53	M. F.	86	S. J.	48	Wild A. M.
48	N. S.	35	M. J.	68	S. R.	75	Wilde A. M.
55	R. M.	87	M. N.	79	Wallace A. G.	79	A. M.
75	Snell J.	71	Tenney L. S.	81	Walton M.	45	S. V.
75	Snow L. A. S.	79	Thacher A. R.	76	Ward H. F.	31	Wilder M. S.
11	S.	86	C. B.	21	Ware A. H.	63	Willey S. C.
79	Somes J. H.	34	Thain M. R.	20	A. M.	73	Williams A. S.
46	Soule C. E.	47	Thaxter L. M.	16	J. L.	48	A. W.
85	Southwick C. E.	40	R. A.	18	M. E.	82	E. E.
78	M. L.	63	Thayer A. A.	15	Washburn C.	75	H. A.
36	M. U. F.	83	A. C.	38	E. C.	67	H. E.
20	Southworth M. P.	55	M. A.	39	F. W. D.	61	I. A.
78	Sparrow C. L.	24	M. H.	49	R. A.	38	M. D.
2	Spaulding H.	59	Thomas E.	1	J. A.	63	M. E.
66	S. A.	36	E. L.	4	L.	10	M. H.
87	Spear C. F.	80	J. B.	63	L.	4	M. R.
17	Sprague A. C.	85	L.	66	L. M.	54	S. A.
47	H. C.	70	L. A.	20	M.	50	Willis L. G.
85	Springer C. B.	71	S. O.	17	S.	32	Wilmarth R. S.
33	M. E.	86	Thompson A. L.	85	S. C.	71	Winchester H. E.
82	Squiers C. E.	52	A. M.	40	Watson C. F.	61	Winn H. P.
73	Stackpole S. N.	55	E.	76	E. B.	73	S. C.
62	Stanley A. F.	40	J. C.	77	Webb C. O.	32	Winning M. F.
74	E. W.	55	M.	12	E. P.	13	Winslow C.
58	Stearns H. F.	80	M. A.	46	F. W.	2	C. H.
76	Steele M.	85	M. E.	39	Webster M. E.	77	E. J.
1	Stephens M.	81	M. F.	85	Weeks L. H.	81	H. W.
61	Stephenson C. L.	49	S. B.	76	Wefer M. E.	7	O. P.
40	Stetson R. J.	52	Tidd O.	32	Weld E. M.	66	Winward E. A.
10	Stiles E. P.	1	Tilden C.	45	S. J.	80	Wiswall A. M.
86	Stinchfield M. L.	74	G.	40	Wentworth J. A.	59	Witherell M. A.
38	Stockbridge A.	63	Tillson A. F.	39	O. F.	66	Wittet S. W.
30	R.	67	Tilly E. C.	32	Westall M.	32	Wood E.
76	Stone M. E.	58	Tinkham A.	70	Westgate M. G.	59	M. E.
33	M. S.	72	A. F.	29	Weston E.	48	P. F.
15	S.	71	Tisdale L. O.	10	E. W.	74	S. M.
77	Stowell M. E.	87	Titcomb M. B.	10	H. M.	34	Woods A. W.
80	S. L.	14	Tower A. H.	70	I. G.	84	Woodbridge M. F.
36	Strange C.	51	Towle S. A.	3	Wethereli M. A.	47	Woodward E. B.
13	J.	84	True S.	83	Wheeler A.	86	Wordell E. S.
17	Strobridge M.	30	Tucker C.	81	A. J.	39	Worth H. A.
73	Stubbert L. M.	17	C. B.	77	E.	77	Wright E. M.
84	Sturtevant C. E.	26	K. E.	84	Wheelock E. F.	70	Wyer L. F.
52	Swain C.	28	L.	69	Whitcomb M. T.		
38	L. S.	5	Turner M.	22	White A. A.	65	Young A. F.
61	Sweeney S. S.			12	A. S.	73	B. M.
48	Sweet A. A.	59	Underwood J.	61	C. A.	77	C. B.
31	L. H.	46	Upham D. M.	19	E. C.	68	C. I.
65	Swift F. C.	86	R. J.	1	H. A.	37	M.
48	M. A.	52	Upton S. M.	78	J.	66	M. A.
31	Sylvester L. C.			8	J. E.		
		74	Veazie E. F.	75	J. L.		

www.ingramcontent.com/pod-product-compliance
Lightning Source LLC
Chambersburg PA
CBHW032149160426
43197CB00008B/833